One *Last* Lunch

A Final Meal with Those Who Meant So Much to Us

EDITED BY

ERICA HELLER

ABRAMS PRESS, NEW YORK

Dedicated to my mother, my grandparents, Mary Lou Shulman, Richard Glass, Catherine Flanagan Stover, Janavi Held, Warren Cassell, Alan Epstein, Arthur Gelb, Dolores Karl, Juris Jurjevics, Ilse Dusoir Lind, Irene Towbin, Lucy, Sweeney, Thistle, and Lola. What I wouldn't give for just one more lunch.

MENU

There will be time to murder and create . . .
And for a hundred visions and revisions,
Before the taking of a toast and tea.
—T. S. Eliot, "The Love Song of J. Alfred Prufrock"

INTRODUCTION

Mr. Eliot's message of loss mingled with memory is achingly clear, but what if, in some cases, there *wasn't* time? Too often, when people are whipped from this earth, they leave behind loved ones who are lost and left fumbling with unresolved issues, without having expressed crucial emotions, secrets, breathless declarations of love, and apologies, troubled by questions, so many questions. Who among us has not dreamt of having just one more sliver of precious time with someone we miss terribly and want—no, *need*—to see again? Sometimes it's in order to tie up loose ends, other times to luxuriate in the divine splendor of their company, linger once more in a loving embrace that was once as warm as sunshine to us on a dark, blustery day?

"I just hope she knew how much I loved her," whispered a tearful friend recently, having just lost her sister.

"The last time we met, we had a tremendous argument. I brutally criticized him, and I'll never forgive myself," a lifelong friend told me this week, in the small, trembling voice of a child, about his brother, who had just succumbed to cancer.

How terrible, I've always thought, to stagger through this life freighted with regrets, with moments lost to us because of stubbornness or fear, all because we always assumed there would be future opportunities.

But leave it to the French to concoct the perfect idiom: *l'esprit d'escalier*—literally "staircase wit"—the predicament of chancing upon the perfect riposte too late, when you've already reached the bottom of the stairs. Well, for our purposes here, let's change it to *l'esprit du cimetière*.

We almost always feel that a loved one's death has cheated us of critical time together. Some people are lucky in that they really *do* have time to say everything. When my saintly but sassy mother was diagnosed with lung cancer in 1994, I quit my job, moved in to care for her, and thus began an honest, ever-ranging conversation with virtually no boundaries that lasted a year and a half. With my father, it was quite the opposite: a call in the middle of the night telling me that he had succumbed to a massive heart attack. Still, I'd give anything to be able to sit around at lunch with one or both of them on a bright, cheerful day. I would laugh and reminisce with my mother, luxuriously cloaked once more in her warmth, wit, and tenderness. With my father, I would finally get the chance to ask the big questions I'd always been afraid to ask, hopefully elicit some rarely exhibited gentleness, and unscramble and decipher some of the constantly crossed wires that helped contribute to a lifetime of cryptic, slow-simmering intolerance from him. It was this lunch, trapped in my imagination but making itself known repeatedly, like a door in the wind that keeps banging away but never quite slams shut, that led me to the basis for this book.

In talking to people for it, I never once heard from anyone that there was *no one* they'd like to have lunch with just once again, if only they could. In most cases, I only had to explain the book's premise and inquire as to whether they'd like to contribute. Most were happy, no, *eager* to participate, but even those who hesitated found that when it came time to create their lunch, the experience they forged tumbled out onto the page almost effortlessly.

Writers, actors, artists; everybody had *somebody* they missed terribly, whose absence was palpable, for what turned out to be a startling variety of reasons. Rain Pryor chose her father, Richard Pryor, to laugh and lunch with. Writer James Grissom longed for one more lunch with Tennessee Williams. Kirk Douglas picked his father, and so on. Amazingly, the current of powerful emotions that ran through all these stories was never the same twice.

What I learned from the lunches was that even the death of someone who means the world to us cannot rob us of two magical things: our memories and our imaginations. Our minds, unchained, are free to wander back any time we like, as often as we long to, to feel comforted or amused or angry or even peevishly annoyed; to rewrite the ending to our own private scenario. Our fantasies, too, often sprint way ahead of us, untethered, to occasions and emotions we might still experience with the person who has been lost to us—to hold on to that person just a little longer and feel as if they're back in our reach and in our life.

Perhaps the most ironic thing about this book is that in each instance, in each fantasy, in order to recount an honest, faithful story, come what may, the person doing the imagining really *did* get to spend valuable time with their loved one, friend, sparring partner, or cherished acquaintance again, if only in their deeply private, kaleidoscopic imagination. One or two lunches we're shown are in fact past lunches, because the writer wanted so much just to circle backward and relive them.

This wish for a definitive denouement is visceral, as old as time. In fact, in Plato's *Symposium*, he imagines an after-dinner conversation between a bunch of Greek luminaries, past and present. *Symposium* just happens to be one of the most famous pieces of writing from the ancient world. And Plato's wish, his fantasy of one last meal with Socrates, was written 2,400 years ago.

But now, please be seated, take a sip of water, and kindly place your napkin in your lap.

Lunch is about to be served.

"I just want you to be happy."

ERICA HELLER (DAUGHTER)
AND JOSEPH HELLER

To imagine lunch now with my father, Joe Heller, it would have to be in spring. Unknowingly reacting to the blooming nature all around him, shoots pushing obstinately up even through the cracks in the city pavement, he was often softer, gentler in spring. Perhaps the tender buds unfurling all around him would somehow leech his own fiercely guarded tenderness to the surface—who knows?

We would meet, of course, at his favorite place: the old Union Square Café. The knowledge that a fuss is almost certainly going to be made about him there is something that he is hardly impervious to. He never was, and this time, he's been gone since 1999.

When I arrive, he is standing outside, waiting for me. He looks healthy, tanned, his majestic crop of white leonine hair, which can easily be spotted from three blocks away, is still surprisingly impressive, like a crown resting atop his head. Both of our eyes fill with tears as we embrace each other, long and hard. "Let me look at you," he says, stepping back just a bit. "You look so beautiful," he says, his damp eyes taking me in. "Are you hungry? I am." He chuckles a bit as we step inside.

Danny Meyer is at the front of the restaurant and rushes over to greet us personally, shaking my father's hand with both of his. We're seated, given menus, and Dad says, "I'm starving, and I know that we should order, but I just can't believe we're here. When I died, I certainly thought I'd never see you again, and it broke my heart." He puts down his menu and takes one of my hands in his. We order, but first he requests his signature drink: a dry martini, straight up, with a twist. His eyes are bright with tears, with pride and, apparently, abundant love for me; this chameleon, who could always turn gruff and biting with a simple, quick, strategic verbal pirouette, seemingly in the space of a single breath.

Great quantities of oysters, pasta, and fish are brought to the table. I am too excited to eat, but he dives in robustly, making most of it disappear with his typical, legendary mealtime fervor. He has clearly caught me unawares, behaving so sweetly, so humbly, and so dear. He laughs, he chatters, he reminisces.

At some point coffee arrives, with a complimentary dessert from a beaming Mr. Meyer. We are talking about paradisiacal summers from long ago, on Fire Island, trips to Nathan's in Coney Island. Suddenly he says, as if in a dream, "I miss her, too, you know," and I know he's talking about my mother, now long gone. A love story for thirty-eight years right up until the cataclysmic moment it wasn't.

Toward the end of the lunch, Carl Bernstein, lunching with friends at a nearby table, strolls over and tells my father how wonderful it is to see him. My father proudly introduces me. "This is my daughter Erica, not just beautiful but brilliant, one hell of a writer." Hours go by, but we are still lost in memories, in laughter, in this golden moment we both know won't ever come again. Dessert, our sumptuous banana tart is but a memory, most of which I ate myself. The restaurant is now almost empty except for the waitstaff setting up quietly for dinner. The light outside is dimming. My father pays the check, stands with his customary grunt, leaves his tip on the table, takes out a Stim-u-Dent from a tiny pack in his coat pocket, sticks one firmly in his teeth, and says, "This is horrible. I never got to say goodbye to you before. Now I do and it's even worse." We step out into the crepuscular late afternoon. Again, we embrace. This time clinging like shipwrecked sailors saying their very last goodbyes.

A loud bus goes by, making his last words almost indiscernible. By now, I am sobbing. I believe he says, "More than anything else, I just want you to be happy. It's really all I've ever wanted," just before I lose him, as he walks slowly down the block, dabbing at his eyes with a handkerchief, until he inevitably blends into the gloomy miasma of teeming rush-hour foot traffic.

I could swear that's what he said, but of that I can never be certain.

"Thanks for the lunch, baby."

CLARENCE MAJOR (FRIEND)
AND JAMES BALDWIN

It's hard to believe, but after thirty-one years, I'm once again back in Nice, France. I taught here from 1981 till 1983. This time my stay will be brief.

Back then, my old friend James Baldwin was living a short distance away, in Saint-Paul-de-Vence.

Today, as I step out of the blazing sunshine into the cool Restaurant Tolentini (Jimmy's favorite restaurant in all of Nice), I see that Jimmy has already arrived for our lunch.

There he is again, with that famous, wide-open smile.

I haven't seen Jimmy since that last dinner party at my apartment in 1983. That was fun, but I am especially fond of my memory of the little impromptu gathering Jimmy; my wife, Pamela; a few other friends; and I had after the formal ceremony when the university here awarded Jimmy an honorary doctorate.

Jimmy stands as I approach our table, and I don't know what I was expecting, but I'm surprised to see that he looks exactly the same as when I last saw him. In his fancy blue dress shirt, black slacks, and black loafers, he looks particularly happy and well. His bright smile always lands me in a good mood. We embrace.

He says, "Hey, baby! Good to see you! The years have treated you well." This is pure Jimmy. He calls everybody he likes "baby." He puts out his cigarette in the ashtray on our table.

I say, "Hey, Jimmy!"

We sit facing each other.

It's great to see Jimmy looking so well. Let's face it, he never had an easy time of it. He preached in a Harlem storefront church from the age of fourteen to seventeen, then as a young man, he moved downtown to the Village, where life was difficult. Finding work was not easy. When he was lucky, he worked as a waiter.

But he was broke a good deal of the time. Sometimes he slept on rooftops. This was in the late 1940s, when legal segregation still existed. Restaurants, for example, routinely refused to serve black people, and public schools were legally segregated by race.

So, in 1948, Jimmy left New York with forty dollars in his pocket. He'd reached his breaking point. And by then he also knew he was a writer and was determined to prove it to the world. A lot had changed since those days: the Supreme Court's ruling on *Brown vs. Board of Education* in 1954, the Civil Rights Act of 1964, and the Voting Rights Act of 1965. But a lot also hadn't changed.

Jimmy moved to Paris, to a hotel, but broke and alone, unable to speak the language, he was very, very lonely. Paris was no immediate panacea. Soon, he was ill. He had no money to pay for doctors or his hotel bill. Rather than putting him out, the elderly Corsican woman who owned the hotel nursed him back to health for three months. This woman was a survivor.

And now, here we were at Restaurant Tolentini. Jimmy knew the maître d', Maurice, for many years. Maurice is an elegant, middle-aged Frenchman with patrician manners. He doesn't miss a beat. You can tell that this restaurant is his ship and he's its captain. Meanwhile, the background music is Mozart's *Magic Flute*. As always, I feel comfortable and pampered here.

Restaurant Tolentini's is airy and plush inside. The white, marble-paved floor is shot through with streaks of green and purple. The restaurant has lots of red velvet drapery, and the tables and chairs are all of highly polished dark oak, with matching red velvet upholstery.

The elaborate crystal chandeliers above us are aglitter with soft light. The wallpaper shows an eighteenth-century outdoor festival with plenty of food and frolicking. The napkins are embossed with the restaurant's name. The railings are gold chrome.

To the left of us there's a big long fish tank on the far wall with a variety of native Mediterranean fish: goby, mullet, skate, blackhead, dory, sardinella, and bass, all swimming around and around in their own private universe. It's lighted like a ship at night, at sea.

The din of voices is rich and low, speaking proper French. We may be in Provence, but this restaurant is no place for provincial rubes.

Maurice strokes his little black moustache.

Jimmy says, "Maurice, this is Clarence Major, a good friend of mine, and a fine writer. He taught here at the university back in the 1980s."

Maurice says, "It's a pleasure to meet you, Monsieur Major."

We're in seats by the window, with a full view of the lush, blooming garden. Maurice places menus before us. He fills our water glasses, leaving the carafe on the table.

Maurice says, *"Puis-je vous commencer avec des rafraîchissements?"*

"Yes," says Jimmy, and we order an excellent dry Sauvignon Blanc. Maurice returns with the bottle and expertly uncorks it, pouring a tiny bit in each of our glasses for our approval.

Jimmy sips; I sip. He nods his approval, and so do I. Dry and slightly sweet, it's an excellent wine. Maurice pours more wine into each glass, bows slightly, then in English says, "We're not so busy right now, so today, I will be your waiter. It's always a pleasure to serve you, Monsieur Baldwin."

Maurice bows slightly and leaves.

"Are you still teaching at the University of California at Davis?" Jimmy asks me.

"No, I'm retired from teaching. I'm writing and painting full-time now."

"I remember when you were teaching there. I remember you telling me about your students, many of them from North Africa, how smart they were and how much you were learning from them. Teaching is always better when you too are learning. We had some good times back then. You finished your novel *My Amputations* here in Nice, didn't you?"

"That's right, and I wrote it on manual typewriter. Hard to imagine nowadays, after so many years of working on a computer, how I ever managed to write novels back then on a manual typewriter."

"I still write in longhand," says Jimmy, leaving me to quietly wonder just *where* and *how* he does this.

"There's a lot to be said for the tactile assurance of longhand. You're in touch with each word on a more intimate basis," I tell him.

Jimmy says, "That's true." He pauses for a sip of wine. "Listen! Things everywhere have changed a lot; not just the widespread use of computers and mobile phones. For example, a lot of European countries are turning against foreigners. Think of all the terrorist killings. I'm sure you've seen it all on TV. They've been rampant in Paris and many of the other major cities of Europe. Over here you never know where the next disaster will happen. It keeps everyone on edge."

Jimmy sighs and shakes his head, then continues. "It's depressing: the frequent police killings of unarmed black men; the constant anti-gay killings; the school shootings, with hundreds of kids dead; the rise of so many new hate groups. The growing mania of the gun culture in America; and, of all people, Donald Trump as president. Don't think I don't follow what's going on."

"I'm sure you do, Jimmy." I pause. "What about gay marriage now being legal?"

Jimmy says, "That's a good thing. It surprised me. If it had happened years ago, I would have taken advantage of it." He drinks his wine. "Seems every time something positive happens in America there's a negative counteraction."

"Such as positive Obama, then Trump?"

"Yes, excellent example. It's the same old backlash every time."

"And were you surprised to see the country elect a black president?"

"Shocked! I admit, I never thought such a thing could ever happen. Most Americans truly believe race is a real thing. But I tell you, Obama will go down in history as one of our best presidents, certainly one of our most intelligent."

"I agree."

Jimmy picks up his menu. "Maybe we should order, huh? What looks good to you?"

I pick up the menu, scanning it. "Remember, Jimmy, lunch is on me."

"Okay, baby," Jimmy says, "Why don't we just order a lot of good stuff and share it?"

"I like that idea."

For appetizers we decide on tapenade with olives, garlic, anchovies, and capers, as well as onion tarts. For the two main courses we select bouillabaisse and lobster with fettuccine Alfredo and fresh green beans in butter. Our two desserts are a ripe fig dish with fresh feta and petite tomatoes, and socca crepes, with whipped cream and almonds.

Maurice returns, and we order.

Jimmy goes on. "As I was saying, things back in your country look grim."

I say, "There's all kinds of delusional thinking. A disturbing number of people in America, for example, don't believe in climate change, don't believe we've messed up the atmosphere of our planet."

Jimmy says, "I know. It's sad. Do we *all* have to perish before they see the light?"

"Did you hear about the Bush administration's response to Hurricane Sandy?"

"Sure did: depressing and shameful."

I say, "I found it depressing that Congress refused to work with President Obama for the good of the country, even when they agreed with what he wanted to do. They started out saying they wanted him to fail."

Jimmy smiles. "Baby, you have to keep the faith; you know that."

"Yes, I do know that. And I try, I try."

"You know, Clarence, I've said it many times: my country was America, and I still love my country, and for that reason I reserve the right to criticize it."

"As well you should. You always felt that it's the business of the writer to disturb the peace."

I'm looking at Jimmy. After all these years I still think of him as a mentor, a big brother, and a father figure, but long before I knew him as a person, I knew him as an ideal writer, and as such, he was for me a beacon and a mainstay.

"I remember one time when I was living here, Jimmy, you left for one of your visits to the States, and at the same time, I also left France. I went to Africa on a lecture tour with stops in Liberia, Ghana, Ivory Coast, and Algeria."

"I remember that. When you came back you told me all about that trip. It reminded me of my first trip to Africa. I wrote an article about it for *The New Yorker*. I had conflicting feelings. I knew I was not returning home. Africa was the land of my ancestors, but America was my home."

I say, "That's what I felt, too."

At this point, Maurice brings out our appetizers and refills our water and wine glasses. There is a pause in our conversation while we start eating.

When we are done with the appetizers, the main course arrives, and Jimmy and I eat for a while, still without talking, just enjoying the food, the music (now the frisky, playful *Eine kleine Nachtmusik*), the ambience and atmosphere of Tolentini's, and of course, each other's company.

Then Jimmy says, "What're you working on these days?"

"A novel."

"Is it going well?"

I say, "Yes, except that I have to keep stopping to do other things, such as take out the garbage, make dinner, and write an essay for a magazine or a foreword to a book I like; you name it. It's life."

Jimmy says, "I remember writing my first novel and discovering in each paragraph things I really didn't want to face, but something in me was driving me to face those hidden realities anyway, and I discovered things about myself by writing that book. I discovered not so much who I *was* at the time but who I was *not*. A lot of it I improvised."

"I hear you."

I notice Maurice watching us from across the room, waiting for his cue.

"Jimmy, your fiction is realistic, it's true, but when I read your novels I can see how you were improvising every step of the way, like a jazz musician riffing. The ostinato is there. The repeated chord is there. There is a pattern to your prose. How is *that* not improvisation?"

"Sure, but in the end you hide all of that to let the story rise to the surface. That is the important thing. The story! If you leave your workings, your improvisations, on the surface, you are likely to be bored, and if it bores you, it's going to bore your reader."

"Touché!" I tell Jimmy. "I've stopped writing things and torn them up because they bored me. Sometimes it was the story, other times, the writing. But I knew there was no point in going on." I pause for a sip of wine. "I got serious about writing when I was quite young, so over time I've learned a lot by practice and by instinct. I've learned to trust my gut feelings and to rely on them to drive what I've learned about technique."

Jimmy says, "As you know, my father's death was a turning point for me. That was the moment I got really serious about focusing all my energy on writing, on making a career of it. At that point I was now the male head of my family, and I was not going to let them down. And more importantly I was not going to let *myself* down."

"I hear you." Jimmy is referring to going to his father's funeral through the 1943 riot–torn streets of Harlem. He was nineteen at the time.

Maurice places our desserts before us. We stop talking and dive into them with unapologetic bravado.

When our plates have been fully ravaged, Maurice returns and asks, "How was your lunch, gentlemen?"

Jimmy beams. "As usual, Maurice, everything was delicious, and *you* were splendid."

I say, "Absolutely delicious!"

"Merci, messieurs!" he says, "Would you like a little digestive drink?"

"I'm up for it; how about you, Clarence?"

"Sure. How about cognac?"

Jimmy says, "Cognac is an excellent choice."

Maurice says, "Cognac it is."

Maurice leaves us and sends a busboy to clear away the dishes, then delivers our cognac. Jimmy and I linger another half hour over it, enjoying the moment, the music, our friendship.

When it's time, I fish out my credit card and pay.

"Thanks for the lunch, baby."

"Anytime, Jimmy. I feel so lucky that we could get together and talk again."

"I will always be here, baby. Never forget that."

I excuse myself to visit the restroom, but when I return, Jimmy has vanished.

What will never leave me, however, is that spectacular smile, wide and warm.

Clarence Major is a poet, painter, and novelist. He is the author of thirty-nine books, and among his awards are a National Book Award Bronze Medal, the National Council on the Arts Award, the Western States Book Award, PEN Oakland–Reginald Lockett Lifetime Achievement Award, and the Stephen Henderson Poetry Award for Outstanding Achievement.

A PLAY IN ONE ACT

BROOK ASHLEY (GODDAUGHTER) AND TALLULAH BANKHEAD

TIME:

The present. Mid-day in a New York summer.

CAST:

The actress TALLULAH BANKHEAD (1902–1968). *Tallulah's famous voice sounds like a bass foghorn burbling through a barrel of warm molasses. That voice, along with her beauty and acting talent, has made her a stage, screen, radio, and television star for five decades. Her off-stage capers include prodigious alcohol consumption, a legion of straight and bisexual adventures, as well as a fiercely vocal opposition to the House Un-American Activities Committee and all forms of racial discrimination. Tallulah can outlast, outtalk, and, most often, intellectually surpass any company she finds herself in. Early in her career, Tallulah was draped with the mantel of "gay icon," and she has worn it proudly ever since. She is a vortex spinning with the energy of dramatic gesturing, political commentary and nonstop theatrical anecdotes. Unlike the contemporaries with whom she is sometimes conflated—Crawford, Dietrich, Davis, Garbo—Tallulah is approachable, maternal, and always witty. Slim, and possessing great gams, Tallulah is surprisingly small but most definitely not elfin. Honey blond hair falls to her shoulders, and her constantly mobile mouth is defined in a deep crimson lipstick the color of Tiptree's Little Scarlet strawberry jam.*

TALLULAH's godchild, BROOK ASHLEY. *Brook's mother starred with Tallulah in* The Little Foxes, *and her father was Tallulah's attorney and occasional lover. She grew up spending long stretches of time in Tallulah's household, observing the panoply of guests and semipermanent residents. Brook has now lived longer than Tallulah, which is a statistic she finds somewhat disquieting. She was a young college student when Tallulah joined (as Noël Coward dubbed it) the "feathered choir."*

DOLORES, TALLULAH's four-pound Maltese. *Dolores has long, silky fur covering her eyes, and it is sometimes challenging to tell which end one is looking at. She remains either at Tallulah's side or in her arms, rather like a living Judith Leiber clutch bag.*

TEDDY, a waiter. *Male, lithe, and slender. He moves with the grace of a dancer.*

SETTING:

The interior of Sardi's Restaurant in Manhattan's Theatre District. Red leather banquettes line the periphery of the room, and brightly colored caricatures of assorted Broadway actors are stacked up the walls almost to ceiling height.

OPENING:

A spotlight shines on the corner banquette, illuminating MISS BANK-HEAD, *who is dressed in a beige shantung silk suit accessorized with a large strand of pearls. The perfectly tailored outfit is a custom design from the early 1960s and remains timelessly elegant.* DOLORES, *her tiny Maltese, is tucked in her left elbow, and that same hand holds a lit Craven A cigarette, from which* TALLULAH *inhales deeply.* TALLULAH *is looking stage left toward Sardi's glass entry door, as it is pushed open by her godchild,* BROOK ASHLEY. BROOK *is wearing a classic, if unimaginative, New York summer outfit of slim black pants, a crisply ironed long white shirt, David Yurman cable bracelets, and black ballet flats. Background noises of street chatter, sirens, and horns are carried in on a warm blast of subway-scented air (exhaust, urine, pavement, and old hot dog water) before the door closes firmly behind her.* BROOK *crosses the stage to* TALLULAH'S *table as* MISS BANKHEAD *speaks without pausing between sentences.*

TALLULAH

Hello, darling! I see you got my invitation. God, what a frightful trip. I think the Celestial Concierge routed me through the hinterlands of Uzbekistan. When I *died*, they gave me a lovely cloud-filled ascendancy with the Mormon Tabernacle Choir belting Handel's *Messiah*. This little return visit was closer to traveling backward in one of those ancient pneumatic tubes that Loveman's department store in Birmingham used for cash payments. And I swear I heard Florence Foster Jenkins screeching "Un Bel Di" in the background.

TALLULAH *takes a breath, stands up from the table, and pulls* BROOK *toward her with her free right arm.* DOLORES *lets out a small yip of welcome as the three of them embrace. Sitting back down,* TALLULAH *looks inquisitively at her godchild and asks with concern,*

TALLULAH
Are you in mourning? Why are you wearing black in July?

BROOK
It's just what people wear now, but you're right—it's a bit dreary. I miss the bright prints from the sixties. (*continuing, a bit hesitantly*) Tallulah, we're talking as if you . . . umm . . . have just been on a brief vacation. There was a note in my mailbox—no stamp or return address—in your unmistakable handwriting asking me to show up at Sardi's today. Do you have any idea how long it's been since you . . . ?

TALLULAH
Passed over? Kicked the bucket? Bought the farm? No, not really.

BROOK
I was just a child!

TALLULAH (*dryly*)
I had noticed a few changes.

BROOK (*speaking rapidly*)

Can you stay for a while? Do you know what's been happening in the world since you left? Would you like a drink?

TALLULAH

No, I can't. . . . Somewhat . . . God, yes! (*Touching the arm of a passing waiter,* TALLULAH *leans into his face and offers a gigantic smile.*) Darling, a bourbon on the rocks, please. Brook will have her usual, and would you be an angel and light my cigarette?

The waiter brings a lighter out of his pocket, takes the cigarette from TALLULAH'*s fingers, and raises it to his own lips. After a few puffs to see that it's lit, he hands it back to* TALLULAH.

BROOK (*astounded*)

But that's how you always liked your cigarettes lit! Mouth to mouth. How did he know that, and why is Sardi's allowing smoking?

TALLULAH

Oh, that's darling Teddy. He hitched a ride down with me and Dolores. There's someone here he needs to meet up with—an issue that never got resolved before the plague of the 1980s took him out. Yes, I know about all that. We welcomed so many beautiful young men in those terrible days. As for the smoking, do you see anyone else in the restaurant noticing us? It's a bit of spiritual wizardry that gives us some privacy, and I do *not* want some tourist from Keokuk asking me for Bette Davis's autograph.

TEDDY *arrives with a bourbon for* TALLULAH *and a Shirley Temple for her godchild.* BROOK, *with an amused glance at* TALLULAH, *picks the bouquet of maraschino cherries out of her ginger ale and deposits them on a butter plate.* TALLULAH *turns to* TEDDY *to order lunch.*

TALLULAH (*to* TEDDY)

Teddy, we'll both have the smoked salmon to begin with, then the Jumbo Shrimp Sardi in Garlic Sauce. It seems to have disappeared from the menu, but would you please ask the kitchen to make the Profiteroles Au Chocolat circa 1966? Brook always adored them. Dolores will have a small plate of finely chopped chicken breast with a spoonful of melted butter drizzled over it. Thank you, darling.

BROOK

Tallulah, I never got to say goodbye. I wanted desperately to let you know how much I loved you. You were so much larger than life that I couldn't imagine you slipping away like an ordinary person. Did you know that your obituary made the front page of the *New York Times*?

TALLULAH

No, darling, I didn't. My, my.

BROOK

May I ask what brought you back? I've always felt that you were still a part of me, that the extraordinary childhood you gave me left a bit of your DNA in my heart. Could the furniture and paintings you willed to me have been a connection as well? I sit in the dining chairs that Syrie Maugham designed when you were the toast of London in the 1920s and imagine your dear friends from that era—Winston Churchill, Lawrence of Arabia—settling their rumps into the same seats. One of the cushions is sprung, and I assume that was Churchill's doing. Sometimes I trace the cigarette burns on your bedside table with my finger, and it conjures all the scorch marks that tracked your movements through my childhood. When I was very small and lying on your carpet with Dolores, I pretended that the pattern of cigarette burns across the living room marked the trail of an exotic animal.

TALLULAH (*tossing her tawny mane of hair, savoring a sip of bourbon, and settling back in the banquette*)
What brought me back? As best as I can make it out, this brief visit with you is rather like *Carousel* without the score. It wasn't the furniture, although I'm thrilled you're still using it. No, it was *you*. I felt I never finished raising you completely. Did I set the right examples, or was I too self-centered to have had a child entrusted to me? God, even up there we still worry about these things. We are allowed one trip back for a final wrap-up, soul cleansing, whatever you want to call it. Frankly, I wasn't even certain if you would show up today.

BROOK
Oh, Tallulah, there isn't a day that I don't think about you. You taught me everything I know about fair play, liberal politics, and the New York Giants. I'm sorry, I hate baseball, but everything else stuck. I didn't even mind being the only child in kindergarten with an "All the Way with Adlai" button, because you showed me how to fight for what I believed in.

DOLORES *gives a slight squeak of indignation, and* TALLULAH *raises the Maltese so that they are face-to-face.* TALLULAH *kisses* DOLORES's *black gumdrop of a nose and addresses the tiny bit of fluff with mock severity.*

TALLULAH

Yes, Dolores, Brook's point about the omnipresent cigarettes has been noted, and I've already apologized to you profusely for that slight conflagration you were involved in.

BROOK (*looking from* DOLORES *to* TALLULAH)
Tallulah, does Dolores actually speak to you?

TALLULAH

Of course. It's one of the greatest benefits we get up there. Dolores has a divine sense of humor. She once pointed out that since dogs have been bred for every conceivable purpose—from truffle searchers to hand muffs—it wasn't too farfetched to consider her destiny as an ashtray to a legend.

BROOK

What was that "slight" conflagration she referred to?

TALLULAH

Oh God, it was the night that the New York *Daily News* immortalized with the headline "Tallulah Is Hospitalized. Hospital Is Tallulahized."

DOLORES *watches intently, as* TALLULAH *continues.*

TALLULAH

According to Dolores—and do remember this is *her* version—she and I went to bed that night without any other company except for my lit cigarette and a few speckled sleeping pills. As she phrases it, sometimes it was a bit "sauve qui peut" for a tiny dog when I had athletic companionship in bed, and she was delighted to have me to herself. I, of course, was only wearing my cropped cashmere sweater—you know how I loathe underwear. Dolores and I were both sleeping soundly when her very efficient nose detected that the tips of her fur were smoldering. She let out a heart-piercing "YIP!" and I woke up screaming, "Oh God, Dolores is on fire!" I grabbed a pillow and began beating at the flames in the dark, somehow managing to shatter the ceramic bedside lamp, which carved an impressive slice out of my arm. Dolores says that I bellowed basso profundo like a rutting musk ox, which seems a wild exaggeration, but it was certainly loud enough to alert the staff. They raced downstairs to save me—darling Robert, who sometimes brought you home from dancing class, arrived in the nude—and then an ambulance, the police, the fire department, and the press were suddenly swarming through the house. It was profoundly disorienting, and perhaps I was a *bit* dramatic in refusing medical attention, but I only wanted to be certain Dolores was unharmed. They prised her out of my grasp and an adorable fireman pronounced her perfectly fine as the medics—absolute thugs— escorted me to the hospital under extreme duress.

TEDDY *the waiter arrives with the first course, and* TALLULAH *motions for him to grind the pepper mill until her smoked salmon is obscured under a thick layer of grit indistinguishable from an asphalt road patch.* DOLORES *sneezes over* TALLULAH'S *plate, and* TEDDY *puts an eggcup of steak tartare in front of the little dog, whispering, "Compliments of the chef, sweetheart."*

TALLULAH *finishes her appetizer, takes a long swig of bourbon, accepts another cigarette from* TEDDY, *and leans in closely as she takes* BROOK's *hand.*

TALLULAH

Brook, darling, this show is running a bit late, and you know I've always had impeccable theatrical timing. I need to find out if, God forbid, I damaged your impressionable psyche while you were under my care. Did the—how do I put this—unconventional and sometimes rather flexible gender situations you observed with me and my guests confuse you? Was it an amusing French farce with the cast flitting between various bedroom doors, or was it a Hieronymus Bosch night terror?

TEDDY *places the main course of Jumbo Shrimp Sardi in front of* BROOK *and* TALLULAH *and an artfully arranged mound of diced chicken next to* DOLORES. *The Maltese is the only one of the trio to try her food.*

BROOK

Tallulah, everything I experienced in your home was enlightening. I was so young that it was like learning a second language without even trying to. Whatever I saw, whoever was doing the flitting between bedrooms or flirting by the swimming pool—it just seemed natural to me. Remember how you told me to go naked if I wanted to and I spent the summer running around wearing nothing but my favorite woolen hat with the pompom? And the hat was only because Gayelord the parakeet loved to ride on my head. Really, the only moment of gender confusion was the evening Gayelord surprised us all by laying an egg, but we still kept referring to the bird as a "he."

TALLULAH

Well, *that's* a relief! What about the afternoon we stuck pins in the picture of Senator Joe McCarthy? I suppose it could have been construed as an inappropriate activity to indulge in with a four-year-old, but that bastard had destroyed the lives of so many of my dear friends. (*wistfully*) If my mother hadn't died at my birth, I might have had better guidelines for parenting. . . .

BROOK

I *loved* doing that with you! No other child I've known has ever been given a hands-on voodoo lesson. Besides, it was part of the continuing message you gave me to fight injustice and oppression. I know you spoke out publicly against McCarthyism and the House Un-American Activities Committee at a time when others were denouncing their friends just to save themselves, and I've done my best to follow your political path.

TEDDY *comes to the table and softly taps his watch twice.* TALLULAH *nods and kisses* TEDDY's *hand before bringing it to her cheek. He clears away* BROOK's *and* TALLULAH's *untouched plates. The spotlight on* TALLULAH *and* DOLORES *begins to dim as* TEDDY *returns and places a silver serving boat filled with Profiteroles Au Chocolat in front of* BROOK. *He blows a kiss toward the table as he backs away and exits stage left.*

BROOK (*anguished*)
Tallulah, don't go yet! There's so much I want to ask you! Are you happy up there? What do you do?

TALLULAH (*faintly*)
Do? We act. What did you think we would do, darling? Run around with harps? There's a perpetual run of *Private Lives*— Gertrude Lawrence thinks *her* performance is the definitive one, but I know that Noël prefers mine. He just won't hurt Gertie's tender feelings. I had to *die* to get a decent run in *Streetcar*, which is rather ironic, as Tennessee wrote it for me, for God's sake! Now, of course, I have to let dear Jessie Tandy play it on alternate nights.

BROOK (*as* TALLULAH *becomes increasingly transparent*)
Do you remember the final lines from your role in *Midgie Purvis*?

TALLULAH
Darling Brook, did you think I could possibly forget them? Or you?

BROOK *reaches out to touch* TALLULAH, *but there is nothing solid left for her to hold on to. Both* TALLULAH *and* DOLORES *are barely visible.*

TALLULAH (*reciting from* Midgie Purvis *as*
she fades from view and into a voice-over)
Do you see those stars up there? When I go I don't want people standing around quietly saying, "We'll pretend she's just stepped out of the room—that's the way she'd want it." Well I *don't* want it that way! When I die I want there to be

24

caterwauling and wailing. I want one of those stars to go out
and NEVER SHINE ITS LIGHT AGAIN!

The scene fades to black as a bright star appears over the spot where
TALLULAH *was sitting. A moment later, an equally bright but much*
smaller star pops up in DOLORES's *place. The only other illumination*
comes from TALLULAH's *abandoned cigarette as it burns a scorch mark*
on the Sardi's tablecloth.

CURTAIN

Brook Ashley is Tallulah Bankhead's goddaughter and spent much of her child-
hood as a participant and observer in the circus of Miss Bankhead's New York
home. Brook made her Broadway debut at the age of seven. After the perfor-
mance, Tallulah rushed to Brook's dressing room, clutched her godchild so fiercely
that the hairs on her mink coat went straight up Brook's nostrils, and proclaimed,
"Get out of your costume, darling. We're going to Sardi's to celebrate!"

— 4 —

"Do people remember my paintings?"

AL DÍAZ (FRIEND, COLLABORATOR) AND JEAN-MICHEL BASQUIAT

It was a few days after my fifty-ninth birthday. I found myself in Reykjavik, Iceland. I was traveling to Basel, Switzerland, and had missed my connecting flight due to delays. Needless to say, I was exhausted and a bit pissed off.

The next available flight was not until the following morning, so I had no option other than to spend the night. I took a room at an airport hotel. It was 11:00 p.m. when I checked in and still broad daylight outside (Iceland is far enough north to have the midnight sun). I crashed onto the welcoming bed the minute I got to my room. About two hours later I woke up, feeling famished. After a quick shower I put on the same clothes I'd been traveling in and went down to the restaurant in the hotel lobby.

The place was two-thirds empty and you could pretty much sit anywhere you wanted. I found a table by a large window and admired the view of the architecturally ambitious airport, with its acutely slanted concrete slabs and precariously leaning curtain walls. I ordered a sparkling water and looked at the menu. Not quite ten minutes had passed when I was spooked by an unlikely yet unmistakable chuckle.

I was slightly delirious from lack of proper sleep, but this was no hallucination. Jean-Michel had already slid into the chair facing me. Disbelief is too inadequate a word to describe what I felt.

We both laughed and made eye contact, an accepted form of greeting between old friends, as if picking up a briefly interrupted conversation. He wore a beret and a US Air Force–issue trench coat that had a rather odd blend of primary and springtime pastel-colored paint spattered all over the lower section. He had on a scuffed-up pair of white bucks. His loose-fitting and weathered pants were held up by a leopard-pattern fabric belt that was way too long.

"Fancy meeting you here, bro," I said jokingly. I was still trying to absorb what was transpiring.

"I must have made a wrong turn back there," he said sarcastically.

"Damn, dude, you haven't aged a bit. Must be treating you right up there, huh? Fuck, I got a shit ton of questions for you." I was feeling slightly overwhelmed.

Jean-Michel assumed a grin I recognized from long ago. An expression of both guilt and defiance. Defiance was a quality that we both held on to stubbornly, and at a very high cost.

"Well, you might as well eat some of this airport hotel food while you're here," I added.

We both checked through the menus for a minute or two. I looked up a few times—as if to confirm that this encounter was *actually occurring*. A rather pale, thin young fellow appeared at the table and asked in perfect English, "What will you gentlemen be having?" This affirmed Jean-Michel's presence, and I was finally able to begin processing the unfolding scenario. I felt a bit sad, but it was mixed with some mild anger. I had long awaited an opportunity such as this, although I never imagined it would be realized. I guess I was still pissed about the abrupt abandonment of what I always thought was a strong friendship as he became more and more famous. The feeling had never been so clear to me until this very instant.

And so I began.

"Seriously, though, when I watch those old video interviews, it seems like you really didn't want to be there."

He seemed disappointed and looked away. "People hang around because they need something you have. They'll squeeze you dry if you let them." His cynicism was evident. One thing his friends would agree on about Jean-Michel (as he became more famous) was how he developed a universal distrust for everyone.

The waiter brought us two plates of haddock with French fries, lackluster portions of a garden salad, and some small dishes with various dips. One was just plain ketchup, and the other appeared to be some sort of tartar sauce.

"*Papitas*," he said, with a goofy grin as as he held up a stubby French fry.

He pulled the plate closer to him and ate slowly, periodically studying the shape of his fry or chunk of battered fish. At one point I noticed some light-colored food flakes at the corner of his mouth, which enhanced his childlike presence. It was difficult for me not to find the charm and humor in this.

People have often asked me throughout my adult life, *What was Jean-Michel Basquiat like?* There were so many contradictions and facets to his personality, which makes that question difficult to answer in a few sentences. Sitting there with him had transported me to a time when we could share nearly anything—obscure facts, feelings, and thoughts. A comparison came to mind. "I was watching a documentary on Quincy Jones. . . . You share parallels with Q. He was very ambitious, very young, also very talented. He was a player, a crazy prolific superstar—but he's still alive. Did you know his mother was schizophrenic?"

Jean seemed to be processing this information and stared into the void for a few more seconds. Then he replied, "I always secretly liked those Frank Sinatra records. . . . Do people remember my paintings?"

"Frank Sinatra was cool. He opened it up for black acts in Vegas, so they wouldn't have to eat in the kitchen anymore. You are as famous as Quincy Jones. Probably not as famous as Sinatra. People think of you as some sort of folk hero. They often refer to you as a 'graffiti artist.'" This made both of us laugh.

I could not help but think about how, when I first met Jean-Michel, he was a sort of homebody who had a few books about MGM films and a crawl space under the stairs for a bedroom. Set against the contrast of Frank Sinatra playing faintly in the background.

Half smiling, he said, "Maybe I should have had Q as my manager. Then I would have been as famous as Sinatra."

I thought to myself, *Enough small talk.* I had real questions. For example, why did he diminish the depth of our graffiti campaign/collaboration in an interview after he'd become very famous?

"Cocaine is a helluva drug. . . ." This was obviously a loaded remark. As well as dismissive. Although we would both separately become heroin addicts, we shared cocaine quite often during the early eighties—and it strained our ability to actually have meaningful conversations.

At this point I knew that I had to pull my reins in, remembering that Jean-Michel was always prone to shutting down in the face of confrontation. Unless of course it was him doing the confronting. Softening the tone of my interrogation, I continued.

"But why now? What brings you around here, to Reykjavik? Here and now, in motherfuckin' Iceland?!"

"I was looking for my mom."

The subject of his mom had always been a conversation stopper. He was deprived of a mother early in his teenage years when she was placed in a psychiatric institution. It became apparent to those of us who were close to him that he hadn't ever recovered from this, or developed any sort of coping mechanism. Instead, he'd act as if he were stalling out when confronted with the subject. The one time I actually met and interacted with Matilde was on a Saturday afternoon in the fall of 1978. She was permitted to leave the institution where she resided for the day, as long as Jean-Michel assumed the role of guardian. She seemed heavily medicated and somewhat confused. His protectiveness and unquestionable love was clear and visible. I am quite certain this pain would forever remain deeply lodged in his soul.

"So much for the concept of heaven. You don't see anyone out there, do you?"

"Heaven? Is that some sort of Nordic mythology? After the lights go out, it takes a while before you realize it's over. Eventually it becomes evident just how alone we always have been."

A long silence followed. I stared out the big window. I thought about the times we had spent at the after-school "drop-in" center called the Door. We'd go there for free meals or to bring girlfriends who needed birth control. I remembered how we lived back then. Free of any worries, responsibilities, and commitments. Just a couple of street urchins, meandering through the universe. Wild-eyed and filled with a lust for living. Believing only in the moment.

The conversation resumed. "People loved you and still do. *You* were the one who fucked that up."

He looked away once more. "Everyone always lets you down."

I responded with my usual optimism. "Yeah, sometimes we fail each other; nobody's perfect. But we try better next time."

"Better to leave an indelible mark; you don't always get another chance," he said didactically.

"Anyway . . . you should know that you are appreciated. You changed the game. A whole generation of creative and ambitious young blacks, Latinos, Asians, Eskimos, Cossacks, those whirling-dervish mofos, misfits, queers, freaks, and what have you . . . they all feel a little more as if they might have a chance at the game. Since you came and went."

"I can't see myself as a guru or like some charismatic-leader type. People should just be inspired from within themselves. It's too much of a responsibility. I don't know. . . ." The obligatory pause and pensive moment followed. There was a brief silence, and he smirked again. "Heh-heh, whirling dervishes . . ."

We finished eating almost simultaneously. After using up the last napkins and pushing the plates aside, we sat back in silence for the remainder of the time. Then, as if like clockwork, the colorless waiter reappeared and cleared away our dishes. I ordered two coffees. Jean-Michel stood up, looked at me, and smiled a knowing smile. I reciprocated with a nod of approval. In an instant he was gone. I looked around a few times to see if he was still there. I stared at his untouched coffee cup as it gradually turned cold. I wished that I had more time to ask the questions we always think of after it's too late, but it was just that. Too late.

By the next evening, I finally arrived in Zurich and continued on to Basel. During my week at the art fairs I saw an immense amount of work, master works: new, old, obscure, iconic. These included quite a few Basquiat paintings and drawings. Viewing them made me think about how and why Jean-Michel had aspired to be included among the masters and earn a permanent place in history.

Meanwhile, I was looking vigilantly for that unforgettable palette of color I'd seen on Jean-Michel's Air Force trench coat in an unlikely Reykjavik airport restaurant.

Al Díaz's career spans five decades. At fifteen he was the recognized subway graffiti artist known as BOMB-ONE. His friendship and collaboration with schoolmate Jean-Michel Basquiat on SAMO© . . . (an avant-garde graffiti project) and the iconic hip-hop record Beat Bop are noted in contemporary art history. A sought-after expert of New York City counterculture art, he appears in publications and films and speaks at universities and museums. His mixed-media work is shown and collected internationally. In 2018, Díaz authored SAMO© . . . SINCE 1978, an illustrated history of his street art legacy.

5

"I was always so busy with Mother, the house, and the cats. I didn't have time to do anything. It took me five years just to find time to buy a girdle."

MUFFIE MEYER (FRIEND, DOCUMENTARY FILMMAKER) AND LITTLE EDIE BEALE

It is a bitter, wintry day in Montreal. I've never been to the Snowdon Deli before, but Edie suggested the place. It's near where she used to live. On the outside, the restaurant is nondescript, in a modernish, four-story building. But inside is a charming Jewish deli, serving traditional Jewish deli fare: smoked meat (what I call pastrami), latkes, coleslaw, matzoh ball soup, overstuffed sandwiches, etc. Even blindfolded, you'd know what kind of restaurant it is by the aromas, that soothing mix of freshly sliced rye bread, pickles, chicken soup, and smoked fish. It is bright without being garish, with rows of booths upholstered in tan leatherette, and Formica tables. I arrive first, install myself at a booth as far from the drafty front door as possible, and peel off several layers of winter clothing. I am early. As I wait for Edie, I order some pickles (a free bowl of pickles is not a Canadian Jewish deli tradition) and muse about *Grey Gardens* and both Edies. I am a filmmaker and was one of the directors and editors of the documentary *Grey Gardens*, which is about a mother and grown daughter, both named Edith Beale—Big Edie and Little Edie—who lived together (with innumerable cats) in a ramshackle mansion in East Hampton, a summer playground for the fabulously wealthy. The Edies were part of the American aristocracy, and it is something of a mystery as to why Little Edie, a debutante and one of the most beautiful and eligible young women of her generation, never married, choosing instead to spend most of her life living with her mother.

Little Edie and I became friends, seeing each other occasionally, writing letters, and talking on the phone from time to time. Usually it was Little Edie in high spirits, calling to announce that it was time to make another film. When I got married, Little Edie came to my wedding and, with a tiny bit of urging from me, sang a couple of love songs for me, Ron (my husband), and the assembled guests.

I help myself to a pickle. I notice that I am both excited and a little bit nervous. What are we going to talk about? One of the great unanswered questions I have about Edie is: What was the relationship Edie had with the many men she obsessed about? Some were suitors, with some she professed to love. Were these love interests fantasies or real? Had she had affairs with any of them? She could be pretty evasive when she wanted to be, and on this topic, she'd *always* wanted to be.

I'm wondering about how I can bring this up with her, when I glance toward the door and there she is. She spots me immediately and, with a big smile, makes her way to my booth. "Muffie, darling!" "Edie, it's so great to see you!". I jump up to help her off with her coat, the same mink that she wore in the *Grey Gardens* movie poster.

She is carefully made up, with delicately penciled eyebrows, a bit of eyeliner, and vividly red lipstick. She is also wearing perfume, a scent that I can't identify but can remember from the old days. She is wearing one of her fantastic Little Edie outfits: a piece of brown wool, unidentifiable clothing (is it a shirt?) wrapped around and serving as a skirt, a tan cardigan sweater over an aqua pullover, a bright blue patterned silk scarf wrapped artfully around her head and neck and pinned in place by a gold broach, stockings, and navy heels. Heads swivel; people are staring. This particular Montreal neighborhood is rather conservative, and the deli's clientele is staid and mostly elderly. Edie doesn't seem to notice and apologizes for her tardiness; she simply did not know where her red wool scarf had gone, even though she had "looked and looked and looked." I say, "Edie, you look fabulous!" And I really mean it. All things considered, she looks sensational. "I'm so happy to see you again." Even though we have not seen each other in more than twenty-five years, we do not embrace. I've always had the sense that Edie did not like to touch.

We sit, and I compliment her on her choice of restaurant, mostly as a way of easing into conversation, "What a perfect place. The food looks delicious, and it's not too noisy." Edie is her usual ebullient self. "Muffie, darling. You're Jewish. How could I go wrong? I knew you'd like the menu. Are you still dieting?" It is so wonderful to hear her slightly upper-class, slightly New York accent once again. She picks up the menu and studies it. I assure her that I am off my diet for the day. We both agree that when you are traveling, calories don't count. I say that I am indulging and having the pastrami on rye, with a side of slaw. Edie seems to be having trouble deciding, so I try to be helpful: "The chopped liver looks really good. Is pâté still one of your favorites?" "You remember! I can't believe it. Yes, liver . . . I'm mad about liver pâté."

Of course I remember. I tell Edie that I have a great memory when it comes to food and that I suspect she still remembers all the ice cream and pâté that she and Big Edie favored in the old days.

We both laugh. "Memories . . . ," Edie says softly. "I think about the past. You know, it's difficult to keep the line between the past and the present . . . awfully difficult." Edie has been gone since 2002. I cannot possibly imagine her "present."

I signal the waiter, who looks as if he's been around since biblical times. He shuffles over and takes our order, with a thick Yiddish accent. What would we like to drink? Edie seems perplexed and searches the menu, so I sing the praises of Dr. Brown's Black Cherry Soda. Problem solved. We both order it.

I tell her that I'm surprised that she moved to Montreal. "I thought you'd always move somewhere warm after you sold the house." Edie replies, "You remember, I did move to Florida for a while. I moved around a lot. I'm so glad you found me. I've always had a myriad of problems with communications. I remember that I had the phone company turn off incoming calls to our phone because I simply couldn't hear the bell! I kept saying that I absolutely *had* to get a phone that rang. I was always so busy with Mother, the house, and the cats. I didn't have time to do anything. It took me five years just to find time to buy a girdle."

I had forgotten how much I loved Edie's enthusiastic soliloquies, replete with wild transitions and whiplash non sequiturs.

Our food arrives, and there is a brief silence as we tuck into our meals with gusto. The pastrami is warm, peppery, and delicious. Edie is clearly happy with her chopped chicken liver pâté. I am relieved that she says she absolutely adores the Black Cherry Soda and wonders how she could ever have gone through life without it.

After a few bites, Edie continues with her monologue: "You have been on my mind lately, and now I know why. I had forgotten that your husband is Canadian. I lived in Montreal almost two years. I never got to England, but I did get to Canada! I speak very little French. I thought Canadians were British people. But actually they are half French–half British. I think Canada is wonderful, but I think the winter is perfectly ghastly. I like hot weather."

I interject, trying to establish a timeline for Edie's peripatetic existence after her mother died and she sold the house: "So after Montreal you eventually moved back to Florida?" That sent Edie into another of her free associations: "I am still a staunch Democrat. I will never forget that election in Florida—when was it? Well, a number of years ago. It gave everyone a nervous breakdown! Al Gore got confused with Pat Buchanan, who lives in Palm Beach County. The butterfly ballots had to be discarded because of the mix-up! George W. was a brave, resilient little guy! He made his own money in Texas. He's in the New York Social Register, you know, Andover and Yale. The Bush family came from Northern England. They were very close to the Bouvier family. I never knew the Bush boys because I was older. Al Gore and Bill Clinton are advanced thinkers. We have lost brilliant minds in government. Will Al Gore run again? I don't know. He makes movies now. When I told my mother that I was going to Tennessee to marry Al, my mother put her foot down. I never met him. It's tragic." She daintily dabs a bit of chopped liver from the corner of her mouth with a paper napkin she handles like French silk.

I seize the opportunity and—trying to be delicate—ask, "Of all the men you knew, whom would you have most liked to marry?"

Edie laughs and exclaims, her voice rising in a kind of mock frustration, "I could never choose." Adopting a more matter-of-fact tone, she continues: "Jacqueline [Kennedy Onassis, Edie's first cousin] was married on the twelfth of September 1953. I think it was a Saturday. In Newport. I had many suitors. How could I choose? And then the war came along. Some of my friends became, well, became nurses. But I had to stay home and take care of Mother. I did the best I could with extremely difficult problems. How is your little girl? Emma, is that correct?" Edie leans forward and in a near-whisper confides,

"Strict religious training is the only answer to today's ghastly world. Our time is limited."

I remind her of the many times she and her mother had argued over her relationship with a married man, a secretary of the interior under Truman and later a businessman. They'd called him Cap Krug. I ask if she was romantically involved with him. Edie does one of her classic arabesques. "I was always mad about Cap. . . . He was darling. But the movie, the movie! I was trying to remember the other day, please tell me again how *Grey Gardens* ever got started? Of course, our film was twenty years ahead of its time. Too much for people to take in, except for advanced study. Well, things have caught up. It's in the right age now: the advanced study of how to stay alive in the apocalypse."

The waiter trudges by, carrying some creamy-looking cheesecake. I have polished off my sandwich. Edie is still eating, but I propose dessert: Do you like cheesecake? Edie responds, "I'm still mad about ice cream." Of course, silly me. "Ice cream it is! With hot fudge?" Edie declares she is also "mad about hot fudge!" Being highly suggestible, I order hot fudge sundaes for both of us. When they arrive, I have no regrets about the cheesecake. A moment of silence descends as we both give our entire attention over to the thick, actually hot fudge, over velvety, rich ice cream.

Edie breaks our little ice-cream reverie to continue her musings. She begins somewhat wistfully. "I always loved weddings, just adored them." And then abruptly switches to her matter-of-fact, practical voice: "You know me, I'm an old-fashioned girl. I'm not modern. Nobody could understand. I was in New York for six years. It was complete, absolute heaven. I loved every single living minute. And then my mother needed me to come home and I never got away again. Regret is terrible. But I couldn't have done otherwise. Muffie, darling, life is nothing but choices. You have to choose; it's either/or."

Edie asks me for the time. She apologizes for not having a watch. It is just past 3:00. The restaurant has more or less emptied out. "Oh, Muffie, I have to get back." She rises to go, and suddenly I realize how much I have missed her and that I do not want her to leave. The world is so much less interesting without her.

I try one more question, to hold her with me just a bit longer. "Edie, do you still have things you wish you could do? If you could do anything you wanted, if you could be alive again, what would you do?" Edie starts to put on her fur coat and then pauses to think for a moment. "I do like the warm weather and the beaches. I'd go back to Florida. Back to the fabulous, tragic USA, of which I still consider myself a patriotic citizen." As she made her way toward the exit, she called out to me, "Thank goodness we'll never again have another president as bad as that dreadful crook Richard Nixon."

She flew through the door, ushering in a strong glacial gust of Montreal winter that blew right through me.

Muffie Meyer is one of the filmmakers of the documentary Grey Gardens *(along with the Maysles brothers, Ellen Hovde, and Susan Froemke), for which she is credited as Director and Editor. In addition, she has directed and/or produced more than thirty major documentaries and series. Her films have won Emmys, a Peabody, and many other awards. She is married to Ronald Blumer, and they have a daughter, Emma.*

6

"Don't shit me just to spare my feelings, Daniel. I'm dead."

DANIEL BELLOW (SON) AND SAUL BELLOW

I was walking my dogs in the tame little woods at the top of Castle Hill like I do every day here in the middle of life's journey. It was November, and the dusk was coming down fast. I came to a fork in the trail, and nothing looked familiar. Ahead, I thought I saw the shadow of a giant wolf on the trail, an inky patch in the darkness. A shiver ran all over me, and my dogs bolted for home. I was about to go after them when I saw the old man hastening toward me through the trees.

"Mercy," I said, for I was sore afraid.

"It is another path that you must take," he said, "if you would leave this savage wilderness."

I would have known that voice anywhere. "Pop?"

"Hello, kid." He gave me that gap-toothed grin. He was dressed for a walk in the country with his mosquito shirt and his old train engineer's cap and red bandanna and his favorite walking stick I picked for him off a beaver dam in the Adirondacks. I threw my arms around his neck. He felt solid enough.

"What are you doing here? You're supposed to be dead. Am I dead? I'm wearing shoes. . . ."

In reply, he grabbed my ass and squeezed it hard until I hollered, like he used to do when I was little. There was no way I could have slept through that, and they say the dead lack sensation, but it still felt like a dream, one I had to keep a lid on before it got out of control.

"I have to find my dogs," I said, trying to cling to what I knew was real.

"They ran off home. Sensible creatures. You always had nice dogs."

"What about your dog?" I pointed up the hill toward the shadow.

"Oh, she's not mine. She comes from Hell, was sent above by Envy."

"Oh. I read about her in a book. You're not going to let her bite me?"

"I think and judge it best for you to follow me."

"How come you're speaking in iambic pentameter?"

"I've got Virgil's old job. Not too shabby, eh?"

"Have you come to take me through the seven circles of Hell?"

"I'm here to take you out to lunch."

"It's dinnertime."

"You took a writing assignment, lunch with your dead famous father."

"I did. I was procrastinating."

"So I'm a little late. Are you coming with me, or what?"

Obviously, I had to go. He took me by the hand, and like a little boy I followed, down the trail in the dark, but instead of the railroad tracks at the bottom of the hill we came out on the east side of Amsterdam Avenue at Eighty-Sixth Street.

To judge by the state of the buildings, the style of the taxis, the rich bouquet of garbage, the exhaust, and the disco beat from an upstairs window, I'd say it was about 1979. Pop was suddenly wearing that double-breasted suit with the psychedelic lining he used to like, and a loud tie. I was still in jeans and a T-shirt and my black leather jacket, so I felt comfortable. We walked into Barney Greengrass.

The waiter, tall and stooped, bald with a greasy comb-over and a nose like a toucan, pointed us to a table in the corner. In the court of the Sturgeon King, it could have been anywhere between 1958 and last week, the deli case with its piles of smoked fish, the mysterious wallpaper with scenes of old New Orleans.

"Pop, where are we?" I asked in a low voice, leaning into his ear.

"Barney Greengrass. Don't you recognize it?"

"Yeah, but how come it's 1979 outside?"

"We're in Hell. Take a good look at the waiter."

The waiter came. "We've got some specials today." He pointed at the spots on the tablecloth. "We've got brisket, and tzimmes, and a stuffed pepper."

"I've heard this joke but I've never been in it before," I said. They both ignored me.

"Have the salami sandwich," Pop said. "They get the good stuff. Best's Kosher from Chicago. Bring us some of those Strub's pickles."

"I'll have a Cel-Ray, please," I said. "With ice." It was a special occasion.

The waiter went away. "Holy shit, it's Philip Roth."

"Yes, this is his job," Pop answered.

"Someone's got a wicked sense of humor."

"He's also married to your mother. She got promoted to Fury last year."

"So if I went home, three blocks away . . ."

"You'd find Philip Roth living with your mother. His fault, the schmuck."

"Oh. Okay."

"There are some things no boy should have to see."

A change of subject seemed in order. "How'd you get this job, leading middle-aged guys through Hell?"

"My entire life was an audition for this job."

"What's Virgil doing?"

"He went back to try his luck again; he made some good films in Japan. Balzac had the job for a while. They need an unbeliever who can tell a story."

"You can come back?"

"Once every thousand times around the sun."

"Do you have a wife, too?"

"Mary McCarthy. Edmund Wilson's ex. You never met her."

"Yeah, but I read her. That famous line about Lillian Hellman— 'Every word she writes is a lie, including "and" and "the."'"

"On *The Dick Cavett Show*. It got her sued."

"She seems like she could give you a run for your money."

"She's got a mouth on her. But she's a hot lay."

"This is not your usual taste in ladies, Pop."

"Hell is here to teach you what you failed to learn in life."

"Like relations with women?"

"I came up short, as I am told and told again. Also being sweet to children."

"You could be sweet."

"Don't shit me just to spare my feelings, Daniel. I'm dead."

"Okay. You were an awful, scary monster, but you could be sweet sometimes."

"When you arrive, you have to watch your whole life on film. Every painful scene, with nothing you can do to make it any better. The movie's made, and now it's in the theaters. Above the screen they write: 'Abandon hope all ye who enter here.' That's when you know you're dead for real."

"Your whole life? Like, every time you take a leak?"

"Just the highlights, but still it takes five years, eight hours a night. You're never quite the same."

"So not quite as bad as being stuck in a hot room with bad décor and two women you can't screw?"

"Oh, worse than that. Look at Philip."

"He always looked like that."

"I'm telling you so you know," he snapped. "Maybe your last reel won't be as hard to take as mine."

The pickles came, in a stainless-steel container on a plate. They were deliciously salty, neither too crisp nor too soft.

"So what do you do all day?"

"Nothing ever happens here in Hell. One day is pretty much the same as the next. The only source of interest is what happens in the world, where things can still be fixed. Everything we see, there's nothing we can do or say about it. I would have warned you not to trust that crooked business partner of yours, and that other putz who started the magazine just so he could shtup his friends' wives in hotel rooms. And you remember when I got into your dream and told you not to be afraid to get divorced."

"Adam laughed when I told him. He said, 'Pop was never afraid to get divorced.'"

Pop chuckled, cocked his head to one side, and smiled an evil smile that somehow included us both.

"Sometimes when we're together and saying bad things it seems like you're there with us."

"I am, but that's you boys talking, make no mistake."

"So you can't act or communicate with us?"

"No. Mostly all I can do is watch helplessly. The wall is very thin, and you can only see through it from this side. Sometimes, when I want a closer view, I come as a dragonfly or a bluebottle."

"So when we went to marriage counseling with the Magic Mama—"

"The time you nearly got sideswiped by that crazy broad who dropped her brassiere straps for you?"

"And the Mama made me do a dance with my wife and said, 'Turn around and look over your left shoulder for your father and your grandfather. . . .'"

"And give us back the burden of Russian Jewish history." He began to giggle.

"Please don't tell me you were both there," I said.

Pop lost it, throwing back his head and roaring like a jackass. "We might have played along," he said, "if we hadn't been laughing so hard." He wiped his eye. "She said, 'Those poor men, they had to leave Russia, everything they knew, and come to a strange land. Oy! Oy!'" He was in stitches and couldn't go on.

"I tried to tell her, no one in my family has ever expressed the slightest regret at having to leave Russia."

"Your grandfather practically had to be carted out." Pop put on the old country accent: "What is this mishegas? Why is he standing still for it?"

"How humiliating! How am I going to make love to my lady with you old bastards watching me?"

"Oh, we leave you be for that. I was never one for dirty pictures. She's a pretty lady, your lady. The last one, too, that little Italian girl, she was sweet. You do all right, kid."

"Shiksas, give me shiksas every time."

"Mine's always entertaining, if not always kind."

I wanted to hear more about married life with Mary McCarthy, but the waiter came and served us our plates from a great height, his eyes averted. The salami was the perfection of salami, just a little dry, wrinkled on the outside. The rye bread was still warm, the mustard Ba-Tampte. I was transported back to his kitchen table on the South Side.

"Food's pretty good here, don't you think?"

"Mmmm. I would have thought bread and water, or pig swill."

"This is the Elysium, and the heroes need their lower chakras taken care of. Down below, it's not so nice."

"So there are hot sulfur baths full of naked investment bankers and politicians, like in the *New Yorker* cartoons? And demons making a trumpet of their ass? Can we go?"

"You want schadenfreude? You should learn to resist it; it's not good for you."

I wasn't so sure about that, but there was no point in persisting. "So if you're Virgil, you get to go wherever you want. What's Heaven like?"

"Just as you'd imagine: nice but dull, like a college town. I go to see my mother. Remember Father Kim?"

"Yeah. Nice guy. But dull. And not too bright."

"He has a poker game on Thursday nights. I used to go, but frankly it's not much of a challenge. It's more fun down here with Delmore Schwartz and Isaac Rosenfeld."

"You guys patch everything up here in the afterlife? They forgive you for the pictures you drew of them in books?"

"Oh sure. They were already dead; they didn't care. That was all a big joke, really."

"Mom didn't think it was so funny."

"Your mother," he said, and then thought better of it. "Allan Bloom rides a motorcycle."

"Has he established the new Bloomusalem?"

"Wears black leather, shaved his head, grew a little flavor-saver on his lower lip. Drives the boys crazy."

"So a fully actualized Allan Bloom."

"He wants to be the Ghost Rider when Johnny Storm retires; he's up your way every weekend, driving fast on twisty roads."

"If you can't be Michael Jordan . . ."

"I wanted to be Michael Jordan. Only other person I ever wanted to be."

"On a page, you could jam. Can I meet my grandfather? Is he really so terrifying? What's he do when he's not hanging out with you making fun of me?"

"Devil's plumber. They call him when the toilets back up. He was always good at making the best of a bad job."

"People take a shit, here in Hell?"

"They use a lot of it downstairs."

"So, Pop, to what do I owe the honor of this lunch here on the edge of the Pit? I mean, it's really great to see you, but I've never had a conversation with you when you didn't have a clear purpose. So what is it?"

"I've always tried to help you. No, really, I have. But I didn't know how. That's one thing I learned from watching the movie of my life. I'd try to wise you up, and you couldn't hear it, coming from me."

"I have made mistakes and later thought, 'Why didn't I listen to my old man when he tried to tell me?'"

"So you see it, too. Good. It's my fault, and I'm sorry. I want to tell you how proud I am you've made a go of your pottery. It really is beautiful, and look at you in all those catalogs and stores. I see how happy you are when you're making things."

"When I was eighteen, you said, 'At least you'll always have a pot to piss in,' and reminded me that Potters' Field is where they bury you when you die broke."

"I knew you'd remember. I like a joke too much sometimes, and I feel bad. If you'd gone to art school, you'd have an easy professor's job. You wouldn't have to scrape to pay the bills the way you do."

"Yes, but if I'd gotten it on a silver platter without the key step of defying you, maybe I wouldn't have wanted it so much."

"You're cutting me more slack than I deserve again. Tell me, do I have your attention? Have I persuaded you I have only your best interest at heart?"

"Oh yeah."

"I'll give it to you straight: you have unfulfilled ambitions to be a writer, and you are not getting any younger."

He waited. Slowly I raised my hand, like a basketball player who has given a foul. He held me in his eye.

"I was so pleased when you accepted this assignment, and when you kept avoiding it and finding other things to do, I got a busman's holiday so I could help you."

"I certainly am all set for material."

"All those years covering the statehouse and writing apple pie features, you've got muscles, kid. What you need is a deadline. Go home and sit down at your keys and don't get up until you're done. Write it while it's hot. You know how."

"Yes, sir."

"And this is the easy one. When you're done, you'd better write that other thing you've been meaning to write."

"Yes."

"Don't yes me!" and suddenly he was my terrifying male parent, Moses down from Sinai discovering the Israelites in idolatry. "We're in Hell! It cost me a lot of favors to get you down here! Don't do it for me! Do it for you! Don't you see?" His voice rose to that pitch and then cracked. "When you're dead, it's too late!"

I put my hand on top of his. I have his hands. "Yes, Pop. For me."

"All right, let's get out of here. Philip! Put this on my tab."

Daniel Bellow, the youngest son of the novelist Saul Bellow, was born in Chicago in 1964 and educated in the finest schools. He worked as a newspaper reporter and editor in New York, Massachusetts, and Vermont, and when that petered out, he went back to his original passion, making porcelain pottery. His studio is in Great Barrington, Massachusetts, where he also teaches high school ceramics, writes an occasional column for the Berkshire Eagle, *and raises large dogs. He has two children, Stella and Benjamin.*

7

"It's in the nature of stars to glow warmer as they grow older."
—Philosopher/scientist James Lovelock, ninety-nine years old,
speaking of the sun, on BBC Radio Four, January 1, 2019

CARINTHIA WEST (FRIEND) AND DAVID BOWIE

"Hey, Rinthy, I'm over here." David waves from a corner table laid for two, on the patio of a small trattoria in Portofino, right at the end of the quay. He is sitting alone, waiting for me. He looks much as I'd imagined him, in black slacks, a white shirt, with a pale blue sweater slung insouciantly over his shoulders. His face seems older, thinner, and more elegant somehow, but not as ancient as the Methuselah character he once played in *The Hunger*, a film with Catherine Deneuve. I had visited him on the London set when he played the first of several practical jokes on me, by pretending to be his own father. "David asked me to look after you," wheezed the virtually bald old man. His makeup was so unbelievably convincing that I shook his gnarled hand until I realized that the rest of the cast and crew were cracking up with laughter. I'd been privileged to be one of a handful of female friends acquired, not through work, show business, or romance but because of my friendship with his longtime personal assistant and closest friend, Corinne (aka Coco). Coco and I had shared some hilarious travel adventures together as well as an apartment in LA, and a friend of Coco's was almost always automatically a friend of David's and trusted by his inner circle. "Rinthy" was David's pet nickname for me. He liked to personalize his friendships by a name no one else would know but him. I always figured it was part of the private uniqueness that was David. Not the public *Man Who Fell to Earth* David, or the *Ziggy Stardust* David, or the *Thin White Duke* David; just David.

I would never dare to call him Dave, though, so when a mysterious postcard summoned me here, to this tiny part of Portofino's harbor, all it said, in David's spidery hand, was "Rinthy—see you at the Italian café for unfinished business. Dave," with a fast-approaching date and time, I was nonplussed but thrilled at the thought of seeing him again. Previously, always respectful of his privacy unless summoned to a concert, film set, or holiday, this time I thought, "I will go to him." The front of the postcard was a faded pastel of a boat, drawn by hand and surrounded by sea. David had owned a beautiful yacht, the *Deneb Star*. Once, it was around 1981, I was one of several friends he invited to spend a week cruising down the Amalfi Coast, taking in small seaside towns and secluded beaches, with a dozen crew to attend to our every need. We moored at bustling Italian ports like Portofino, sampling the small tourist shops and designer boutiques that lined the quay, or simply sunned and swam, but like myself, David always got antsy just sitting on his yacht, and he would find every excuse to go on shore—a packet of Marlboros, a *Herald Tribune,* or to make a phone call from the local post office—for we were sailing in a time long before mobile telephones and WiFi and emails and satellites, still sending postcards from each port we visited.

The "Italian café" for today's lunch was shorthand for the restaurant we all liked best, as none of us ever remembered its real name. I knew exactly where to go. How like David to have chosen a place where he had once felt so carefree. The café itself was a bright splash of white, brilliant light, exotic potted plants, colorful tiles on the floor that sometimes turned intimate conversations into virtual shouting matches, so loud was the hubbub of background noise. But the crisp white tablecloths were an instant giveaway: this café had a distinctly chic air that set it high above the other cafés along the quay.

Patting the seat beside him, David thanks me for coming. I have given up cigarettes, so I am nervous about seeing him after all this time, but I notice that he is now smoking an e-cigarette. He seems calm, occasionally pushing away a strand of reddish hair peeping through gray with his free hand. Slowly, I become adjusted to this new version of David. Zoning in between time frames and trips, highs and lows, triumphs and disasters, loves and hates, he free dives into memories and friends we share, what he calls the "unfinished business" we never had time for on the boat. He wants to know what I have been working on and about certain friends (a polite curiosity always was a great part of David's charm).

There is a waiter whom I vaguely remember, who brings us each a menu and a glass of Orvieto, gesticulating that the wine is "on the house," and curiously, he does not speak or seem surprised to be serving us. We order mountainous plates of Caprese salads to toy with, with mozzarella that would melt in our mouths. A buzz of muted conversation has gone up from the ghostly presence of the *passeggeri* crowd I perceive to be just outside the restaurant, and I can tell they are aware that "Boweee" is inside, but with a nonchalance long born of iconic stardom, he appears not to notice. His blue eye is turned to me intensely while the brown one seems to dance in dreamlike delight. They change color all the time, the result of a punch from his best friend in a teenage brawl over a girl. He'd been told he was going to lose his sight, but with true David aplomb, he always credited his friend, now long forgiven, as giving him a kind of "mystique." Sometimes one eye looks to be an azure blue, the other a dark green or brown demonic dot, and I notice that when we are talking in spiritual terms, the green/blue iris takes on a shimmering light, and when we are being practical, like ordering from the menu, then the darker eye becomes predominant. There is no doubt that this David still has chameleon eyes.

Right now, he is in an expansive mood. Just to be here—in the sun, by the sea, with one friend to talk to—seems to be enough for him. "Remember that trip to Cornwall?" he questions. "You had that weird boyfriend, what was his name? Earl somebody or other? He had a Rembrandt on the wall in his dining room, but he wouldn't pay for that pub lunch, and he wanted me to play some festival he was organizing, but when I found out he had a bull's head buried in the middle of his maze, I backed out? Too weird, even for me!"

"Yes," I say, reminding him of the name. "My mother wanted me to marry him, not for snobbish reasons, but because she had once dated his father! That was a lucky escape!" "You've had a few," says David, in an avuncular manner, affectionately patting me on the arm, "God, the English upper classes, they are so eccentric! I could have told you he wasn't a safe bet for any girl—and that's me talking!" We laugh a lot at this as we joyfully hack away at our salads, naturally segueing into a discussion about another mutual friend, a performer whom David was very close to. He has a theory about their friendship. "He sees everything through the eyes of physicality, dance, movement, sensuality, and that's what makes him such a brilliant entertainer, but I think my style is a more cerebral one, perhaps because I studied mime. I love women, as you know, and men, too, sometimes, more as brothers in arms. But I never had the desire to own and conquer, and I believe it made me a better friend and companion to women." I can't dispute this theory, as David was only ever the most sensitive of friends to me. He was, by nature, a generous, thoughtful soul. We go on to discuss a mutual female friend as our waiter refills our glasses. She is involved in an abusive relationship, and we both agree it isn't likely to end well. "The problem I see so often with women," David observes, "is that they never believe a man when he tells them who he is. If you listen closely, men will always tell you their true natures. The problem lies with women never believing them. They think they can change the man they're deeply in love with. It's always a delusion."

I store away this nugget of gold for future use, and sensing that at any moment David might vanish as swiftly as he came, I change the subject and remind him of the *Hunger* incident. David laughs. "Yeah, I used to love to play jokes like that," he says. "You could really catch people unawares. I loved dressing up as a waiter or a chauffeur and watching how rude people could be to someone they perceived as just there to serve them. Then when they found out it was me, they became all smiles and ingratiation. Sad, really."

We discuss how precious were the times on *Deneb Star* and traveling on it. In between tours and making albums or recording, like other stars of the time, it was the only real relaxation—even in those days of no social media . . . yet here we are reflecting in our dream world—no bodyguards or anxious personal assistants. "Did you like my postcard?" David says jauntily. "I drew it of *Deneb* from this very spot just outside. I thought you'd enjoy that. Or at least puzzle out who sent it from the beyond. One of my little jokes."

We move on to the subject of art and the precious place that owning and collecting paintings once took in his life: David Bomberg,

Wilhelmina Barns-Graham, Frank Auerbach, German Expressionists, to name a few. I reminded him of a visit the two of us once took with Coco to the studio of Francesco Clemente in New York, and of the day he came with his art dealer to meet the painter Richard Kidd at my family home in Warwickshire. Being an excellent painter himself, it was apparent from both visits how trained and exceptional David's eye was by the way he looked at other artists. "Yes, that day was a lot of fun, but I am glad that I asked my estate to sell most of my collection at Sotheby's and let go. Everything about life is in the letting go eventually." I was surprised by this thought. David never seemed the faintest bit mortal, but then neither did many of us from the sixties and seventies. Our lives had been so haphazard, so idealistic, compared to the "sensible" generations that followed. As if reading my mind, he says, "It's always been easy for me to make money. I think it's because I never pursued it. It's in the pursuing that people make mistakes—that desperate need to consume and collect . . . better to let go. . . . But letting go of *everything* is not so easy. I still miss my family very much."

As if on cue, David leans forward and softly sings a few lines in my ear: "Look up here, I'm in heaven, I've got scars that can't be seen, I've got drama that can't be stolen. Everybody knows me now." And as I hear the sound of his chair scraping back, I feel so grateful to have had these minutes of private time to hear his lyrics straight from his lips, his insights, and, above all, to have his trust. "By the way, I meant to tell you earlier, this place we called the Italian café is called La Dolce Vita." He grins broadly and winks at me with his left eye, the one that never quite closes, and puts a finger to his lips. As I watch him gradually fade, until nothing more is left of him, I reflect that, sadly, no one will ever again call me "Rinthy."

But his secrets are safe with me.

Carinthia West is an English photographer and journalist whose writing cred-its include Marie Claire, Harper's *and* Queen, Harper's Bazaar, Tatler, *the* LA Weekly, *the* Independent, *the* Telegraph, *and* Saga *and* US *magazines, covering travel, lifestyle, humor, and (her least favorite subject!) the celebrity interview. As a photographer, she has grown up in the presence of, and been friends with, some of the twentieth century's greatest names from music, film, and society. Anjelica Huston, Mick Jagger, George Harrison, Ronnie Wood, Robin Williams, Paul Getty Jr., Neil Young, Helen Mirren, David Bowie, Paul Simon, Carly Simon, James Taylor, and King Hussein and Queen Noor of Jordan are just a few of those she photographed at casual, private, intimate, and poignant moments in their lives.*

8

"Bill and I are eating our lunch on the new roof.
We're having a naked lunch."

AVIVA LAYTON (ALMOST FRIEND)
AND WILLIAM BURROUGHS

It was in the late fifties when I arrived in Paris from Montreal to be met by the man I was living with, later to become my husband, the Canadian poet Irving Layton. Irving, who was the recipient of a Canada Council for the Arts poetry grant, which enabled us both to travel, greeted me at the airport with an exuberant poem "The Day Aviva Came to Paris" and the news that we were going straight from the airport to have lunch with William Burroughs (whom we'd never met), with a stopover at Shakespeare and Co. I thought I'd died and gone to writers' heaven. Jet lag? Shower? Breakfast? Who cared? I had arrived in Paris not as a mere tourist but as a privileged insider.

When we arrived at the legendary bookstore, the owner, George Whitman, invited us upstairs, which I'd heard was a rare privilege. He ushered us up the rickety wooden ladder to the famous upper room, where he told us to make ourselves at home among the low divans and stacks of books, but only after Irving had checked that his books were prominently displayed (they weren't) in the downstairs store. There was a window at the end of the room, which looked over a corrugated plastic roof several feet below us.

We lolled on the divans like pashas, while George brought us coffee on a brass tray and sat down to fill us in on our lunch. It turned out that Burroughs was withdrawing from a heavy heroin habit and was being looked after by his friends, among them Allen Ginsberg and Peter Orlovsky, all of whom were living in a nearby ratbag hotel on rue Git-le-Coeur. We were slated to take over from them at Burroughs's bedside for two hours, and Allen was going to leave us our lunch of baguettes and cheese, which we'd eat while making sure that Burroughs didn't make a bolt for it. After our shift had finished, we'd meet Allen at La Coupole, sip absinthe, and generally behave like the literary celebrities we so clearly were.

A few minutes after George left, Irving started grimacing and grabbing his stomach. "I think I need to use the toilet," he said with a moan. He started swaying around the room like a drunken sailor. "Aviva, I need a toilet. Where is it?" he shouted, his voice strained and urgent. I looked around the room. No toilet. It was obviously downstairs, but Irving was in no shape to negotiate the narrow ladder. By now he'd turned a pale shade of green and was sweating profusely.

It was clear he couldn't wait a second longer, so he did the only possible thing he could do, which was to hurl himself out the window. First I heard the sickening thud of his body landing on the corrugated roof, followed by an ominously loud cracking sound. Rushing to the window, I saw that the weight of Irving's plunge had created a ragged hole through which his bottom half had fallen in mid-shit, while his upper half was trapped above. He was wedged tight. There were horrified shrieks from below, where, it turned out, the owners of a chic gallery had been preparing for a vernissage that evening.

Above their shrieks came the sound of George thundering up the ladder. "You filthy pig!" he shouted at the famous Canadian poet whom he'd welcomed so warmly only a short time ago. His pale, thin, rather aristocratic face was suffused—understandably—with rage and disgust.

My memory of the next few minutes has, mercifully, been erased, but I have vague images of venturing out onto the cracked roof to help Irving clamber out and clean himself up as best he could. What

I do remember with great clarity, though, is Irving and me trudging through the industrial wasteland of some Parisian suburb, dragging a huge sheet of newly bought corrugated plastic through dreary streets, unable to fit it into either a taxi or a bus and delivering it to the still-enraged George. Gone was the William Burroughs lunch! Gone was the warm welcome at Shakespeare and Co.! Gone was La Coupole! Gone was the best part of our holiday budget! We left Paris shortly afterward for Rome, where we had to stay in a rat-and-cockroach-infested hostel because it was all we could afford.

All of this happened well over fifty years ago, when we were young and beautiful. Irving died at the age of ninety-two, George Whitman at ninety-eight, and William Burroughs at eighty-three. I'm still here, which is why at the ripe old age of eighty-five, I've decided to finally give myself the gift of having the lunch with William Burroughs I so ignominiously missed out on. Having once said that an imaginary world is the one in which he would like to live, I don't think he'd mind, so this is our lunch. . . .

It's a gentle spring day in Paris, and Bill and I are eating our lunch on the new roof. We're having a naked lunch. Never mind the metaphorical meaning of the title of the book he'll write a year later—we're literally buck naked, both our bodies sun-kissed and silky and indescribably perfect. The plastic roof has transformed itself into a glass one, which sparkles in the soft Parisian sunshine. Through the glass we can see the gallery below, its proprietors lifting delicate flutes of champagne to toast us. Irving is sitting by the window, quietly writing another love poem to me; Allen and Peter are noisily making love on one of the divans in the corner while Bill and I are blissfully sipping the nectar of the gods. We drank, we gabbed, we ate, we laughed, all as if we were old friends newly reunited.

And that is my naked lunch with William Burroughs. At last, and well worth waiting for.

Aviva Layton has taught literature in universities, colleges, and arts schools and has reviewed books for newspapers, journals, and radio in both the United States and Canada. She is the author of a novel, Nobody's Daughter, *and several children's books and has had essays published in four previous anthologies. She currently lives in LA, where she works as a literary editor.*

9

"The world might end. I don't know. I went to heaven, not to Delphi."

BENJAMIN CHEEVER (SON)
AND JOHN CHEEVER

The promise of barbecued spare ribs routed any misgivings I might have had about seeing my father again, though I hadn't met with him—outside of dreams—since he went and died on me back in the spring of 1982.

I was surprised and pleased by the eagerness with which he accepted my invitation to lunch at the China Bowl, at its original location, 152-4 West Forty-Fourth Street. This social victory was given considerable heft by the theory that the approval of a parent is all a child needs to make her-or-his entire life a triumph. Though the theory is patently false, it's wildly defended, and even when said child is fully grown and said parent, a feast for worms.

Besides which it's fun to socialize with the dead because they know so little about what's happened since they left.

There's no WiFi in the afterlife, no newspapers or magazines. It's a house rule St. Peter implemented after so many worthies had had their heavenly bliss spoiled by a mixed obituary or—what's much worse—a missing obituary.

If nothing else, heaven is supposed to be just. Which is not how it looked when Judas got thirty pieces of silver and front-page notices around the world.

Iscariot made matters worse, of course, by having his write-up laminated and taking it with him everywhere. "There's no such thing as bad publicity," he said.

St. Peter finally had to deputize Samson to beat the shit out of Judas and put the clipping in the recycling.

Damming the current of current events turned out to be a truly heavenly policy. It also swelled the ranks of those interested in the *One Last Lunch* program. The dead were ignorant and therefore curious, while the quick were in a position to amuse their forefathers and foremothers with floods of trivia. Also, some artifacts were permitted. I heard about one boob who didn't know Rome, Italy, from Rome, Ohio, but he still astounded Caesar with his iPhone 7. Julius couldn't believe that it was water resistant.

The trouble with meeting Daddy in 2018 was that I was certain to confirm his most serious complaint about his self-pitying oldest son. "So, you're happy?" he liked to ask, whenever we came together. "I suppose the old world is running like a clock?" Daddy took my sorrow personally, as if it were a blot on his own copybook.

And in 2018, national politics were making it hard to put on a happy face. Plus, I had a lot of friends who wanted to know what my father might have thought about rumors of the coming Rapture.

I could imagine him rolling his eyes.

I miss Daddy, but if it hadn't been for the China Bowl, I might have cancelled. That was another great feature of the *One Last Lunch* program, since you could eat with people who were no more, you could also meet them at eateries that were also gone.

My father was as fickle about his restaurants as he was about his lovers, but my father was faithful to the China Bowl for decades. He liked the acres of white tablecloth, the heavy napkins. He claimed the mirror in the bathroom made him look taller and that he had once been shown to his table by Madame Chiang Kai-shek. This I always doubted, although the empress of China did live in Manhattan until she was 105. There was no arguing with his assertion that the martinis were cold and the mustard was hot.

Toward the end of his life, John Cheever used to lunch at the Four Seasons, though this seemed ridiculous even to himself. "You pay fifty dollars for a piece of lettuce," he would say. I'm guessing that would be $125 in today's money.

Walking west on Forty-Fourth Street, I could see the clothes people around me had on were changing in style, while the cars took on a comforting vintage look, the clangor of horns faded, and the engines had a full-throated roar. I knew the magic was working for sure when I picked out the bowl-shaped sign on the roof. On the street, I saw a brown-haired, smallish gent, in one of those suits from Brooks Brothers that were ingeniously designed to fit no man.

I'm always glad to see the people I love, because I have trouble reconstructing faces. I can summon the way they feel and smell. I can re-create the ring of a voice, but the facial features are a blur. My father could beam at you with such force that it was a surprise, and he was beaming now as he approached me on the sidewalk. I held the restaurant door for him, but he insisted I go in first. He'd lived at a time during which those with the greatest authority always went through a door last. When he went to Russia, he learned that it was safe for males to embrace, so thereafter, we embraced, though awkwardly.

When we got to our table, it wasn't clear who should sit first, so we both stood ashamed behind our chairs. Finally, and at the same moment, we both gave up and sat down.

"We used to eat here when we came to town to buy you toys," he said.

"If that's how you remember it," I said, not wanting to tumble immediately into a familiar squabble.

"I distinctly recall leaving a racing-car set with the hat check girl, because it was gigantic, almost as big as you were then and far too large to hide under the table. We bought the last one in the store, and they had to take it out of the window."

"You bought me toys," I allowed, "but the ostensible purpose of the trip was Christmas shopping, which we did for the entire family. Especially for Mummy."

The arrival of a waiter reminded my father of those chilled martinis, and we both ordered one. "You remember, of course, that I was sober for the last five years," he said. "But now it doesn't matter."

"Amazing," I said.

"You did like to buy things out of the window," I said. "There was a store in Orbetello, near Rome, that had a dollhouse full of pet mice set up in the window, and you bought it on the spot."

The drinks came, and he sipped carefully from the lip of his glass.

"That's right," he said. "I must have offered what seemed like a lot of money, and the man who owned the shop had to shake the thing violently to get the last female mouse out. 'La donna,' he explained."

My father was never one of those tiresome alphas who couldn't be teased, but when he took another pull on his drink, I could smell the tobacco smoke that had for decades accompanied the astringent taste of gin. He settled in his chair with a confidence since lost to literate American males.

"The state of the nation?" he asked, and I reached wildly for my own martini. I drank deeply, ate all three olives, and put the toothpick in the saucer for my teacup.

"If only you'd wanted to meet me for lunch during the Obama era," I said.

Of course, he'd think I invented the Trump presidency as an excuse to feel sorry for myself. I considered lying.

I had lied to him, when I banged up the Studebaker. That falsehood was never discovered since his station wagon had had so many previous collisions that not even his guilt-ridden son could tell in the cold light of morning which one had occurred the night before. I don't remember much at all about that night, except that I was with a girl, a pretty girl, who had blue jeans with a busted zipper.

She couldn't close her pants, which turned out not to be a good sign, although we liked each other as friends and all.

That next morning, I told him about the zipper, but not about the ding on his car. Now I was tempted to lie again.

"Let's order first," I said, since the waiter was back at our table, this time with a pad and pen.

"Well, that much is easy," he said. "If we get the family dinner for two, we can have wonton soup, egg rolls, the barbecued spare ribs, and pay extra for the lobster Cantonese."

Both the waiter and I nodded in mute agreement.

"So, state of the nation?" he asked again.

"Donald Trump gets into an elevator and a gorgeous model gets in with him?" I said. "Have you heard it?"

"If I heard the joke, I've forgotten," he said.

"When the elevator doors close, she puts his hand on her left breast. 'We've got a minute,' she tells the Donald. 'Can I please, please give you a blow job?'"

Just then, the soup and egg rolls arrived, and my father reached out, touched one of the egg rolls. "Ouch! Hot!" he said, and pulled his hand away.

"Wrap it in a napkin," I said, but he'd already speared the offending appetizer with a fork, moved it to his plate, and was cutting off a piece.

"Back to the joke," I said. "So, the model asks Trump what he's waiting for. 'I'm trying to figure out what's in it for me,' he said."

This got a smile, but not a laugh. "I don't know why you're talking about Donald Trump. I wasn't all that interested in him when I was alive. I'm going to the restroom," Daddy told me, "and if you encounter the waiter, order another martini for me."

I nodded and was delighted to see that when he stood and walked, he wasn't favoring his right leg, the one that had been riddled with cancer.

"I don't know what Donald Trump has to do with anything," he said, when he got back. "I *am* curious though about the state of the republic."

"Let's start in with idle chatter," I said. "Why does an all-powerful God allow suffering?"

"There are dozens of excellent books on the subject, most of which—I daresay—you haven't bothered to read," he said. "I don't want to spend our only lunch together in twenty-five years mulling over the problem of pain," he added, cutting into the noodle in his soup with the side of a large, stainless-steel spoon. Then he brought the steaming wonton to his mouth, blew across the surface, and swallowed.

I held my peace.

"You're not going to ask me for money again," he said, and took a pull on his martini.

Again, I said nothing.

"There's no cash in heaven."

"Yeah," I said. "I heard. You can't take it with you."

"Well, if you're not broke, why did you arrange this lunch?" he asked. "Don't tell me it's for that book that Heller girl is putting together."

"Erica's her name," I said, "and that's certainly the genesis of this lunch, but that's not why I set it up."

"Okay," he said, and used a knife to separate out one of the barbecued spare ribs. This he dipped in hot mustard and took a bite. His eyes filled with tears. He took three long pulls on his water glass, then another slug of gin.

"Are the ribs as good as they used to be?" I asked.

Daddy nodded, took another bite, put down the rib, and wiped his lips with an impossibly thick white napkin. "Heavenly," he said.

"What's it like in heaven?" I asked.

"What leads you to conclude that I'm in heaven?" he asked.

"I just assumed," I said. "You wrote like an angel. No burn scars."

"Do you honestly suppose that people coming up from hell all look charred, as if they'd been hamburgers taken off the grill too late?" he asked. "And do I catch disappointment in your voice? Were you picturing your poor old father dancing around on a bed of charcoal briquettes, while horse-faced creatures with cloven hoofs lashed at him with bullwhips?"

"Not disappointed," I said. "Nor surprised. I'm delighted. I loved you. Love you. And by the way, you look great," I told him, as I finished slurping my soup.

"That's the thing about the dead," he said. "We always look the way people remember us."

"I hadn't thought it through," I said, "but you do look a lot like the way I remembered you, only somehow filled in, more corporeal than when alive. And of course, you're in a suit. At home you were in a crewneck sweater, often torn at one elbow. And wash pants. Remember the ones they sold at the Army Navy store with the patented grow feature, which was a nip they'd taken at the waist, a nip that you could let out?"

"Yeah," he said, "the only way you could grow was fat."

"Maybe it's the gin, but you seem to have a glow about you," I said.

"I'm down from heaven, for Christ's sake," he said. "Of course I'm numinous. I'm not in hell, though I can't exactly thank you for that. I mean, the stories you detailed in therapy—"

"That's therapy," I cut in. "You're not supposed to be fair in therapy."

"Nor accurate either?" he asked.

"As a master of fiction," I said, and this made him blanche. "As a master of fiction," I said, enjoying the fact that the second reference also made him blush. "John Cheever of all people should understand that accuracy is something we search for, not a series of facts that have been established." I took a rib.

He remained silent while I chewed and swallowed. "I'm still not a homosexual," I said. "If *that's* what you're worried about."

"I'm no longer worried about that," he said. "That was what they call a projection of me onto you."

"You're right," I said. "Just as my yearning to be a great writer was a projection of me onto you."

My father began to crane his neck, apparently looking for a waiter.

"I've missed you," I said.

Silence.

"Of course, I'm pleased," he said, "though not entirely convinced."

"Sure, I miss you," I said. "Remember you'd be in your armchair when I came back home at night from a date, and you'd ask if you were a disappointment as a father?"

He nodded. "I was sometimes a chore."

"Sometimes," I agreed, "but I was also flattered. And you'd say that you weren't like an ordinary father, and I'd say that I didn't mind, because ordinary fathers were crashing bores."

He smiled, though weakly. "You were always adept when it came to saying what was wanted."

"I mean it," I said. "I understand you, because I'm lonely, too. You remember when you took me and my first wife, Lynne, to London, and gave her fifty pounds to go shopping, so that you and I could be alone together?"

He looked vague. "Remind me."

"You and I walked around the Serpentine in Hyde Park. You weren't drinking, but you encouraged me to have some silly drink. A plimsole?"

"You mean a shandy," he said.

"That's right," I said. "A shandy. And then you said that you sometimes experienced a species of loneliness so intense that it felt like intestinal flu. This was during one of the most successful phases of your career. And I thought how odd it was that a man so much admired could be so lonely."

He was peering around now and seemed to have stopped listening.

"I didn't know the kind of loneliness you were talking about then," I said, "but I do now. I often feel that lonely myself."

He cleared his throat. "I'm sorry to hear that," he said, but he didn't look at all sorry.

"Your writing has kept other people from being lonely. I've met women who saw you speak forty years ago and are still vibrating. They were in the back of the auditorium and you were at the podium. You said that good prose could cure a sinus headache or athlete's foot, and the woman in question would never afterward have a single doubt about her life or work. I only wish you'd given me that sort of encouragement."

He smiled vaguely. "Did I say that about athlete's foot?"

"I'm not sure," I said. "You can look it up in the biography."

"I haven't read it," he said.

"It's a masterpiece," I said.

"I'm glad," he said. "I'll take your word for it."

Our waiter appeared, took our order for more martinis, and another man came to the table with a chafing dish. He took off the cover and gave us each some lobster Cantonese. Daddy insisted I take the big claw. The waiter looked at us for some sign of approval, and we both nodded and watched politely, while he put the scoops of white rice on our plates.

We both leaned forward and ate in silence for a time.

"So, what's the problem?" he asked.

I gulped down some more martini, cleared my throat, and began: "We have an orangutan in the White House. Trump! People are afraid the world is going to end," I said. "There's a lot of talk about the Rapture, which alarms me."

"*What's the matter with Benjamin Hale?*" he said.

"*He cries enough to fill a pail*

"*Oh, what's the matter Benjamin Hale?*

"*He cries enough to float a whale.*"

I sensed that our time was almost up and signaled to the waiter, who brought the chit, and I asserted the authority of the living by putting my platinum American Express card in the fake-leather pocket designed to receive it.

"I remember that poem," I said. "But you have to believe me when I tell you that there's lots of trouble down here. People more naturally cheerful than I am are losing sleep."

The waiter came back, and I added the 20 percent tip, signed, and put my card back in my wallet.

"I don't know if this will shed any light," he said, "but they've closed purgatory. Freed up a lot of space, which we are in need of, especially if they decide dogs have souls. It's going to be so crowded, nobody will be able to lie down."

"But why don't you need purgatory anymore? Wasn't that mostly a Catholic thing?"

"It was," he said. "But they found that the time spent watching the TV news was painful enough, and in just the right way. They found that when they came up with a soul that owed time in purgatory, he or she had already suffered eons in front of the screen."

"Interesting," I said.

"So that's my answer," he said. "If you think the world is going to end, then turn off the television."

"So, I should tell my friends that if they turn off the TV, the world won't end?"

He pulled out his chair, stood, and grinned. "The world might end. I don't know. I went to heaven, not to Delphi. What I do know, though, is that if you turn off the TV, you'll have a better time until it does end. Which is enough, don't you think?"

"I guess," I said.

By now, we were standing in the street, about to part.

He shrugged and beamed. "We should do this again soon," he said. "I've really missed the lobster Cantonese."

Benjamin Cheever has written for the New York Times, The New Yorker, *and* Runner's World. *He illustrated craven moral flexibility well before it was in vogue by contributing to the* Reader's Digest *and the* Nation *within the same five-year period. He's published four novels and three nonfiction books. He has taught at Bennington College and the New School for Social Research, and lives in Pleasantville, New York.*

10

"You're no longer alive, but you're definitely immortal."

SARA MOULTON (PROTÉGÉE, FRIEND) AND JULIA CHILD

We worked out all the details over a Ouija board. Julia would meet me for lunch at the Summer Shack in Cambridge, just five minutes by car from the house on Irving Street where she and Paul had lived for decades. It was her choice—she'd always been a huge fan of Chef Jasper White—but I was happy to go along with it. Our reservation was for noon. By 11:55, I was sitting in a booth waiting for her. At the stroke of 12:00, the clock by the register in the front of the restaurant started tolling. As the last gong faded away, Julia started fading in on the other side of the booth.

She was smiling, of course. "Dearie, how *wonderful* to see you," she said, in that famous strangled foghorn of a voice. "I'm so glad you found the time to meet with me."

I was just as delighted to see her. "Oh, come now, Julia. I wouldn't have missed it for the world."

She looked terrific—much better, in fact, than in her bent-frame later years. She held herself erect, and even though she was sitting, I had a feeling that she was once again every inch of six foot two. She was wearing a simple blue shirt covered by a green cardigan, a black skirt, and some "sensible" shoes. Her gaze was direct, her skin clear, her energy high. Come to think of it, she looked very much as she had when we'd met in 1979, when the grand dame was a mere sixty-seven years old. Given that I myself was now sixty-five, I felt a new appreciation for her legendary vitality.

I had a thousand questions for her. "Julia, what's it like on the other side?" I said. "Are you happy there? Do you get to see Paul?"

"I'll tell you one thing right off the bat," she said. "The Germans had it right—in heaven there is no beer. Even worse, there is no *wine*. I promise I'll answer all your questions, but first let's put in at least a part of our order."

She'd no sooner spoken than our waiter, Sal, was at our side. "How can I help you, Julia?" he said.

"Sal!" she said. "Still on the job—and still keeping fit, I see." It was just like Julia to engage the veteran waiter as a friend. She was the least snobby person I'd ever met.

Sal, a modest man, blushed, but in fact it was true. He worked out religiously and stayed ripped. "How 'bout some wine, Julia?" he said. "A glass of Sancerre, as usual, or would you like to try some of this new California Chardonnay?"

"You know me too well," Julia said. "The Chardonnay sounds lovely, and it will give me a chance to see what they're up to in California these days. And some oysters, too. What's on the menu today?"

Sal ticked 'em off, one by one: Cotuits, Wellfleets, Sandy Necks, and Standish Shores from Massachusetts, Pemaquids and Glidden Points from Maine. Her eyes gleaming, Julia ordered half-a-dozen each of the Wellfleets and the Pemaquids.

As Sal strode off in the direction of the kitchen, Julia folded her hands in front of her and looked back at me. "What's going on in the food world, dearie?" she said. "I want to know all about it."

I wasn't sure where to start, but then I figured I might as well give her the bad news right up front. "Well," I said, "French cuisine isn't at the center of the universe anymore. Chris Kimball is as busy as ever, and he tells everyone that the new model is international cuisine. Salt and pepper in every single dish has got to go. Pepper, in particular, is a spice like any other and shouldn't be added willy-nilly."

"Nonsense," huffed Julia. She was clearly offended and sat up even straighter. "What does that even mean—*international* cuisine? There's got to be a *base*—and nothing and no one beats the French." I replied that I'd begun working alongside Chris on a broadcast for National Public Radio and that we tussled over this question week after week. "Believe me, Julia, I defend the French way every time," I said.

Truthfully, I had a ton of respect for Chris. He'd been working in the trenches of food magazine publishing for decades, first at *Cooks Illustrated,* then at *Milk Street,* both of which he founded. He could be prickly, but he was an empiricist. When it came to cooking a particular recipe, he accepted nothing as given. In effect, every article was a test of the given recipe in a quest to determine whether that way was in fact the best way to make it.

And it's not like Julia was very different. Jasper still likes to tell the story about what happened during one of his guest appearances on Julia's show. He chose to complement the dish they'd prepared together with a handful of Vermont Common Crackers purchased from the Vermont Country Store. Julia was shocked. Surely, she believed, a decent cook could whip up a better product at home. With that thesis in mind, Julia assigned a team of cooks the task of reverse engineering the recipe for the common cracker, which has been a staple in New England country stores since 1828. When she and Jasper sampled the final version of the dozens produced and rejected by her team, the two of them agreed that it tasted exactly like . . . the commercial product.

Of course, I loved and subscribed to Julia's empiricism and her never-ending search for excellence. It was because of my devotion to her method of "boiling" eggs that I ended up meeting her in person.

One day in the late seventies, during the brief period I worked for a catering operation, a colleague and I were boiling and peeling seven hundred eggs. I did it Julia's way. You didn't actually boil the eggs. You put them in water and brought them to a *near* boil, let them sit for twelve minutes, then chilled them in ice water. The result was a cooked egg with an admirably tender white surrounding a yolk that wasn't marred by the ugly green line that invariably encircles it when you boil eggs the usual way.

Turned out my young associate knew all about Julia's method. Her mom was a personal friend of Julia's. After I'd finished regaling this young woman, she asked if I was interested in working with Julia. Was I? Was she kidding? The next day I found myself on the phone with Julia herself. "Oh, dearie, I've heard all about you," she said. "Tell me—do you *food style*?" Food styling was then in its infancy, but I was familiar with the term and I certainly knew how to land food on a plate in an appetizing way. So I lied and said yes, I was very good at food styling. She hired me on the spot to work on *Julia Child and More Company,* the series she was then making for public television. I worked behind the scenes there and afterward helped with the food styling for the cookbook that bore the same name. A few years later, JC started appearing on *Good Morning America*. I'd already moved to New York and volunteered to help Julia on the set of that show. Eventually, the folks at *GMA* thought it might be a good idea to put me in front of the camera. That gig led to a tryout at a brand-new venture called the Food Channel. I ended up hosting several series there over the course of a decade.

So, what was Julia to me? First a teacher, then a mentor, always a dear friend. I never stopped learning from her.

Back at the Summer Shack, Julia was partly mollified by my flag-waving on behalf of the primacy of French cuisine. "Well, then," she said. "What else is new?"

"Food bloggers are the new stars," I said. It was more bad news, but I knew she wanted me to give it to her straight. "A few of them are excellent, but most of them have no training, as you know. You remember their websites? They just repurpose other people's recipes and take the advertiser's money." Julia shook her head but continued listening raptly. "Maybe it all comes down to these new easy-to-use digital cameras. The bloggers shoot every step of the prep," I continued. "Anyway, they're the ones with the brands these days, so they're the ones who get the big cookbook deals."

"What do you mean, *brands*?" said Julia.

"It just means that they're good at self-promotion," I replied. "You were pretty good at it yourself."

Julia squinted at me in mild annoyance. "I promoted French cuisine and home cooking," she said brusquely. "I happened to be a good teacher, but it was never about me personally."

Abashed, I apologized. "Of course not," I said.

But Julia was fired up now. "Speaking of bloggers, whatever happened to that dreadful Julie Powell?" she said. The very idea of Powell's *Julie and Julia* blog had pissed her off. How in the world was this *stranger* allowed to make money off Julia's name?

Nothing to do but plow ahead. "A year after you died, Julie Powell gathered her posts into a book, which Nora Ephron turned into a big Hollywood movie starring Meryl Streep as y-o-u," I said. Personally, I thought it was a very lovable film, but I decided not to say so to Julia. Instead, I mentioned that the movie had goosed sales of *Mastering the Art of French Cooking* . . . and, more broadly, that it introduced Julia to a new generation of young people who might not otherwise have heard of her. "I remember you telling me that everyone forgets you when you're no longer on TV," I said. "You can't be mad, about *Julie and Julia*. They put your story on the big screen. *Meryl Streep* trained herself to talk just like you. You're no longer alive, but you're definitely immortal."

Julia was not impressed. I decided to double down. "And it's not just old media, Julia, it's new media, too," I said. "On the internet a company called Twitch has made every episode of *The French Chef* available to the zillions of young nerds who typically visit that website only because it's where they play their virtual war games. I know it might seem weird, but your old show is acquainting young people who definitely don't cook for themselves with the joys of cooking."

Now Julia seemed at least slightly intrigued. "Well, Americans weren't cooking when we launched our show in the early sixties either," she said. "Why bother cooking when there were TV dinners in the freezer?"

Speaking of TV, the woman who essentially invented food television now wanted to know about the state of the art. Again, I took a deep breath and plunged in. "None of the network execs care about cooking shows," I said. "If you're a chef and your mission is to *educate*—if you want to show the viewer how to make a recipe—you're gonna do it on public TV or you're not gonna do it at all." Julia took a none-too-delicate gulp of her Chardonnay but otherwise held her fire. "Food TV today is all about competition," I continued. "The model seems to be pro wrestling. Think Bobo Brazil."

"Who?" Julia said, clearly annoyed. "Was he a wrestler? The first and last wrestler I ever knew by name was Gorgeous George."

"Sorry, Julia," I said. "I've never heard of Gorgeous George. But I'm sure it's all the same. Food TV today is mostly chest-beating and the spectacle of humiliation. There aren't any headlocks, but there're plenty of peacocks."

Suddenly Sal—who did indeed know Julia's preferences—reappeared and landed an overflowing lobster roll in front of each of us. "Wonderful!" Julia said. "Jasper makes the best lobster roll I've ever eaten." She took a hearty bite of the sandwich and chased it down with another sip of wine. "Seen any good movies lately?" she wondered. Same old Julia. As much as she meant to the world of food, she was never a foodie. Her interests were too broad.

"I don't get a chance to go very often, but my husband, Bill, went to the theater recently to see *Dunkirk*," I said. "He thought it was a good movie, but very old-fashioned. The Brits were self-sacrificing angels; the Nazis were faceless devils. The thing ran for one hour and forty-six minutes and you never saw a woman or a person of color. It seemed to come straight out of the fifties."

"I don't understand," replied Julia. "The Brits *were* angels. The Nazis *were* devils. Believe me, I remember the Battle of Dunkirk. It helped FDR start to persuade Americans that it was time for us to get into the war. By the time Pearl Harbor happened, I was already volunteering for the Red Cross. After Pearl Harbor, I tried to enlist in the WACS, but they told me I was too tall. Luckily, I wasn't too tall for the OSS, so they gave me a job." She took another bite of her lobster roll.

"Lovely," she said. "But tell me all about Washington. Who's the president these days?" she said.

I smiled sweetly and replied, "Oh, I don't think you want to go there, Julia. Much better for you to rest in peace." Julia looked at me quizzically but decided not to press the subject. I meant to move on but found myself blurting out: "Planned Parenthood is under attack and hanging by a thread but definitely fighting back!" I couldn't help it. Planned Parenthood was Julia's favorite charity.

"Bravo," said Julia.

It was getting late. Sal had cleared our dishes and the restaurant was emptying out. But now, finally, I had a question for Julia: "If you had your life to live over, what would you do differently?"

"Paul Child and that sole meunière in Rouen changed my whole life for the better," she said with her typical firmness. "If I'd ended up back in Pasadena, I probably would have married a Republican and become an alcoholic." She took a last sip of the Chardonnay. "Piaf had the right attitude—*Je ne regrette rien.*"

And with that Julia began getting hazy, vanishing, a piece at a time. Her smile was the last thing to go. I kept looking at her as long as I could, not wanting to lose her, but soon there was nothing to see.

As ever, I'm going to miss her.

There was only one Julia Child.

And this time, she was really gone. For good.

Sara Moulton hosts the public television show Sara's Weeknight Meals, *now in its eighth season, co-hosts a weekly segment on* Milk Street Radio, *and is the author of four cookbooks, including, most recently,* Home Cooking 101. *Sara was the executive chef of* Gourmet *magazine, food editor of ABC's Good Morning America, and the host of several well-loved shows on the Food Network during that channel's first decade.*

"What do you want me to say?" he asks. "That I love you?
That everything will be all right? That you have a Father in Heaven?"

THE REV. GEORGE PITCHER (ANGLICAN PRIEST) AND JESUS CHRIST

He's late. It's past lunchtime. It's Friday, and the usual crowds have dwindled. The sun, low now, is shining in on me at my window seat. It's a place I come when I want to be on my own. They know me here. It's a good place. A thin place.

I've drunk a little wine as the hours passed. Red, then white. I'm a little heady but not pissed, listening to the rhythms of words, outside in the street and inside me. Like a prayer.

A waiter comes and stands by my table, between me and the window. He's in a bright white smock, and I squint up into the light.

"Why are you waiting?" he asks.

"I'm waiting for my friend," I say.

"I said why, not who," he says, not unkindly. "How long are you going to wait?"

"He'll come."

"But why are you waiting here?"

"I booked this table. Name of Pitcher."

"George," he murmurs. And he slips in to sit opposite me. He's looking down at his hands on the table. Like suddenly he's waiting to be served himself.

"Have you just started working here?" I ask.

"No, I've been working for ages." Still, he doesn't look up. And I remember now. I've watched him, cleaning tables, bringing food. I just hadn't looked at him.

"Thank you for being here, George." Strangely, it's a voice that I find I recognize.

"Rabbi?" I say, and now he looks up.

"Shalom," he says with a smile, and I start back from the table edge.

"Come on. Don't be afraid." He takes a bread roll from the basket, breaks it in half, and holds a piece out to me.

He shrugs. "Shall I say grace?" he asks.

* * *

Yes, I know you want to know what he looks like. But there's the thing: Familiar is all I can say. Like someone you've always known but, as in a dream, won't be specified. The light falls and he's dark, then fair in the setting sun. Younger, then older. Is the hair long or tied back? I can't remember. Rough, then pretty. Giotto or Caravaggio. You or me? You *and* me.

I suppose I should say that when he looks at me, it's as if he's always known me, or it's like he's looking right through me. That his eyes are like doves. That he's gentle, like a mother. But none of that works. He's simply here, present. There's no impression to be made beyond that. Sorry.

"I'm thirsty," he says, and I pour some water from a pitcher. Then more wine.

"We were meant to have lunch," I say. "It'll be time for supper soon."

"Call it lunch," he says. "It's meant to be lunch, right? We're in my time." And he looks out into the fading light. "It'll soon be Sabbath."

"Shabat," I say.

"Call it what you will. Tell me what you want."

"I wanted to eat with you. At your table."

"You do that all the time, George. You're a priest. Isn't that what you say? 'Come to this table.' But this is your table. Why have you called me to your table?"

"It's for a book. We get to have lunch with someone we love who's dead. They asked me to have lunch with you."

"Do you love me?"

"I don't know—I'd like to try. I got ordained, so I must a bit. Someone has to feed your lambs."

"And do I look dead?"

"I told them you weren't dead. You're the only one in the book who isn't."

"Awkward."

"But you were dead once, right? Really dead."

He stares at me. "George. Do I look one thousand nine hundred and eighty seven years and eighty-four days old?"

"No."

"Good. Then I'm alive. But I've been dead. Is that so hard?"

"Well, yes, actually," I say. "At any rate, it does put you in rather a different category to the other subjects in the book."

"So far. So they asked you to interview me because they think I'm dead? Interesting."

"I know," I say sheepishly. "It's a category error. One that's easily made by people who haven't met you, I guess. The editor said she's a lapsed Jew. I told her, well, you're kind of a lapsed Jew, too."

He smiles again, like he really is a category error. Then he holds out his hands, white and strangely feminine: "Touch me."

I slowly take one hand. It's warm. I feel for the hole in the palm. It holds mine.

"I have to ask," I say. "Do you really *need* to eat?"

"I'll have the fish," he says.

* * *

And we talk. We talk endlessly, as it gets darker. About friends, about what we've done, about what we love to do, about joyous stuff and very dark things. It comes easily. Except that I realize afterward that he doesn't tell me anything about him—it's all about me. When I ask questions about him, it's just turned around.

A line from a musical comes to me.

"Are you who they said you were?"

"I am. Are you?"

"That Mary from Magdala. Tell me about her."

"She gives her love to you. What will you give her?"

"The stories—are they really true?"

"Someone once asked me what is truth. What do you think is true?"

I persist: "But were you . . . accurately reported?"

"You were a journalist before you were a priest. Do you believe everything you read? Or just the truth?"

And so I do all the talking. Or rather, I do all the telling, while he eats with his hands. I wonder if he's there or if I'm imagining him. But the other waiters fill his glass. And I notice a woman, who sits on the bench seat at the next table, glance at him and move her bag a little closer to her. I want to shout, "This is the living Christ, for God's sake! He's not going to steal your purse!"

"I might, George. They always thought I was a criminal."

"Of course. You knew what I was thinking," I say. "Why do you want me to tell you about me, if you know it all already?"

"I want to know if you know it."

"But you'd know that, too." The waiter brings more bread. Had he asked for it? Weird.

Then, suddenly, he takes the conversational initiative: "Was the lamb good?"

I hadn't noticed what I'd been eating.

"Yes. Very good. Thank you."

"It is finished," he says.

I look down at my empty plate.

"Oh, that's terrible," I say. "Truly terrible." And he laughs for the first time, a guttural chuckle, full of life.

* * *

"It's time you got on," he says eventually. "It's getting late. And I have people to serve."

"You're going to be a waiter again?"

"No."

"Forgive me," I say. "Yes, I'd better go. I'll get the bill."

"I've already paid," he says.

I look at him hard, but he doesn't recoil. "Will you stop that?" I say.

"Stop what?" he says.

"Stop it with the double meanings. . . . The Son of Man isn't meant to do one-liners, dreadful puns."

"You haven't been listening closely enough. Where do you think you get them from?"

I'm feeling resentful now. "I thought you'd have something to tell me."

"I do."

"What?"

"I've already told you. You're the vicar, remember? You're the expert on what I have to say."

I look at my own hands. "They always say: 'What would you ask him if you had just one question?'"

"Well?"

Slowly I say: "My question is—what do you want to tell me?"

"What do you want me to say?" he asks. "That I love you? That everything will be all right? That you have a Father in Heaven?"

He's speaking quickly now. This is what he's come to say. "Do you want me to make everything all right? Is that it? I can't take away what you've done, all the stuff you've brought to this table tonight and haven't told me, the life you've led that you won't confess even to yourself. I can't stop people hating you for it. But they hated me before they hated you. Remember that, George. Shit happens."

"I didn't think you'd talk like this."

"It's your voice, George. Language you understand. Quite Pentecostal, no?" A calmer beat. "So, again, what do you want me to say? That I'm really here?"

"No, I suppose not."

"And why would that be?" Suddenly he's leaning in, looking for my answer. Like a teacher.

I pause for a moment, looking into his eyes, before answering: "Because I already know that."

"Because you already know that," he repeats slowly. "Now go and write this up. And try to tell the truth for once."

A pause, then barely audible, a voice in my head: "Write it in peace. Write it as a prayer."

We sit for a moment more in silence as I try to think of something to say.

"Thanks for coming," I say eventually.

Another pause, and he says softly: "Now you're doing it, y'see."

I stand up and wonder if a hug is in order, but it doesn't seem necessary.

"*L'chaim*," I say, and he nods.

"Cheers," he replies.

At the door, I see it's dark outside. I'm not going to turn around, because I'm pretty sure he won't be there. But I do. And he is, still watching me.

I raise a hand in salutation and he raises his, the first two fingers together and pointing upward, the next two folded down into his palm, touching the thumb, like in a painting.

George Pitcher has been an award-winning Industrial Editor at the Observer *and Religion Editor, a columnist, and leader-writer at the* Daily Telegraph. *He also co-founded, built, and sold an innovative PR agency, before being ordained a priest in the Church of England. He served his curacy at St. Bride's, the Journalists' Church in Fleet Street, and is now rector of a rural parish in East Sussex, having spent a year as the Archbishop of Canterbury's public affairs adviser. He is today involved in a long-term project with Dow Jones, publisher of the* Wall Street Journal, *to develop a new model for media ethics in the digital era. He is the author of* The Death of Spin, *an indictment of our spin culture in business and politics, and* A Time to Live: The Case Against Euthanasia and Assisted Suicide. *His first novel,* A Dark Nativity, *was published by Unbound in 2017.*

12

"This life is designed to overthrow you. No one ever masters it."

DAVID LAYTON (GODSON)
AND LEONARD COHEN

The harbor, lined with tavernas and fishing boats, was a good place for lunch. The Aegean Sea, cool even in the height of summer, offered a refreshing breeze, and best of all, my sister-in-law and her husband ran the best restaurant on the island of Lesvos.

About twenty or so outdoor wooden tables sat on marble paving stones. Several were taken by tourists seated under oversize umbrellas that shaded them from the sun but did not block the ruffled sea and the hills shrouded in the milky-white haze of summer heat. The rest were locals still lingering over their morning coffees, one of whom I thought I recognized. He was seated at the far corner, next to the water, and had on a dark suit with an open collar, tailored to fit a European gentleman who'd reached respectable retirement. He wore ruby-tinted sunglasses. Approaching, I noticed a Panama hat seated on the chair next to him. He wasn't a local; he was my godfather, Leonard Cohen.

"Leonard?"

"Hello, my friend," he said, as if expecting me.

"What are you doing here? *How* are you here?"

"I'm not sure. You tell me."

Shocked to see him, I took a seat at his invitation. He looked about the same since I'd last seen him in Los Angeles, which had been a few years earlier, and as I'd done back then, I wondered how such a large presence could fit inside such a small, almost fragile frame.

"Shall we order?" Leonard said, greedily scanning the menu of familiar dishes.

"Sure," I answered. He may have died in 2016, but as Leonard used to say, Greece was where the magic happens, and so it felt like the most natural thing in the world to see him here with fishing boats bobbing behind him.

My sister-in-law came to our table, and Leonard rattled off a voluminous series of dishes and wine.

The first plates arrived within minutes, laid down on the white cloth with the quick efficiency of a card dealer. The plate of taramosalata, its pale pink color subtly suggesting that this Greek restaurant was of a higher quality to those serving overly bright concoctions, was placed beside a plate of white tzatziki, a black olive on top. Warm pita bread sat in a basket. Next to it was a Greek salad, its slab of feta set atop glistening red tomatoes.

Leonard stared at the untouched food.

"Aren't you hungry?" I asked.

"Well, I haven't tasted this for a while," he answered.

"What do they feed you where you are now?"

"Ambrosia."

"Ah," I said. 'The food of the gods."

"But I prefer this," said Leonard. "I'm glad you brought me here."

"I didn't bring you."

"Well, I wouldn't be here right now if it wasn't for you."

"You sure?" I asked, surprised that I had the power to conjure him up from another realm.

"That's the way it works."

My sister-in-law returned with a bottle of Metoxi, one of the finest bottles of wine that they had, and poured us each a glass. "Drink," she said. "Eat."

As if he'd been waiting for her orders, Leonard tore off a piece of pita bread, dipped it into the taramosalata, and took a large hungry bite. He then washed it down with a glass of the white wine made by the monks of Mount Athos. A wolfish grin spread across his face.

"I miss this," he said.

"What's the story you used to tell about living in London when you were young and depressed?"

"Before I became old and depressed?" Leonard said, still smiling. He popped the black olive in his mouth and chewed it as if it were the size of a plum. "It was one of those gloomy, overcast days. I went into a bank to change some money and spotted a teller wearing sunglasses. I liked his excessive optimism and asked where he was from. When he told me Greece, I booked a ticket the following day. A little while later, I wrote to your parents inviting them to Hydra."

"My parents always said you found Greece for us."

"I didn't find it. It was always there."

We'd arrived when I was a baby. In my mother's mind it was Leonard who did the summoning. Fifty odd years later and here I was, still returning to Greece.

"The funny thing is my wife was born in this village and we now live in London. I suppose neither would have happened without you. I'm not the reason you're here. You're the reason *I'm* here," I told him.

"I'm pleased to have contributed."

"What's it like where you are?"

"It's a bit like Greece. It must have been very special in the beginning, but it's crowded now and much like everywhere else. People are still searching for something, even after there's nothing to search for. But the light is very beautiful."

More food arrived, and this time my sister-in-law was helped by her husband, Theo, who looked annoyed at being pulled away from the grill. They brought us lamb, potatoes, giant beans in tomato, beets in yogurt, grilled eggplant, and octopus.

"What fish do you have today?" Leonard asked Theo.

Theo said he had fresh snapper, sardines, and small anchovies.

"I do like sardines," said Leonard, considering. "I'll have everything."

We tucked into the food, poured more wine, and eventually I asked, "Have you run into my father, by any chance?"

"No, not really."

"Not really?"

"It's hard to explain."

"Did you wonder why I wasn't at his funeral?"

Leonard had been there. I'd seen the newspaper photos of him holding aloft my dead father, Irving Layton, Leonard's poetic mentor and his closest friend.

Leonard was one of the pallbearers. I was not.

I still found it odd to think of myself as the son who had failed to attend his own father's funeral. It sounded so dreadful and final, as if I was making an unavoidable statement when, in fact, I'd only been supporting my brother's decision to stay away. One loyalty had clashed with another, which I suppose was statement enough. But I'd taken some of my father's ashes and spread them in the very sea that lapped beside us.

"You see that, my boy? That's how it ends," my father would have told Leonard, and Leonard might have answered in the same words he'd once used on another occasion: "This life is designed to overthrow you. No one ever masters it."

Leonard, once he started eating, had an almost inexhaustible appetite. One dish followed another, including the fish, and watching Leonard eat, I pictured him and my father still on Leonard's patio in Hydra, cracking open poems, speaking of war and romance, the two of them discussing people who were long dead as if they were still alive, while occasionally treating those who were actually seated next to them as if they were ghosts. This was a habit of my father's, a man who was unafraid of death but obsessed with immortality.

Finally the table was cleared to make room for a plate of honey-soaked baklava.

The last time we'd sat at a restaurant together, Leonard had insisted on paying the bill, becoming so agitated at any suggestion otherwise that he began to strike his forehead with the open palm of his hand. He never wanted anyone else to pick up the tab, but he had nothing to pay with now.

"I'm getting up now," said Leonard. "And I'm not coming back."

The finality of those words saddened me, but I knew they were true.

"I guess I've never had a chance to thank you. For all of this," I said, nodding in the direction of the sea and sky.

"You know when I said that where I am is a bit like Greece? Well, it isn't. There's beautiful light everywhere, but no cracks. Do you understand?"

"I think so."

"Enjoy the imperfections while you can. Believe me, you'll miss them when they're gone."

"Goodbye, Leonard," I said.

Leonard picked up his hat and used it to wave goodbye. As he stepped onto the ancient cobblestones, I watched him begin his upward journey toward the crumbling castle that sat over the village like a king's crown. On the parapets, a Greek flag fluttered briskly in the wind, and beyond that lay the impossibly blue sky that Leonard now belonged to.

David Layton has had short fiction and articles published and anthologized in various literary journals, newspapers, and magazines, including Penguin, *the* Daily Telegraph, Condé Nast Traveler, *and the* Globe and Mail. *He is the author of* Motion Sickness, *a memoir. His latest novel,* The Dictator, *was published by HarperCollins in May 2017. He teaches creative writing at the University of Toronto.*

13

"What did you think of me becoming an actor?" Pa grunted.
"I liked you in that movie where you played the boxer."

KIRK DOUGLAS (SON)
AND HERSCHEL "HARRY" DANIELOVITCH

The only time I remember eating lunch with my father was in the first grade. I was six years old, and it was 1922. I did a play that people liked. My father was in the audience, but I didn't know it. He grabbed me after the play and took me to his favorite saloon. He had a drink, and he gave me some loganberry juice. I was very surprised. I never had lunch with him, even at home. I would like to have had a regular lunch with him, because maybe then we could have talked about things we never discussed before.

Years later, I found out that he was very proud of me. But he never shared that with me. If we could have lunch together now, I would ask him a lot of questions—for example, what did he think about my going to college? He never gave me any money to pay my expenses, but I heard later, much later, that he was thrilled that I had graduated. Maybe if we had lunch together now he would express his pride? That would be very important to me, because I had six sisters; I was the only boy. An only son carried a tremendous burden in those days. When Pa came home each afternoon with his wagon loaded with junk, I often ran after him and jumped on the wagon, climbed up, and sat beside him. He never seemed surprised. He got off the wagon when he reached the corner of our street. He didn't say anything to me and always gave Bill, our horse, a slap on the rump. Bill trotted down the street with me holding the reins. At the end of the street, he turned up the small hill in front of our house, stopped, and I got off. My mother was waiting to give me lunch. My father went off to the saloon. But, what if . . .

"Issur!"

"Yes, Pa?"

"Come with me." He gestured gruffly but never slowed down. I waved goodbye to my mother as I followed my father down the street. We stopped at his favorite saloon. I followed Pa and slid next to him on a stool at the bar.

"Two glasses of vodka."

(It's my fantasy, and I would prefer that to loganberry juice now.)

The bartender placed two glasses in front of us. Pa sipped his glass, and I sipped mine. Delicious.

"Pa, what was your life like in Russia?"

Pa took a deep breath. "Hard."

"Why?"

"That's a stupid question. If it was easy, I would have stayed there. Why do you think I came to America?" He continued sipping his vodka, slowly.

We sat in silence. I mustered the courage to ask him another question: "What did you think about me going to college?" I braced myself for a harsh response.

"I was very proud of you."

"Really?"

"Yes, very proud."

"What did you think of me becoming an actor?"

Pa grunted. "I liked you in that movie where you played the boxer."

"*Champion*?"

"Yeah, I shouted at the screen when you were fighting. I wanted you to win."

He put down his glass and looked at me. "You are my only son. I had six girls and only one boy—you. I was thrilled to see you succeed."

I was so happy I didn't know what to say. My father was *proud* of me, what I'd always wanted more than anything from him—a pat on the back. Here at last I had the validation from him I felt I had spent my whole life chasing.

"Pa—"

But he didn't seem to listen; instead, he turned to the waiter and ordered me a great big bowl of vanilla ice cream for dessert. My favorite.

Maybe it was to stop my questioning.

I'll never know.

Kirk Douglas was born Issur Danielovitch. The archetypal Oscar-winning Hollywood movie star of the postwar era, Kirk Douglas built a career with he-man roles as soldiers, cowboys, and assorted tough guys in more than eighty films. Douglas was also a Tinseltown innovator and rebel, as one of the first A-listers to found his own independent production company. Douglas also effectively ended the 1950s practice of blacklisting Hollywood talent suspected of communist ties when he insisted on crediting famed screenwriter Dalton Trumbo for his script adaptation of 1960's Spartacus. *He began a second career as a writer and focused on the philanthropic efforts of the Douglas Foundation until his death in February 2020.*

14

"**Who do you work for**—*her or me?*"

JESSE KORNBLUTH (SITUATIONAL "FRIEND") AND NORA EPHRON

I have five thousand "friends" on Facebook, but not really—I actually know just a few hundred of them. And I could say I was Nora Ephron's "friend" from 1974 to 1982, but I was really just a friend-once-removed—for a few of those years, I was living with a writer who had been dating Carl Bernstein when he met Nora, and Carl, never strong on the one man/one woman thing, asked Nora for dinner, so Nora called her friend and asked if it would be okay for her to go out with Carl, and it was, which cleared the path for the debacle that was Nora and Carl's marriage and the romance that put me in Nora's orbit.

I wrote a piece for Nora at *Esquire*. I was in the horse-drawn carriage Carl commandeered and overturned after a drunken dinner at Le Cirque. And when Nora left Carl—as any wife might if her husband had an affair while she was pregnant—we both lived in the Apthorp, the baronial apartment building on the Upper West Side. So, okay, "friends." In the specific, situational, Manhattan meaning of the word.

And then Nora wrote *Heartburn*, a novel about a Washington-based political journalist who has an affair while his wife is pregnant.

The idea to do a piece about Nora's intensely autobiographical novel was a no-brainer: I'd toss some questions to my friend, and she'd hit two thousand words over the fence. I could have placed that Q&A anywhere, but I was a contract writer at *New York* magazine in that decade, so I pitched it to Ed Kosner, who assigned it. And then I called Nora.

Nora said she would only be doing interviews in the cities she toured, and then only on the day she was in those cities—there would be no previews of the book, no glossy press. And then she delivered the line that chilled: "I forbid you to do this piece."

Ed Kosner's reaction: "Who do you work for—her or me?"

Gee, now that he put it that way . . .

I called Nora. I said I was doing the piece and that I'd tell everyone that she had declined to be interviewed.

We never spoke again.

"Scenes from a Marriage" was published in March 1983. It presented a Nora Ephron radically different from the charmingly opinionated survivor in her book—I'd interviewed many of her friends, and, to my surprise, they'd not only failed to kiss the ring, some had expressed astonishment at the mere existence of *Heartburn*. (As it happened, my story wasn't the worst for Nora. Leon Wieseltier, writing under the pseudonym Tristan Vox, took on the morality of the book in *Vanity Fair*. "Here is Carl Bernstein and adultery; there is Nora Ephron and child abuse," Wieseltier wrote. "It is no contest.")

I didn't see Nora for twenty years. Then, at the Aspen Ideas Festival in 2004, she turned a corner and there I was. It was a movie moment. She didn't gasp, but close. Clearly there was no statute of limitations on the crime I'd committed against her.

Nora Ephron died in 2012. But for her legion of fans, she's astonishingly present, eternally alive in her writing and her movies. Why, just the other week I read a piece that asked, "What would Nora do?"

Good question. What *would* Nora do if, by the magic of literary conjuring, she were yanked back from the beyond to have lunch with me? She wouldn't be pleased by her companion. But as even her friends will admit, Nora was one of the greatest control freaks on the planet—who but Nora would, in her terminal year, have the presence of mind to befriend the new "It" girl, Lena Dunham, knowing that she could place her account of their friendship in *The New Yorker*. She might loathe me, but she'd use me to burnish the identity she'd brilliantly created: accessible icon, chatty neighbor, career romantic.

What could I ask that would get her to go beyond the quips and opinions that made her name? How could I make our lunch matter? More to the point, why did I want it to? Why couldn't I, as I hoped to do three decades ago, serve up questions she could easily hit out of the park?

My method as an interviewer is to read everything and write a hundred questions—and then throw all that away and play the moment. But as I walked into Michael's, the media lunchroom, gloom descended. In the cosmic pecking order, I realized, nothing had changed. We'd be as we were: Nora, born to the A-list, eternally confident, and me, a nail-biter, B-list to the core.

Ah, there she was, seated at a good table in the front room of the restaurant, like a Dickens ghost, seen only by me. In a lovely memory piece, her son Jacob described her uniform: "Chanel flats and her cream-colored pants and her black-and-white-striped blouse." That is exactly how she looked. Unchanged.

"This is . . . beyond amazing," I said. "You look great."

"You couldn't think of anyone else?"

"Like someone from history?

"I hear Michelangelo was a fascinating guy."

"I thought of Oscar Wilde and George Bernard Shaw, but the deal was that I had to have actually known the person, and you and I had unfinished business, so . . ."

"I died, Jesse. Our business couldn't be more finished."

"For you."

"Oh, dear. You want to unwind the clock, make it right?"

Whatever I'd had in mind, this wasn't it. Nora had turned the tables. She was interviewing me.

"In the sixties, I was a ferocious journalist, fearless, confrontational, exciting to read. In the seventies, I lost my nerve. I trimmed my outrage, I wrote nice profiles. And then you came along. I had to do the piece, but it didn't have to be so . . . honest."

"Oh, is that what it was?"

"You lived it; I wrote it down. After, I remembered that was what good journalism is. And for the next few decades, that's how I wrote. So . . . I owe you."

"I'm happy to have helped," she said, though by the way she delivered the line, I wasn't so sure.

"I'm curious: What was it like for you to read that piece?"

"I didn't read it."

"Bullshit."

"I cried."

"Why?"

"You caught me in the act."

"Writing it, I thought: This woman is as scared and insecure as I am."

"Or more. I had two small children, and . . ." She caught herself. "Your life worked out. And you're still living it."

"Jealous?"

"You cannot imagine."

"What's it like . . . over there?"

"You wouldn't understand."

"Try me."

"I can't. Words are inadequate."

Imagine that: a description of eternity eludes a writer who had something to say about everything.

"Forgive me?"

I didn't mean to ask that, but as soon as I did, I knew this was why I'd wanted this conversation with Nora. All these years later, I still felt her power, still hoped for her approval.

"Death is nothing but forgiveness."

There's a moment in a conversation when the exchanges aren't strategic or social, a moment when two people are, simply and sincerely, saying what they believe to be true. Was this that moment? Was there more to say?

I felt a spectral presence behind me. Nora brightened. My ability to see the dead extended only a few feet, so it wasn't until the presence was standing directly beside me that I recognized him: Mike Nichols, looking as suave as ever.

"Just a minute, Mike," Nora said, and I realized that she and Mike often had lunch at Michael's, and our conversation, this once-in-a-lifetime communication with the dead, was far more important to me than it was to Nora. For me, she was a window into eternity; for her, I was a chore. Ms. Ephron simply didn't dwell on unhappiness.

I pushed back my chair, stepped aside for Mike Nichols. Nothing, really, had changed. Nora got the last word. Nobody got the last laugh.

Jesse Kornbluth has been a journalist (Vanity Fair, New York *magazine*) *and an internet executive (Editorial Director of America Online). He is now a novelist and screenwriter* (Married Sex), *a playwright* (The Color of Light), *and a cultural concierge (HeadButler.com). He lives in New York.*

15

ELWOOD H. SMITH (FORMER STUDENT) AND NANCY BOYER FEINDT

Lunch at the Martindale Chief Diner
By Elwood H. Smith

I was sitting alone in a classic diner shortly after noon
on Route 23, just off the Taconic Parkway, waiting for my
spinach, tomato, and cheese omelet. I was studying the clots
of cream in my coffee when she appeared. I looked up, and
there she was, Mrs. Feindt, sitting across from me, fidgeting
with the torn edge of the menu's yellowed plastic sleeve.

She smiled at me and looked back down at her menu.
I was restless all night long, in anticipation of our luncheon
rendezvous. I finally fell asleep and when I awakened, I rolled
out of bed and stumbled toward the bathroom door and
crossed directly into the Martindale Chief Diner.

Nancy died in 2003. I
visited her at her home
in Toledo, Ohio, two
weeks before cancer
took her life. I sat on
an ottoman at her side,
holding her hand.

She was lying in an old leather recliner, puffy from the effects
of chemo and heavy drugs, but she was aware of everything:
her two fat, lazy cats, the dishes being scrubbed in the kitchen
by an old friend. I was thanking her for the umpteenth time
for being my mentor, my saving grace, my link to the outside
world, when she squeezed my hand and told me I was the
most stubborn student she'd ever had.

I remembered being a model student, eager to learn, a hungry
sponge. I soaked up the Skira prints she gave me, works by
Daumier, Van Gogh, and Chagall. Eventually, she slipped
Picasso and Francis Bacon into the mix. Mrs. Feindt was an
endless font of magic. I was enthralled and overwhelmed.

"I could see great potential," Nancy said, "but your focused,
inquisitive nature constantly wrestled with your mile-wide
streak of skepticism and stubbornness."

Mrs. Feindt, Alpena High's new teacher, was as tenacious
as I was cautious. In two years, she managed to breach
my sturdy wall of resistance, bringing with her riches
from worldly experience.

Throughout my childhood,
I studied the great cartoon
strips of the forties and fifties.

I absorbed the characters in Barney Google, Pogo, and Popeye.
I studied Norman Rockwell's *Saturday Evening Post* covers.
Nancy found ways to honor my keen interests, while steadily
steering me into unexplored waters.

Nancy Feindt, my mentor, my old friend, had changed. She was
no longer the solid, sturdy woman I'd known over the years.
She was, this day, vaporous, almost not there.

"Just coffee," she said to the waitress. "Black, please."
Then she looked at me and said, "I can't stay too long,
I shouldn't be visiting you."

"I am so happy to see you, Nancy," I said, but I was too chipper.

"If you are expecting tales from the other side," she said, "stories of horrific landscapes from Hieronymus Bosch or a schmaltzy heavenly street paved with gold by Thomas Kinkade, you're at the wrong diner on the wrong day."

I reached across the table and placed my hand gently on hers. "I'm not expecting anything, Nancy," I said. "I'm not even sure this is happening."

She smiled and said, "I always knew you'd make it, you know. I think about those days in Alpena with great fondness. My Michigan memories, and those of my happy times in Europe have enriched my life, my afterlife."

"Why are you here?" I asked.

"Why are you here? That is the better question," she said.

Nancy didn't wait for an answer.

"You are here," she said, "because you need help. I am here because you think you don't. You do. You are not following your compass. You are near your destination, but you are off course."

Nancy was right about my unreliable sense of direction, in my life and in my art. Her voice has always been, I realize at that moment at the diner, an internal guiding light throughout my entire adult life. And now, here she was, ready once again to barrel through my stubbornness, my unwillingness to listen.

"You think you came up with your latest idea to abandon your trusty pen for a simple graphite pencil in an attempt to reinvigorate your art?" she asked. I looked down and picked at the soggy spinach leaf peering out of my cold, rubbery omelet.

"Remember the necklace, the one I wore at my seventieth birthday party?" she asked. "You know, the colorful pencil stub necklace Helen Eustis mailed to you after my death?"

I did remember it. It's in a drawer somewhere.

"You didn't hear it speak to you, but it did!" she said. "You don't always listen, but you somehow manage to hear important messages when you are ready. The necklace spoke to you just before you began your 'Death at the Circus' drawings. You listened then. Open your ears; messages are being sent to you each day like thunderstorms. Open your windows, my stubborn boy, and let in the light, let in the rain.

I laughed aloud. Here I was, a seventy-seven-year-old man being scolded by his deceased high school teacher. Nancy smiled and said, "Okay, I think we are finally getting somewhere."

Nancy was a feisty apparition, I'll give her that. She reminded me that she had to get back before she was found out. She swallowed the last of her burnt coffee and stood.

"Find that necklace and hang it close to your drawing table,"
she said. "It will speak to you, so open up your stubborn ears
and listen. It will guide you back to the true path. In fact, my
friend, you have been more or less off-track since you were
that small child soaking up the Sunday comics."

"You were genuine then. Listen to the necklace, it will lead you
back to the truth. Yeah, I know I'm sounding like a new age
spiritual guru, here, but trust me, that cheap colored pencil
stub necklace is a talisman. Follow it back to the truth."

I promised I'd pay close attention to the talisman. BLINK!
Nancy Boyer Feindt was gone. I paid the check and drove
back home. I could feel the rain on my face.

*Elwood Smith, an internationally acclaimed advertising and editorial illustrator,
has also written and illustrated numerous children's books, two recently for the
Creative Company,* I'm Not a Pig in Underpants *and* How to Draw with Your
Funny Bone. *Elwood currently lives in Great Barrington, Massachusetts, with
his companion, Janice Kittner, and his three unruly cats.*

16

"And then he was gone. I never even heard the door slam."

DAVID BREITHAUPT (FRIEND, COLLEAGUE) AND ALLEN GINSBERG

It sat on the table, a round, green tangle of green twigs about the size of a strongman's fist. It was fragrant, and I felt better just for smelling it. But this could only mean one thing.

He must be around here somewhere.

I am sitting in Allen's old kitchen, East Village, New York City, East Twelfth Street, sorting through old cassette tapes, making notes. Reading his spidery writing on the tiny labels makes my eyes sore. It is an art I have mastered at last. Allen left behind a flotilla of material to be organized when he died in 1997, when liver cancer took him away. I started helping his staff catalog the videos and recordings of his yearly readings, back in the early 1980s, for eventual storage at Columbia. It was an annual event, like a harvest, hauling his years' worth of wisdom to the collegiate archives. They have since moved to Stanford, who apparently had the money to purchase the hoard. In any case, the worker ants are still cataloging.

I also smell tongue from the Ukrainian deli around the corner on First Avenue, yet another sign. Rimbaud stares from the wall, that portrait of which looks like Verlaine just pissed on his shoes, which he may have.

On the other side of the doorway hangs Whitman, gazing down, as if keeping an eye on young Arthur. I look at the laundry hanging on lines outside the kitchen window. This could be a view from 1910, a Jacob Riis shot. How the other half lives.

I hear a cough, and Allen walks in, bespectacled and suspendered. Mildly potbellied and palsied-eye, short beard peppered with gray. Same as when I last saw him with his measured gait, almost as if he were walking in iambic pentameters. He could be anybody's Jewish uncle.

"I knew you were here," I say. "I saw your green stuff sitting here."

Allen bows slightly, sits. "Green tea. A gift from Weiwei. Not like what you buy here. Would you like some?"

"Yes, please." Allen's old friend Weiwei, the revolutionary conceptual artist from China, always had the best tea.

Allen rises and places the kettle on the burner atop the old white stove. His movements are slow and deliberate. Above the stove hangs a large black-and-white cityscape by Berenice Abbott. A Mothers Against Drunk Driving sticker adorns the side of the stove. I smile whenever I see it, thinking of hectic rides Allen had with Neal and Burroughs's wife Joan Vollmer.

I wait for the kettle to whistle. It's strange to see him alive after all these years.

"How've you been?"

"I'm fine," I say. "But what about you? Do you have TV in heaven? Do you know what's going on? The times, they been a-changin'."

Allen nods knowingly; he's chewing something he removed from the fridge. "Tongue. Want some?"

"No thanks."

It still looks like tongue. Gross.

"Not really heaven. More like a leisure spa at the end of the Bardo. I saw you here and thought I'd say hello." The Bardo was an after-death state for Buddhists, a journey they took until they reached their final state. I never imagined a leisure spa as an option for the final result. They must have liked Allen.

"Climate change, Obama, the Twin Towers . . . life has marched on since you've gone. . . ."

"I know."

I don't know how he knows, but it's probably one of those next-world things. I sip my tea. It's wonderful.

"What do we do?"

"Meditate."

"I knew you'd say that."

Allen chews. I ask, "How do you eat that shit?" I feel freer with my opinions now that he is living in the next world.

"Acquired taste. Jewish Eastern European DNA. We eat animal parts."

"I don't know if even enlightenment can save us," I offer. I don't want to talk about tongue.

"Think back. History. We've suffered much worse. World wars. Police actions. A blueprint is in place."

"Fight, resist, raise a stink?"

He nods.

"Sit on the railroad tracks?"

Again, affirmative.

"Damn. I thought you'd have an easier answer since you've been in the beyond. Like a magic pill or something. Or a ray gun that removes bad people from office."

"Tried and true is still the best. Power of the printing press. Don't forget Trotsky on St. Marks Place."

I remember. Trotsky once had a secret printing press in the basement at 77 St. Marks Place, where Auden later lived.

"Okay," I say, resigned.

With his permission, I scrounge in the fridge for something to eat. I pour some oil into a pan and sauté some garlic and ginger. Then I chop off the ends of some bok choy and separate the leaves. I toss them in the pan and put a lid on. It smells fantastic. We are both drinking green tea. There is one slice of cheesecake left. I'm not touching that.

I remove the lid and sprinkle some low-sodium soy sauce and sesame seeds on top. I serve us both. We eat in silence, lost in our own thoughts.

"You shall prevail," he says with a wink. No easy chore with that palsied eye. I wonder if he knew something I didn't, *living in his bardo spa.*

"Gotcha."

He puts his dishes in the sink and straightens himself.

"Good to see you," he says. "I must be getting back." I don't argue; it's strange seeing him again. It's sad. It's happy. Not bittersweet but sad and happy.

He walks away, eyed by Whitman and Rimbaud. "Keep the tea," he says. "Oh, and finish the cheesecake." Before he vanishes, he turns and says, "Remember, the key is in the sunlight."

I nod. Of course. How could I forget? And then he is gone. I never even hear the door slam.

David Breithaupt is a child of the cold war, born into a small, conservative town in the Midwest. His work has been published in the Los Angeles Review of Books, *the* Rumpus, Exquisite Corpse, *and the* Nervous Breakdown, *as well as the anthology,* Thus Spake the Corpse: An Exquisite Corpse Reader. *He has edited* Hand on the Doorknob: A Charles Plymell Reader. *During the 1980s, he worked as an assistant archivist for Allen Ginsberg. He lives in Columbus, Ohio, where he helps edit two sports magazines, one dedicated to the Cincinnati Reds and the other to OSU collegiate sports.*

17

"I'm fine, Bama. Really fine," he says.
"I don't want you to worry. It's all cool."

PHYLLIS RAPHAEL (GRANDMOTHER)
AND MAX GLEZOS-CHARTOFF

My grandson Max, who died in 2012 at the age of seven, has agreed to meet me at La Caridad, the Spanish/Chinese restaurant next to my apartment building on the Upper West Side that was his favorite place for a takeout lunch.

He's there before I am, waiting on the bench next to the kitchen, dangling his legs. His face lights up when he sees me. Mine does, too. I can feel my heart beating faster, and I wind my arms around him. Alive. So alive. "Oh, Max," I say. "I'm so glad to see you."

I've promised myself not to cry and I'm not going to. He looks beautiful. He's wearing the gray zip-up fleece jacket I'd bought him in the Patagonia store. All the ravages of his illness are gone, and he looks just as he did before the brain tumor made its inroads upon him.

His skin is white, and his hair is dark and shiny and wavy. His eyes are their normal shade of gray/green, and the one that was crossed (the first sign of his illness) no longer is. If this is what happens in heaven, it can't be too bad.

"So what will it be?" I ask (as if I didn't know).

"I'll order," he says. "Boneless chicken with yellow rice," he tells the stone-faced waiter who wears a white short-sleeved shirt and clear glasses and is all business.

We sit on the bench waiting for our order. The palm of his hand in mine is unbelievably sweet, and I give his hand a quick kiss on the knuckles. The restaurant is full of lunchtime diners: taxi drivers, West Side workers, a pair of lovers, boys from the exclusive Collegiate School around the corner. But I can't take my eyes off Max. He's so beautiful.

"How are you, really?" I ask.

"I'm fine, Bama. Really fine," he says. "I don't want you to worry. It's all cool," he says, leaning his shoulder against me.

"Okay," I say. "If you say so."

"I do," he says.

There are a million questions I could ask him, but somehow I don't want to. Where has he gone? What is it like? Answers will just beget more questions. It's enough just to be here with him, the two of us together. I'm happy just being with him to share a lunch. I don't want anything more.

The bag with our food is set on the counter, and Max jumps up. "I want to pay," he says.

This is total Max.

"Are you sure?" I ask.

"Yes," he tells me. "Then you can pay me back."

This, too, is Max. I should have known there would be a catch.

He's into money. He saved the dollars he wheedled from me, from his step-grandfather—my husband Bob—and from his California grandfather, and his banking skills display the workings of the mind of a future Wall Street power broker.

One afternoon he and his best friend Nikki tried to sell their paintings in the lobby of their apartment building. The prices were exorbitant, but Max wasn't worried. He said, "Don't worry. My grandma will pay." And I did.

He produces a grown-up leather wallet, a gift I recognize from his aunt Jen, from the pocket of his jacket, and together we take out two ten-dollar bills. He hands the money to the counter man, who misses the humor of being paid by a seven-year-old with a Ferragamo wallet, and I take the change, and Max takes the warm plastic bag that holds our lunch and carries it close to his chest. Once at my building, he waves to our gateman, who hollers, "How's it going, Max?" as we ride the elevator upstairs to my apartment. In our formal dining room he takes his customary seat on one of the French chairs at the head of our long pine dining table. I put down the place mats that I brought back from India.

"I like those," he says.

"I know," I say.

"No red stuff," he warns me as I dish out the chicken and yellow rice.

"You think I could forget?" I say as I pick out the strips of pimento from his serving, and we both dig into the warm food. One order is enough for a family of four, and there's crusty bread and pats of butter.

"I've read all your schoolwork, all the stories you wrote," I tell him. "They were really good."

"I know," he says. (Modesty was never his strong suit. The boys in his class used to fight to see who would sit next to him in the lunchroom. When his mother asked him why he said, "Because I'm famous.")

"I don't know which story I like best," I say. "It's a tough choice. Maybe 'How to Walk My Dog.' I like when you say, 'Find a tree.'"

"You don't have to pick," he says. "You can like them all."

He's looking at me earnestly, and I have the wish that this moment would last forever, just me and Max and our chicken and rice.

I spoon out a second helping of chicken and rice and butter a piece of bread for him.

"I like what you wrote about money," I say. "'Children should be paid to go to school, like thirty dollars,'" I read. "'Why don't they get paid?'"

But Max has lost interest. He's finished his chicken and rice and is on his way to the kitchen freezer and is soon back with a carton of Häagen-Dazs ice cream and two bowls and spoons. That's my cue to get the sprinkles—not chocolate, the rainbow sprinkles are the ones he likes, hot pink, green, blue, white, yellow, orange, and red. He sprays them over his mountain of vanilla ice cream, so thick the spoon is dense with them as he fills it up. I pick some sprinkles off his lip, and we sit looking at each other and eating ice cream together.

Our spoons are scraping the bottoms of the bowls. Lunch will soon be over and he'll have to leave. I feel a wave of anguish wash over me. Our time is coming to an end. "You know that La Caridad may soon be gone, don't you?" I say. "It's going to be bulldozed to the ground. A high-rise will be going up where it is now."

"I know," he says. "But I'll never forget it. Will you?"

"Never," I say.

Max takes the bowls into the kitchen, and when he comes back I hold him tightly, my lips pressed against his cheek, hearing the soft sound of his breath and feeling his bones against my chest as he slips away.

"I love you, Bama," he says.

"Oh, Max, I love you, too," I say.

I walk him out to the elevator. The door opens, and he's gone.

Standing in the empty hallway I have a sudden recollection of Emily Gibbs in Thornton Wilder's play *Our Town*, learning how painful it is after death to go back among the living. Just as unbearable, I think, for the living to have one last chance to be with the dead.

Phyllis Raphael is the author of the memoir Off the King's Road: Lost and Found in London. *Winner of a PEN Award for short fiction, her stories and essays have appeared in* Harper's, *the* New York Times, *the* Village Voice, Vogue, Boulevard, Creative Nonfiction *magazine, and the Norton anthology* The Seasons of Women. *She has taught creative writing at the New School, at New York University, and in the undergraduate creative writing program at Columbia University.*

*". . . she had become a global culinary superstar. The Beyoncé
of Bolognese. The Adele of Antipasti. The Rihanna of Risotto."*

STEPHANIE PIERSON (STUDENT, FRIEND)
AND MARCELLA HAZAN

I know this will come as a surprise to her husband, Victor, and their
son, Giuliano, but from the time I was about twenty-six until my early
thirties, Marcella Hazan wasn't just one of the most influential women
in my life; she was like a mother to me.

The job was open since my own mother basically abdicated early
on. ("What changed the most for you once you had children?" someone asked her. "I could no longer afford designer shoes," my mother
replied, without even a touch of irony.)

Marcella was rarely described as maternal. If anything, quite the
opposite. Just Google "someone who didn't suffer fools gladly," and
Marcella's name will probably pop up.

And yet the "Author Who Changed the Way Americans Cook
Italian Food" (from her *New York Times* obit) changed the world for
me. I do not think I thanked Marcella for all she gave me when she
was alive. And by the time I would have told her, she had become a
global culinary superstar. The Beyoncé of Bolognese. The Adele of
Antipasti. The Rihanna of Risotto.

I first imprinted myself on Marcella when I signed up to take
cooking classes in her New York City apartment in the early seventies.
I was neither famous nor forthcoming. Many students in the class
were both. Just how unfamous and reserved was I? When Marcella
announced to us that she would be teaching a cooking course in
Bologna, I remember telling her, "Count me in. I'm coming." She
looked at me and said, "You?"

"You?"?! Ouch. I went to Bologna, where we got to know and really like each other. It could have been my zeal at the stove under her watchful eye, or it could have been the warmth of many glasses of grappa after a dinner one night on a class trip to Parma. Because Marcella could be cranky, critical, short. (A student stirring a stockpot in our class in Bologna: "Marcella, how do you know when this will be ready?" Marcella: "When it is done.") But after my trip to Bologna, she was never anything but kind to me.

In short, my mother fed me. Marcella nourished me.

She gave me my first taste of fried zucchini blossoms, Jerusalem artichokes, cranberry beans, the best bollito misto in Bologna. I would say you can't top that, but actually I can: Marcella introduced me to Julia Child and blood orange juice on the very same day. She taught me magic tricks: stick two lemons in the cavity of a chicken—don't add liquid, don't baste, don't do a thing—and you will get the sweetest, juiciest, most sublime chicken you have ever tasted. She taught me simplicity: to make her rich, thick tomato sauce, all you do is put canned tomatoes (the best canned tomatoes) in a saucepan with a halved onion and butter and simmer for forty-five minutes.

She taught me patience: peeling fresh chestnuts. (Enough said.) She taught me exactitude: rolling pasta. She taught me the proper disdain for what isn't honest and authentic. Re: commercially grated parmesan cheese: "It is of no interest whatever to Italian cooking" (from page 15 of *The Classic Italian Cookbook*).

From Marcella, I learned how to chop, how to turn out evenly sized crespelle (well, to even know that crespelle existed! A wonder! Right up there with grappa!), the difference between tortelloni and tortellini. She beamed when I cleaned the squid perfectly. Praised me when my risotto simmered away happily, not too dry, not too wet; not too low a heat, not too high. The day I learned to caramelize? Marcella gave me a hug.

Now, almost fifty years later, my Marcella cookbooks are dog-eared, ragged, ravaged by small red stains from cabbage, dried traces of grease from frying an eggplant, the soft imprint of a grain of Arborio, the tiniest crumb of I-don't-know-what on the recipe for Spaghetti with Tuna Sauce.

The Invitation.

"Dear Marcella, come to lunch from the Great Beyond, if you can manage it, so I can thank you properly. I hope you're free."

"Dearest Stevie. It has been forever. Yes! And could I ask you to bring me something?"

Our Lunch.

Well, I couldn't possibly cook for Marcella. (I actually did, just once. A dinner party at my New York apartment. Afterward, Marcella told me how much she disliked my opera stage manager husband and how much better she had liked my journalist ex-boyfriend. Unprompted. Duly noted. I made a James Beard roast, one I had cooked to perfection a million or so times before, but somehow, that night, it took more than three hours to be done. We ate around 11:30 p.m. How do you say "disaster" in Italian?

"Dear Marcella. Let's go to Marta. It's on East Twenty-Ninth Street, right off Park. We'll have fun. We can reminisce. I will never forget when our class picture was on the front page of the biggest newspaper in Bologna. I think the Italians were floored—where were our nonnas? Why did we have to pay to learn to cook?! Do you remember that?"

"Dearest Stevie. Of course. And I will never forget the first moment you walked into the big kitchen in Bologna. You were so shocked to see that Maria, our beloved New York cooking assistant, was there to be our pasta-making expert. You ran to her, hugged her, and burst into tears."

Back then, I was soft. Marcella was al dente.

A table for two at 1:00 p.m. Marta, Twenty-Ninth Street right off Park Avenue. Italian but not the kind of American Italian that Marcella hated. Fresh ingredients. Nothing complicated. Presentations that weren't meant to be Instagrammable. Everyone was Danny Meyer–friendly. The food was Danny Meyer–satisfying.

The place was full. I was waiting by the entrance. An ooh and aah of foodie acknowledgment when Marcella walked in. We hugged. Self-assured, as sleekly blond as ever, with that disarming, slightly crooked smile that I loved. Marcella was wearing a pale blue cashmere turtleneck with a black pencil skirt. A double strand of pearls lit up her face. She gracefully sat down on the banquette across from me, taking in everything, seeing what was on every plate, in every glass, not missing a thing. The waiter handed us menus.

A glass of Frascati for me. A Jack Daniel's for Marcella. And we ordered appetizers. To share. Crisp zucchini fries. Tomato risotto croquettes with mozzarella. Grilled baby artichokes. Wood-fired mushrooms.

"How lovely to be here," Marcella said. "And with you! And I am starving! But why now? I haven't seen you in so many years."

"Well," I said, "I wanted to thank you. I didn't get a chance earlier." We toasted.

"For everything. By teaching me to cook your food, you changed my life. I came to life. I grew up at your table. Everything was foreign, and then nothing was. Food became everything it should be. Love. Discovery. Confidence. Contentment. Empowerment. Passion. Joy. Giving. And you gave it all to me."

"That is a lot," said Marcella. "I had no idea.

"And, Stevie, I hope you brought what I asked for. My *New York Times* obituary."

"I did," I said, and took it out of my handbag.

"Maybe it's vanity," Marcella said, "or curiosity. But I want to hear what it said about me. And by the way," she added, "this food is delicious!"

"Not as good as yours," I ventured.

"Oh, not at all!" Marcella agreed. "But maybe we should try the chicken meatballs with ricotta. . . ."

Of course. After we ordered that, I told her that Kim Severson had written the obit. Kim, who I had interviewed once for an article. A gifted writer who was as down to earth as Marcella.

"A good choice," Marcella said. "Read it to me."

"The headline," I said, "is 'Marcella Hazan, Author Who Changed the Way Americans Cook Italian Food, Dies at 89.' Frankly, it's a rave. A total rave. Lidia Bastianich called you 'the first mother of Italian cooking in America.'"

"Not in the *world*?" Marcella asked. "Just America?"

"Oh, Marcella! America is a big country!" I laughed, scanning the page. "Kim went on to say that you 'embraced simplicity, precision and balance' in your cooking. And she said that you 'abhorred the overuse of garlic in much of what passed for Italian food in the United States, and would not suffer fools afraid of salt or the effort it took to find quality ingredients.'"

Marcella asked, "Did she say that I hated when people put lemon peel in their espresso? That Italian coffee should never be reheated? That I wrote in one of my cookbooks that in most parts of this country it is easier to find a unicorn than a really good piece of veal? And in another, I said, 'If an olive oil brand has become familiar to you through advertising, stay away from it.'"

"No," I replied. "But Victor . . ."

"Aah, how much I miss Victor," Marcella said. "The love of my life."

"In the obit," I said, "Victor is quoted as saying, 'A lot of people had encounters with her because she knew in her mind, in her heart, exactly how things were supposed to be. That is what made her cooking great. Marcella wasn't easy, but she was true. She made no compromises with herself with her work or with her people.'"

"What is that expression?' Marcella asked me. "'She took no prisoners'?"

"That's it," I said. "You took no prisoners." And I added, "People loved you for that. For your honesty and integrity. And, Marcella, there weren't just obits. There were so many tributes and celebrations. The day after you left us, the *Times* asked cooks what their favorite Marcella dishes were. You cannot believe how many people responded."

"Really," said Marcella, with a smile on her face. "And the dishes?"

"Oh, everything," I said. "From osso buco to your pesto to your tomato sauce to lasagna to your Bolognese sauce to Roast Chicken with Lemons. And, Marcella, they *got* you. Who you were. Your candor. Your caring. Your dry wit. The way you could totally demolish something but with good intentions and a good heart . . ."

"Uh-oh," said Marcella, "that sounds intriguing. What do you mean?"

"Well," I said. "Here's what a woman in Indiana wrote to the *Times*." I read it out loud. "She said, 'Marcella Hazan has been my hero since I started cooking seriously in my twenties. Many of her recipes remind me of my Italian grandmother's dishes, which were never written down. I own six of Marcella's books and have prepared about one thousand of her recipes over the years. I agree about her Bolognese and Roast Chicken with Lemons, which I make regularly. Two of my current favorites are the Friulli-Style Vegetable Soup and Broccoli Potato Soup from her *Marcella Cucina* book, which is among her best."

She went on to say, "One last thing, I had the good fortune to meet Marcella twice. The first time, we sat together at a food and wine event where she was being ignored as everyone buzzed around the trendy chefs. She picked up a crab leg, took one bite, looked at me, and said, 'There's nothing good to eat here.'"

Marcella leaned back and roared with laughter. "'There's nothing good to eat here!' I remember that! Let's take no prisoners! Let's eat!"

She smiled. By that time Marcella was eating the pizza with everything fabulous: sopresatta, guanciale, pork sausage, mozzarella, Grana Padano. I was enjoying the pizza with very little—the Margherita. After that, an arugula salad. We ate slowly. And happily.

"Oh, Marcella," I said, "I feel like you should know this. Growing up, our dining table was a battlefield. My mother would leave in tears after an argument with my father. When we were very young, my brother, Sam, and I were often sent away to eat in the kitchen since Sam was too antsy to sit still in the dining room. When we were older, well, it didn't get better. Every night we had soup. One night we were eating cream of tomato soup. 'None for me,' I said. Silence. My father looked up and said: 'You like tomatoes, don't you?' Yes, I replied. 'You like cream, don't you?' Yes, I said. 'Well then,' said my father, banging his spoon down in a cold fury, 'you like cream of tomato soup, goddamn it!' And he made me eat the soup."

"Another glass of Frascati," Marcella told the waiter as soon as she could catch his eye. "I'm sorry," she said. "You didn't deserve that. How awful."

"Oh, Marcella, I know I didn't. But I'm fine now. The happiness and beauty of your food healed me."

Marcella took my hand and held it.

"Dearest Stevie," Marcella said. "A splendid lunch. I loved every bite and every word written about me. Maybe by now it is easier to find a good piece of veal than a unicorn. So I would edit that out of the next printing—maybe you could see to that?"

I nodded.

She went on. "But I can't see you again. You know that. Just know you have made me very happy. And I am so proud of you. They could have served the pizzas a little hotter."

Oh, Marcella! A declaration of love. After all these years.

"Dessert?" I asked her.

"I'm full," Marcella said.

"Me too," I told her, taking her hand in mine. "Me too."

And then she stood up, and left so quickly I didn't have time to give her a kiss or a hug or cry. (I'm still soft.)

I watched as she rushed out of the restaurant and hailed a cab and disappeared.

And then the waiter said, "Just so you know, she's taken care of everything." How did he know?

Stephanie Pierson is a New York advertising copywriter and journalist. She has written lifestyle, design, and food articles for the New Times, New York *magazine,* Atlantic Monthly, *the* Huffington Post, *and* Food52. *After she fell in love with Marcella Hazan's cooking, she found herself inexplicably smitten with brisket. She wrote the definitive (it's the only) book about brisket:* The Brisket Book: A Love Story with Recipes, *published by Andrews McMeel. She knows that everybody has the best brisket recipe ever. And that you have the best brisket recipe ever!*

19

"And honestly, did I really want to see my mother, dead by her own choice since 2003, over a Cobb salad or an omelet? No, I did not."

MARGARET HEILBRUN (DAUGHTER) AND CAROLYN HEILBRUN AND HER PSEUDONYM, AMANDA CROSS

My mother, Carolyn Heilbrun, always liked to sleep well into the mornings and never met anyone for lunch. I didn't even consider suggesting that she and I have lunch together, so well were my mother's absolute ways of living familiar to me.

True, she was now dead. Would she, in death, prove more amenable to lunch? It seemed to me unlikely. And, honestly, did I really want to see my mother, dead by her own choice since 2003, over a Cobb salad or an omelet? No I did not.

Over hard liquor was how we used to meet each other in her latter days. At a bar near my parents' Upper West Side apartment. I used to work nearby, and she and I would meet just after 5:00 p.m., when no one else was in this particular dive. She'd order a gin martini with olives, and I'd get a whiskey sour, a kind of drinking that neither of us indulged in at home.

But I didn't really want to meet my dead mother for drinks either, truth be told.

On the other hand, her pseudonym, Amanda Cross, author of fourteen mystery novels involving Professor Kate Fansler, was in many ways my mother's foil. No, Amanda Cross was more than that. She was the manifestation—and creator—of what Carolyn yearned to be: a WASP author writing about an elegant, slim, decidedly childless WASP academic who was an amateur detective, contentedly married, after some persuasion, to a partner whose name and ring she did not accept.

It followed, then, that Amanda Cross would agree to come to lunch with me. She did.

She suggested that we meet on the Upper West Side and that I should pick the place. I proposed lunch at the Utopia, a coffee shop near the Seventy-Second Street IRT, one of the rare holdouts from my childhood in the area. I was in the mood for eggs over medium with a buttered English muffin. Fried eggs are never as satisfying when I make them at home, perhaps because of the prospect of having to clean the frying pan.

On its Amsterdam Avenue frontage, the Utopia now declared itself a "Restaurant" but it had changed little inside. Although I was early, Amanda Cross was already there, in a booth along the edge. She saw me and raised a hand in greeting, an odd gesture with no flexion in the wrist. Rather like the queen, I thought. Carolyn was the same age as the queen and, until she grew out her curly hair and pinned it back—and grew herself out a bit as well—they had looked somewhat alike and had carried the same kind of purse.

Amanda Cross stood up, and we offered each other a peremptory hug, our kisses glancing off each other's cheeks—her skin was as soft as my mother's. Settling down in the booth, we both spoke at once—"You're looking well"; "It's very nice of you to come."

Service is on the mark at the Utopia. Amanda Cross ordered a BLT on white toast and an iced tea, while I ordered my eggs, English muffin, and coffee. It's funny how one can grow nostalgic about lousy coffee with free refills.

Let me interject here that, as you may have noted, I find it necessary to refer to Amanda Cross by her full name. My mother—she of the absolutes—had told me when I was in fifth grade and obliged to read *Tom Sawyer,* long before I knew of Amanda Cross, that "you cannot refer to Mark Twain as 'Twain'!" I took this as an admonition about all pseudonyms.

For years, I took all my mother's declarations as gospel. They carried such conviction. It was decades before it dawned on me that they should at the very least be run through a filtering process, if not disregarded entirely. (I also took the words of my father, Jim Heilbrun, to heart, but he was less prone to declarations and admonitions. Our morning, evening, and weekend caregiver when we three children were young, he once stated emphatically, as he and I read from *Minute Sketches of Great Composers,* that he disliked Mahler's music. So I abjured Mahler, admittedly not a tricky task. Years later I found him preparing to record a live Mahler program on WQXR. My father had changed his mind but had forgotten to tell me.)

Our lunch arrived. Some coffee shops don't manage "over medium," preferring the efficiency of sunny-side up or the routine of over easy, but the Utopia's over mediums were delicious.

"How have you been?" I asked Amanda Cross as she negotiated her BLT. She was backlit by sun from the front window, so it was hard to make out her face too closely.

"You know how I've been," she said. "Shall we call it limbo? And by the way, you don't type nearly as fast as Carolyn did."

So Amanda Cross knew that I'd been trying to write a book by her. I'd wondered about that. It's hard to tell with pseudonyms. Perhaps she'd read that *New York* magazine article, published some weeks after Carolyn's death, in which I told the journalist that Carolyn had agreed to embark on a coauthored Amanda Cross with me.

It was when Carolyn and I were at that dive bar. "I've come to the end of my writing life," she said after we'd taken a few swallows of our cocktails and had agreed that the weather was far too humid. I wanted to think it simply another of her declarations that I could now, with acquired facility, set aside. Yet it had the ring of consequence, of defeat, about it. She had pulled out her compact and was blotting her face, damp from her walk to our rendezvous.

Now I looked up from my eggs. "It's funny. The scent of her face powder lingered in her study for months after she died."

"You sound like a James M. Cain novel," said Amanda Cross.

"Really, though. Whenever I found myself in her study afterward, I could still smell the face powder. It stayed for weeks and weeks. Then one day it simply wasn't there."

"How's the Amanda Cross coming?"

"Slow progress."

That last time at the bar. Carolyn, having declared the end of her writing life, was fiddling with her martini olives, stabbed together on a cocktail pick. The bartender, a sweet woman who remembered us from visit to visit, had not bothered to cue up any music yet. The place was empty, save for my mother and me. A long and narrow aquarium, which served as a divider between the bar and the haphazard upholstered seating where we were, bubbled away. An artfully broken Bacardi bottle was nestled on the graveled bottom, with a little aerating deep-sea diver anchored nearby, ceaselessly ready to explore it. A small, whiskered gray fish suctioned algae off the glass.

"Of course it's not over," I insisted. "Think of all the things there are to write about!"

"I proposed a book to my editor and she turned it down," said Carolyn. She had sounded more emotional about the weather. She munched an olive.

"Well, let's write an Amanda Cross together!"

"Okay."

Her ready acquiescence to my whiskey-soaked suggestion astonished me.

My eggs and muffin devoured, I looked up at Amanda Cross. "I guess she knew she was going to kill herself in a few weeks. She wasn't really committing to any other project." The waiter came by to refill my coffee.

"Who knows, Marg."

Only my parents and one gym teacher had ever called me Marg, such an unimaginative nickname.

Amanda Cross was looking at me, a solemn stare from the shadows that I found unsettling. I was not up to the task of matching her gaze, so I resorted to my iPhone, faceup on the table next to me. With sidelong glances and one roving finger, I idly checked the time, texts, Facebook, Twitter, and the status of an Amazon order.

"Explain Twitter to me."

"Well, you share anything you want. It used to be limited to a hundred and forty characters of text, but now it's double that."

"What on earth does one say? I suppose it's like a postcard."

"Then everyone who follows you—"

"Like lemmings?"

"—can see it."

"'Having wonderful trip. Wish you were here. Weather fine.'"

"Well, not really like postcards . . ."

"P.S. I love you." She quietly half-sang the line from Johnny Mercer's song.

"'The journey is over. Love to all. Carolyn.'" I said the words of my mother's suicide note as if reading from a list. "That fits really easily on Twitter. I've seen it there. Also in Spanish: '*El viage ha terminado. Amor para todos.*'"

With a red plastic straw, Amanda Cross was shifting the diminishing ice in her glass. Rattle, rattle, rattle.

I persisted. "She could have gone on a bit longer, don't you think?"

"Sure. Two hundred and eighty characters, you say?"

"I mean in the note itself. On her letterhead. Left on the bureau in the foyer. I thought maybe there'd be a follow-up letter from her in the mail. One to each of us—her kids; Jim, who was out of town when she killed herself—but there wasn't."

"Well, you never know with the post office. It may yet arrive."

That made us both chuckle. I leaned back with actual delight, and the booth creaked. A memory caught hold of me.

"Remember the laundromat that summer in Oxford?"

"St. Bernard's Road, 1973."

"We'd taken our laundry to a place on Walton Street—remember?—and we were on a bench inside near the front waiting for the dryer to finish—"

"We leaned back against the wall—"

"—and it leaned back with us—"

"Into the liquor store next door!"

"Wine and Spirits!" I briefly clutched her wrist across the table and felt it stiffen.

"Remember how the proprietor glanced up?"

"Unfazed! I don't think we were the first to come through that wall."

"Then we sat back up, into the laundromat."

"—where nobody noticed what had happened!"

We were both laughing now.

The waiter placed the check between my mother and me on the table.

I grinned and stretched in my seat. The booth creaked again, and we both laughed again. Carolyn took off her glasses and wiped them on a napkin. "I remember how we used to get lost on highways—"

Funny, our urge to turn a solitary memory into a pattern of recurring moments. "Yes! That time in Connecticut! Where were we going?" I was actually scratching my head, trying to recall.

"I can't remember. You were supposed to be navigating, but then you collapsed in giggles with the map. That set me off, too, and I had to pull over."

"On a breakdown lane outside of Torrington. Or was it Waterbury?"

"Well, I must go."

"To Connecticut?"

She smiled indulgently. "You know what I mean, Marg. It's been fun."

"I'll get this," I said, standing up with her and surveying the bill to do the math for the tip. "Shall we?"

She was gone.

I left a twenty on the table and meant to move the coffee mug to hold the check and money in place, but I moved a small, flat circular hinged case instead. I opened it. The face powder was entirely rubbed away from the center, but there was a nice rim of it all around the edge. It smelled like heaven.

Margaret Heilbrun has been an archivist, curator of manuscripts, library director, and magazine and freelance editor in New York City. She has curated exhibits as well as published on topics relating to the city's history. She now lives in a former railroad passenger depot in western Massachusetts.

20

"It was my idea to light my guitar on fire. . . . Nobody else's."

JOE LEWIS (ACQUAINTANCE)
AND JIMI HENDRIX

Lunch with Jimi? How could I ever have thought that possible? He'd been gone a long time; then again, our whole connection had always seemed strangely otherworldly to me.

Amazingly enough, I almost forgot the first time I met Jimi. It was 1967; I was fourteen and studying rhythm guitar with Hal Waters. I began hanging around this little smoky basement dive called Steve Paul's Scene on Forty-Sixth Street and Eighth Avenue in Manhattan a few nights a week to watch Hal. On one particular night, I heard there was going to be a jam session, and rumor had it Jimi Hendrix was going to play. Damn! Jimi Hendrix was God. There is no contemporary equivalent to the position he held in the music world. He played the guitar upside down and backward. *Axis Bold as Love* is one of the only records I ever actually bought.

That night, the Buddy Guy Trio was the headline act and a great performer. But, Buddy was no Hendrix. No comparison. Hal played an acoustic second set, I sat in with him on "Water Boy," and then BAM! The backroom door opened. Out walked Jimi, and surprisingly, he joined us onstage, dropping right into the groove. About halfway through the song, he leaned over, quietly asking me, "Am I playing too loud?"

I was fourteen years old and suddenly playing with Jimi Hendrix, *and he asked me if he was playing too loud!*

After Hal's set, roadies rearranged the stage, tweaked the massive columns of Marshall amplifiers and house drum gear in preparation for the jam session. The scene immediately packed with some of the best musicians in town. They started with a scorching up-tempo twelve-bar blues. But when Jimi stepped up, the music exploded in his presence; and his solo was so loud it shook your dental fillings loose. He didn't just play the guitar; he *became* the guitar.

That night, Jimi had transported us somewhere into the cosmos and then suddenly, he blacked out and fell off the stage. Quickly, the house bouncers untangled him from the crowd and carried him to a small round table in the back corner. I thought, here's my chance, slowly threaded my way over to his table, pulled up a chair, and in no time, we were face-to-face. He was slouched down and leaning heavily to the side with his hair and face picking up colors from the room's psychedelic lighting. I got down closer to the table and said, "Jimi, can you tell me just one secret of the universe?" His eyes were blurred and crossed, but he managed to raise up a bit and looked me squarely in the face. He began to speak, and then vomited all over me.

I was fourteen years old, and Jimi Hendrix had just vomited on me.

His handlers rushed over, cleaned him up, and spirited him out of the club. Occasionally after that, when he was in town, precocious, music-possessed kid that I was, we'd bump into each other at parties, in one of the rock clubs, or performance venues like the Fillmore East, Nite Owl, or Cafe Wha?. When we did, he'd always give me a nod, a wink, or a slap on the back. On September 17, 1970, Jimi Hendrix died—three years after that jam session at the Steve Paul's Scene. Since then, rarely a day goes by that I don't think about something Jimi, especially his music; a potent elixir that continues to improve as the years pass.

And now, here we were, about to lunch at Robert, a fancy minimalist American restaurant, on the top floor of the Museum of Arts and Design, high above Columbus Circle. It had wide, expansive views of Central Park. It was just a few short blocks from the formally elegant

Wellington Hotel on Seventh Avenue, where he used to ensconce himself. With a big smile, we met in the museum's lobby. "Joe!" he said. Guitar in hand, he was attired in his signature style, sporting a tailored, royal blue velvet jacket edged with gold ribbing and buttons, boisterous silk paisley shirt and scarf, large gold chain belt, with pointy snakeskin boots and a wide-brimmed hat dramatically perched on top of his giant Afro. Jimi never disappointed. Looking around he said, "I love the street sounds of this city!"

The hues of his vibrant couture accentuated the sleek modernist overtones of the restaurant's deep purple and maroon décor. We caused quite a stir among the people power-lunching. Just imagine Jimi, the flower-powered-dandy, juxtaposed with the stiff, tieless, single-button executive crowd.

Arthur, the maître d' and an old friend, seated us front and center with an uninterrupted view of the park and uptown Manhattan. Almost immediately, a score of men seated close to us started snickering, loudly parsing thinly veiled bigoted comments and primitive innuendos our way. I thought Robert was the perfect setting for us to talk about changes and innovations in music, but this interaction momentarily blurred my vision. Jimi was a lot statelier than I and said with an effortless smirk, "I guess things haven't changed that much, now, have they?" Arthur was aghast at the table's behavior and apologized profusely to us after diplomatically excoriating the suits.

I wanted to laugh, but the menu snagged my attention. Arthur intervened, "Mr. Hendrix, may I suggest, for starters, the Papaya and Goat Cheese Salad—arugula based with Crottin de Chavignol, radishes, and Key lime drizzled vinaigrette; and for your main course, Tiger Shrimp Stew in a rosemary-fennel butter base. And for you, Joe, your usual?" "Yep, Lobster and Steak Frites, black and blue." *Just like Jimi's music,* I thought; seared black on the outside and cold and raw in the middle. Greco di Tufo, a fresh, unoaked white wine freely flowed into Jimi's glass as I drowned myself in Arnold Palmers. The wine loosened Jimi up; he was notoriously tight-lipped—unless you were female, and then he had the gift of gab—always with guitar in hand. And sure enough, as our meal progressed, he was besieged by female corporate types with iPhones. They gathered around our table after finishing their lunches, asking him if he wouldn't mind taking a picture with them. They didn't look old enough even to know who he was; I guessed they sensed, unlike their male counterparts, that he was a very famous somebody. Then he'd flash that famous smile—the broadest grin I'd ever seen.

It took a while for the amalgam of their flowery and musky perfume base notes to dissipate; then, we became the last patrons in the restaurant on top of the architect Edward Durell Stone's controversial trapezoidal bonbon, anchoring the southernmost corner of Columbus Circle. An architecturally designed building ahead of its time, hosting a musician the future was still trying to catch up to.

Jimi was blown away by all the gadgets performers used to generate the sounds he created by twisting the volume or tone switches back and forth with his pinky while playing his Fender Stratocaster, upside down and backward to boot. While gazing devotedly at his guitar perched on our table, he said, "And it was my idea to light my guitar on fire at the Monterey Pop Festival. Nobody else's." Just as I'd always thought.

I had already decided, feeling nostalgic for those long-ago days, not to remind him of how we'd first met. "What do you think about the business of music, Jimi? There are a lot of stories about how your management tried to control you by sabotaging various band configurations, messing with your money and copyrights." "All true," Jimi said. "The business was truly evil. Dangerous, backstabbing, and greedy." I interrupted, "My dad had an office in the Brill Building and published music, as a Black man, during the 1960s in Tin Pan Alley.

Even as a child, I knew you could get your legs broken in the music industry." "Your dad published music in the Brill Building! Damn. Then you know . . ." "Yep," I said. Jimi carried on, "All I ever wanted to do was make music. I built Electric Lady Studios to capture all the stuff going on in my head. I had plans but never got to implement them. I hated touring and the constant requests for certain compositions; playing the same song over and over. Man, I never understood why people couldn't just come and hear me play like they did for, you know, Coltrane, Monk, Parker."

I so wanted to ask him to kick out a few riffs from my favorite songs—"Spanish Castle Magic" or "Little Wing"—but his candor quickly made me realize I would take those requests to my grave. So I switched gears. "You know, your music changed the DNA of everyone who listened to it; especially me." I gave him a copy of my first CD. "Cool cover art," he said. "Hey, you play left-handed, too?"

Arthur came by again, and I said, "We're just about to leave." "Oh, no, take as much time as you like." And magically, two Upside-Down Peach Cakes with Rhubarb Caviar and Almond Tuiles appeared on our table. "I am so embarrassed by that table's behavior this afternoon, please, lunch is on me." I said, "Arthur . . ." "No, no no. It's all right, Joe. Indeed, my pleasure." I asked Arthur to join us.

Jimi focused on the unusual amorphous shapes of the Tuiles adorning the tops of our desserts. We sat drinking cappuccinos, and he savored some Hennessy X.O for another hour or so, telling stories about our life's many foibles, covered in high-decibel, side-splitting laughter about them. (Given its own space, failure can be kind of funny at times.) Jimi's laugh was a full-bodied, light-headed eruption that left him seeming unexpectedly helpless and vulnerable. The waitstaff began setting up for dinner. Jimi and I thanked Arthur for an unforgettable lunch. He told us that his restaurant was our restaurant, to come back anytime.

When we got outside, Jimi jumped into a yellow cab. But before it screeched down Central Park South, he opened the window and said, "Joe, man, I'm really sorry I threw up on you that time. Definitely not cool." And off he sped. Then it hit me: I hadn't taken a breath all afternoon. As the taxi's image blurrily vanished in the distance, I remembered that I had forgotten to ask him the most critical question: What is it like being a god?

A few months later, I was in London on business and found myself standing in front of 23 Brook Street, the building where Jimi died. Did you know that a single wall separated his apartment from George Frideric Handel's?

Some people think Jimi was the reincarnation of Handel.

Not me. I know that gods never die.

Joe Lewis is a nationally known artist, educator, author, musician, and professor of art at the University of California, Irvine, where he served as dean of the Claire Trevor School of the Arts from 2010 to 2014. He was also the dean at Alfred University and FIT in New York, and co-founding director of Fashion Moda. Currently, he is the president of the Noah Purifoy Foundation, Los Angeles/ Joshua Tree, California. He has written for Art in America, Artforum, *and* LA Weekly *and was a contributing editor for* Artspace *and a correspondent for* Contemporanea, *an international arts magazine. His essays regarding art, technology, and society have appeared in anthologies and peer-reviewed journals.*

21

"But when [his words were] projected by that marvelous voice—
together with a wicked smile and naughty, flashing eyes—
they soared to new heights to delight friends and terrify foes."

HUSSEIN IBISH (CLOSE FRIEND)
AND CHRISTOPHER HITCHENS

I arrive at the Bombay Club restaurant at noon, per the arrangement. It is a beautiful, mild day in Washington, sunny but not too warm, probably in the late summer but possibly spring. Under the circumstances, it's hard to be certain. He's already there. Christopher Hitchens, my dear friend, is sitting at one of a small cluster of outside tables. There aren't any other customers yet, but, I think, it's early. Still, this has the feel of a Lafayette Square weekend, not a bustling workday.

I know the Bombay Club and its immediate surroundings intimately. My office was located in the same building—815 Connecticut Avenue—for seven years and then directly across the street for another four. I am somehow quite sure that it's Saturday, though for some reason I do not know it, exactly. Even more strangely, the Bombay Club doesn't serve lunch on Saturdays. Yet here we are. Christopher—it's never "Chris," and although I never made that mistake I saw people who did be corrected gently and not-so-gently, depending on various factors. As I approach, I can see he's already smoking and has gotten a drink. At a glance I can tell that, as usual, it's Johnnie Walker Black, with just a splash of water. Uncanny as it is to see him, I grin broadly. I've missed him desperately, and this is a rare, unexpected opportunity to reconnect. As I get closer, he sees me, too, and beams.

When I arrive at the table, he rises to greet me. We approach each other and, as always, exchange a long hug and two lingering kisses on each cheek. I'm nonplussed to see him, because, of course, he passed away years ago. He seems much less confused about all this than I do, though. On the contrary, he's relaxed and, as usual, appears to have everything under control. "Christopher—" I begin to say. He interrupts me: "Oh my dear . . ." I begin to struggle for some broad, existential remarks, but again he stops me, deliberately turning the conversation in a more familiar and quotidian direction. "I hope you don't mind sitting outside, dear boy," he drawls, "but this smoking repression seems to have gotten rather worse since I've been away. Had the devil of a time convincing them to let me puff a little ciggy out here, let alone in there." He waves in the direction of the restaurant's interior.

When the smoking ban in Washington's restaurants started, it had been a real blow to Hitch, a passionate smoker who dined out frequently. One of his solutions was to convince old haunts in which he was a known and valued quantity to figure out how to make an exception for him. The Bombay Club used to put him in or near a private room, but, he says, this time they had only grudgingly agreed he could discreetly smoke at an outdoor table. Frankly, I was surprised they had even granted that. Since there were no other customers seated outside yet, there was also no one to complain, so that obviously made it easier. "I see you people haven't yet appropriately addressed the smoking question," he observes, in a mocking and semi-accusatory tone.

We sit at a table in the shade, enjoying the sunny, mild early afternoon. He looks wonderful. Christopher has returned appearing as he was just before he fell ill, a robust, slightly puffy, but oddly youthful and even cherubic middle-aged man. When he was sick, at least in my presence, he never lost spirit, lucidity, or determination. But he lost his hair, a vast amount of weight, almost all his energy, and most of the sparkle in his eye. That was all back now, somehow.

Even his sonorous, mellifluous speaking voice—one of the most potent weapons in his formidable personality arsenal and one that could seduce or demolish with equal efficacy and speed—which had suffered so greatly during the latter parts of his illness, was back in all its majestic, resonant glory. His words were invariably superbly crafted, and in writing he'd been one of the great nonfiction stylists of his generation. But when projected by that marvelous voice—together with a wicked smile and naughty, flashing eyes—they soared to new heights to delight friends and terrify foes.

He lit another cigarette, drawing on it deeply and exhaling in evident satisfaction. "Still smoking, I see," I observe, recalling how, even when he was very ill, both Christopher and his wife, Carol, used to "sneak" cigarettes when the other supposedly wasn't paying attention or aware, swearing third parties like me to a faux secrecy that didn't really exist and wasn't needed. He grunted, plainly enjoying the cigarette. "Do you smoke"—I ask, struggling for words—"where you . . . are?" He shakes his head vigorously from side to side. "Sorry, dear boy, can't get into any of that. You know that." I suppose I did. But I had to ask. There's almost no doubt that smoking had contributed to Christopher's cancer, but there was no point in bringing that up now. Many things had contributed, including drinking and, of course, genetics, since his father died of the same cancer, though at a much more advanced age.

The double doors of the elegant Indian restaurant open, and out floats the suave, graceful Turkish maître d' in his always impeccable dark suit. Funny, I think, he hasn't worked here for years. But things were now not as they are, but as they should be, or might have been.

"Greetings, Mr. Hussein," the maître d' purrs, as emollient and deferential as ever. Before I can order, Christopher points at his own tumbler and says, "I'll have another of those." I say I'll have a coffee. "Coff-coffee? *Coffee???*" Hitch sputters incredulously, choking on the last drops of his rapidly disappearing dram of Johnnie Walker. "Oh, come now!" I explain that I haven't been drinking much these days.

He reiterates, as he has insisted many times before, that periods of abstinence are not only useful but also essential to the truly committed drinker. However, he tells me, I could and should make this meeting an exception because, as he somewhat cryptically puts it, "no harm can come of it, I assure you."

I relent and order a glass of champagne. "That's more like it," Christopher says with some satisfaction. "Now, would you like it served room temperature, as usual?" I assure him that I prefer it cold, indeed ice-cold. In his company I had been willing to drink large amounts of bubbly unchilled, because, while he usually had champagne, like most other forms of fine potable alcohol, readily at hand, it usually wasn't already chilled, and I wasn't willing to wait. Carol, who was often the only other person joining me in preferring sparkling wines over anything else, frequently repeated the comforting conceit that the French somehow *prefer* to drink champagne at room temperature, the same way the English really do like bitter beer cool but not cold. I knew that wasn't true, and she probably did as well, but, like many a dubious factoid, it served its purpose.

Christopher explains that he's already ordered a number of dishes because he knows what he wants.

"You know, the usual . . . tandoori chicken, rogan josh, various tikas, chicken biryani with loads of that yogurt stuff, plenty of naan, lots and lots of mango chutney, and, oh yes, that splendid yellow daal. Thank God they've got that. I'm not keen on the brown muck, as you know," he explains. He urges me to get anything else I might want, but I tell him it sounds perfect, except that "I would like some brown muck, thanks," and I order a portion of their excellent dal makhni. The waiter serving us is an affable, thin Moroccan who always speaks to me in barely comprehensible Maghrabi Arabic, and it occurs to me that he hasn't worked there for years either.

I look at Christopher carefully, and it really is the old Christopher back again, inexplicably in the flesh. "We've really missed you," I say, somewhat hesitantly. He snorts. "I should *think* you have. You're making a proper mess of things back here, aren't you? A real pig's breakfast . . . No, I'm afraid you've really let the side down this time." "It's not my fault," I protest. "I did my best. I'm not sure what more I could have done. The country—" He interrupts, waving aside any suggestion of advice, "Not having to participate in such sanctimony and squalor is one of the advantages of my present circumstances. Worked hard to get here," he drawls languidly. "Came by it honestly, too. Not giving that part up for love or money, dear boy."

There was a clear understanding, achieved in the same occult and enigmatic way that the lunch itself had been, for want of a better word, "arranged," that the circumstances and details of his current existence—if any—were not to be discussed at all during this unexpected and inexplicable new conversation. The experience, I was given to understand in a manner that I cannot lucidly describe now and which I am sure will always remain ineffable, was contingent on accepting the mystery and unresolved, unknowable character it was bound to have. At what, if any, level this lunch and the whole experience was "real," or this figure was or was not in any meaningful sense Christopher Hitchens, or what is implied about anyone other than myself, were all questions that wouldn't really be addressed, let alone resolved, at the lunch or in the account of it here. But I couldn't resist wanting to broach the topic anyway.

Helpfully, just then the food arrives, looking familiar but particularly delectable. Another round of drinks is ordered, naturally, but with Christopher switching to red wine, and we tuck into the charcoal-grilled meats and steaming, unctuous curries. After a minute or two he looks up in great satisfaction and asks, "Why does anyone ever eat anything else?" He plainly means it literally. I knew how much he, like many Brits, adored Indian food in general, and appreciated the Bombay Club in particular.

As Christopher got sicker and became increasingly less inclined or able to get out much, I would frequently get big bags of Hitchens family favorites—although the restaurant is an elegant, white-linen affair rather than a takeaway joint—carefully packed to go and deliver them to his Kalorama apartment around suppertime. By that stage, he wasn't eating much, sometimes virtually nothing. But this gave him the option, and everyone else who was with him had to eat, too, and no one wanted to cook much. At this uncanny new lunch, between big bites, long gulps, and endless puffs—sometimes all three magically and mystifyingly combined, just like in the good old days—he tells me that he'd really missed "this sort of thing." But he then shoots me a penetrating glare that said, in wordless but no uncertain terms, that I wasn't to inquire further into any of that.

Lunches were always an important feature, and frequent setting, of our friendship. It was only well into our friendship that I learned just how important some of his own regular youthful lunches, as recounted in his excellent memoir, *Hitch-22,* and elsewhere, with a group he called the "Demon Lunchers of Fleet Street" had been to the formation of his mature persona, worldview, and style. The informal gang that lunched on Fridays in London in the 1970s included Martin Amis, Ian McEwan, Julian Barnes, James Fenton, Robert Conquest, Mark Boxer, Clive James, Peter Porter, Craig Raine, and Terry Kilmartin, among others, sometimes even including Kingsley Amis and Anthony Powell. Now *that's* a lunch. And Hitch had been part of it, for years. There's no doubt that these lunches were a key to his informal training and ad hoc education in his early professional years. For Hitch and these others, the usually quotidian mid-day meal could, and did, assume meanings, depths, and heights that the rest of us can only imagine.

Hitch and I first encountered each other at what began as a lunch but took on a life of its own in an organic but remarkable manner that defined a good deal of our evolving camaraderie. Christopher and I met shortly after I arrived in Washington, DC, in the fall of 1998, an obscure and unknown "all-but-dissertation" graduate student serving as communications director and spokesperson for an only slightly less obscure and unknown Arab American civil rights group. My predecessor in that job, Sam Husseini, had been skillfully researching the bombing of a medicine factory in Sudan by the Bill Clinton administration in response to the Al Qaeda attack against the USS *Cole* off the coast of Yemen. Christopher had contacted him in the course of researching what was eventually titled *No One Left to Lie To*, his brutal and brilliant evisceration of the Clintons, which one of the book's various subtitles describes as "the worst [as opposed to the first] family."

Being an honorable man, Sam apparently felt it was part of his role to acculturate me to Washington and make sure that I met a few interesting people before he totally disappeared. "How would you like to join me for lunch with Christopher Hitchens tomorrow?" he had nonchalantly asked. I tried to maintain the general atmosphere of sangfroid with an equally casual "sure," but, in fact, I was thrilled. I'd long admired Hitchens's speaking and writing in general, and his iconoclasm and take-no-prisoners style in particular.

I went to the lunch as a third wheel and, initially at least, tried to be respectful of the fact that the whole point was for Christopher to interview Sam to help build the case against the attack on the factory. So, during the first half hour of the meeting, I kept reasonably quiet, but that didn't last long. During the second half hour, I abandoned my shell pretty completely, and the literary allusions, snide and snarky comments, crude humor, and militant iconoclasm were flowing as freely as the drinks.

It appeared to me that what had, for Christopher, begun as a pleasant though somewhat tedious chore had turned into some good fun. I admired the man but hadn't expected to hit it off with him so immediately and powerfully. After about an hour and fifteen minutes, Sam—who had long since faded from a conversation that was rapidly moving away from anything in which he was even remotely interested, and which had now, for instance, turned to the relative merits of various lesser-known P. G. Wodehouse novels—politely but dryly observed that he'd better head back to his office in the National Press Club building on Fourteenth Street. Christopher and I both thought we might be able to choke back one or two more cups of the needful, particularly since his publisher would be paying for this "vital research project."

The restaurant, La Tomate, was just down the street from Christopher's apartment, just behind the "Reagan Hilton," so-called by many Washingtonians because of the attempted assassination that had taken place there in 1981. We were exulting in the company, the food, and the conversation when, just before five in the evening, Carol and their daughter, Antonia, walked by and spotted us. They joined us for about half an hour, the first of countless times I was to enjoy their company (as I still do). But at our first meeting, when it was almost 6:00 p.m., and the then very young daughter needed her supper and bedtime, Carol took Antonia home amid a mixture of pleasantries and Christopher's promises to be along "very shortly."

Four hours later, around 10:00 p.m., she called him up and told him that he had been talking and drinking with me for almost ten hours and that was probably enough. He somewhat sheepishly explained that family life could occasionally prove somewhat constricting. After we briefly chortled over the scandalous size of the bill we'd racked up for his publisher, he staggered up Connecticut Avenue toward home while I stood at the corner flapping my arms around in hopes a taxi driver might take pity on me.

I'd had hangovers before, of course. Many of them much worse. But hangovers were frequent, indeed typical, consequences of evenings with Christopher, and these had their own special characteristics. Because Christopher was generous with drinks and kept a well-stocked bar, not only was ample, and perhaps even excessive, consumption typical, but also an arguably ill-advised mixing of various distillations and fermentations of the juice of the grape and the grain could be hard to avoid. On most occasions, I made no effort to avoid it, knowing full well the probable consequences. But Hitchens-induced hangovers tended, at least for me, to be strikingly free from the ghoulish specters of regret, recrimination, and remorse that haunt so many other mornings after.

Less than a week after our extended introduction I received my first invitation to a dinner at Christopher's home. The first of many, it solidified what was an already rapidly developing friendship.

Many years later, only a week or so before he was diagnosed with stage 4 cancer (as he pointed out, "What's most significant about stage four is that there is no stage five,") after a terrible incident in New York, he once again demonstrated his enormous friendship at another key lunch meeting. I was undergoing an emotional crisis over a disastrous romantic entanglement with a severely disturbed woman, and I reached out to him on the phone for counsel and comfort. I explained my situation, and he told me that he had just arrived in Chicago to begin a book tour but that I should give him a few minutes and he would call me back. Evidently he could tell from the briefest call that my poor little brain was struggling to deal with an assault of, literally, mania from the lady I was breaking up with.

I needed help. I needed a friend. I hadn't said anything of the kind, at least explicitly, but he certainly seemed to get the message clearly enough. A few minutes later, he rang back and told me that he was canceling his next event, would be flying back to Washington that night, and that I should meet him for lunch (where else?) at the Bombay Club the next day.

"No wives and daughters this time," he averred. "Just us boys." In any event, he spent four hours with me, patiently listening to my whining, offering wise observations and largely very good advice, and generally talking me down off an emotional precipice.

He'd always taken an interest in my relations with women, for whatever reason, and one of his nicknames for me—"Mount Ibish"— was a play on both my vast bulk (for much of the time I knew him I weighed between four and five hundred pounds, though I'm now half that size, and he liked to say, "You came by that honestly") and a sly double entendre given that I wasn't exactly starved for attention. Now, for the first time, it had gotten me into a rather deep hole, and he was kind enough to want to help me out of it, which he certainly did.

He even paid for the meal, beyond having already done that in several ways, by canceling his event in order to babysit my wounded ego, changing his travel arrangements, and in several other obvious and not-so-obvious ways. It was particularly touching because while Christopher had a very generous streak, as I've noted, he also took money very seriously. He was more than willing to lend cash, but he wanted to be paid back, and I took care to never borrow any from him. Though he would have gladly lent it, I'd seen unpaid debts come, at least to some extent, between him and other mutual friends, and I didn't want that to happen to us.

Now, today, the platters of steaming food kept coming at us with great rapidity, and, up to the task, we quickly demolished them, all the while still drinking our respective quaffs. (Christopher was especially besotted with Johnnie Walker Black, which he said he had deliberately cultivated a particular liking for because it was both very good and universally available, including in most war zones and throughout the Islamic world—with a couple of rare exceptions.)

At first, being a perennial guest at his home, I suspected that his apathy regarding red wine held, or at least powerfully articulated, opinions possibly based on some overwhelming economic realities. Great wine can be very pricey, and most people can drink a lot more of it much more easily and carelessly than they can knock back Scotch, for example. Financial ruin could have been a foreseeable consequence hosting so many people so frequently and with such emphasis on keeping the company well lubricated, if he'd ditched the boosterism of plonk. Over time, however, it became clear to me that he deeply believed in this opinion. I began to suspect that constant cigarette smoking had, perhaps, blunted my friend's taste buds to the point that "the house plonk" really was sort of indistinguishable from a complex Bordeaux, a subtle Pinot Noir, or a profound Priorat.

But that clearly wasn't true, because I had seen him demonstrate that his palate was actually in remarkably fine working order, at least when it came to certain flavors. At the beginning of the meal, as always, he had ordered a double Johnnie Walker Black with a tiny splash of water. His first sip sent him into paroxysms of outrage: "What the fuck is this?" he bellowed. "It's . . . it's fucking lemonade!" The waiter, the bartender, and then the manager were imperiously summoned, in that order, to discover how and why an excellent and innocent Scotch was being forced to impersonate some "fucking kiddies' lemonade." A brief investigation determined that the little splash had come from a pitcher of filtered water. All DC residents know that, if you can possibly avoid it, Washington tap water is strictly undrinkable—unless one likes to quaff lashings of chlorine and God knows what else.

Hitchens not only shared this view but took it a step further: he would also cook with only bottled or strongly filtered water. At the bottom of this benighted pitcher, which was rapidly being recast as a veritable anus mundi, was discovered a lone, thin, and entirely forlorn slice of lemon. That villainous shard of fruit, it was universally agreed, must have been the interloper and culprit. In other words, one thin sliver of lemon had imparted the merest hint of flavor to almost a gallon of water, less than a tablespoon of which had then been poured into a double Scotch. From that, and with just one sip, the whiskey was declared to have been so adulterated as to become, in effect, "lemonade." That's a great many things, both good and bad. But it is *not* a crippled palate in action.

The men's room at the Bombay Club is all the way in the back of the restaurant on the right-hand side. I walk through the front door, past the bar, across the dining room, and into the men's room. In spite of everything else about this strikingly uncanny afternoon, I am still taken aback by the fact that, while everything is perfectly in place for a normal lunch service—even though this is, I somehow feel certain, a Saturday, and they normally only serve dinner on Saturdays—there are no other customers at all. All the tables are perfectly set, but no one else is there. As far as I can tell, only the Turkish manager and the Moroccan waiter are present, though I do see a light faintly glowing in the kitchen. Other than that, the place is eerily deserted. I don't mention this when I return to the table.

Much of our discussion is, naturally, about politics. We revisit old agreements, most passionately about the evils of religious politics in almost every form and guise. But we also revisit old disagreements, most notably the 2003 invasion of Iraq. We agree that Obama mishandled Syria dreadfully by ceding the field to Iran, Russia, and Hezbollah, and therefore also to Al Qaeda. We also agree that current circumstances are, if anything, worse in Syria rather than better.

But we also discuss art, films, and literature. An old fan of Bob Dylan, he nonetheless scoffs at his winning the Nobel Prize for literature. "How many Dylan songs could you really not live without, under any circumstance?" he asks me pointedly. I reel off a long list, most of which he dismisses. A few, he allows, are masterpieces. But he thinks the oeuvre as a whole is overrated and that a more critical second look at Dylan's catalog is warranted. Moreover, he reels off a list of his own: American fiction writers who much more richly deserve a Nobel literature prize than Bob Dylan.

Soaking up the juices of our once-mountainous plates of food, we dragged our triangles of excellent naan through what little food was left. We agree that it's amusing that the Nobel committee appears surprised that Dylan would snub the ceremony and seem so utterly disinterested in the award. "Who the fuck did they think they were dealing with?" he chortles, gleefully. "Did they sleep through the sixties?" He says he hasn't seen any recent films, and as far as I can tell, the same applies to the most recent novels. He appears to be aware of recent things, but not, perhaps, with the kind of detail that close reading would require. In that sense, it's a little different than talking to the old Hitch, at least about new things, but it's hard to put one's finger on precisely how or why.

After a few more hours of drinking, talking, and continuing to nibble, he tells me our time is up. He won't discuss it any further, and he won't use any other phrase. "Time to shove off, I'm afraid," he insists. I offer to pay, or at least to split the bill, but he won't hear of it. The Turkish maître d', who's been lurking helpfully by the side of the patio for most of the afternoon and providing us with typically excellent but unusually attentive service, pointedly tells me, "Your money's no good here, sir." It occurs to me I've heard that phrase somewhere before, but I can't quite place it.

I rise, and we embrace warmly. I notice the stain of curry on his shirt. Three lingering kisses on each cheek punctuate the afternoon, and with many affectionate remarks and mutual appreciation I turn and walk toward the Farragut West Metro station to take the train home. About ten seconds after I start walking away I realize that, for some inexplicable reason, I haven't asked him the most important question of all. How could it possibly have slipped my mind? I spin around to trot back a couple of hundred yards and rectify the oversight. But he's gone. The maître d' is gone. The tables and chairs are gone. The lights are off. The door is locked. And there is no sign that the Bombay Club was ever open for lunch that Saturday.

Hussein Ibish is a senior resident scholar at the Arab Gulf States Institute in Washington. He is a weekly columnist for Bloomberg Opinion *and the* National *(UAE) and a regular contributor to many other US and Middle Eastern publications. Many of Ibish's articles are archived on www.ibishblog .com. Ibish previously served as a senior fellow at the American Task Force on Palestine, executive director of the Foundation for Arab-American Leadership, and communications director for the American-Arab Anti-Discrimination Committee. He has a PhD in comparative literature from the University of Massachusetts, Amherst.*

22

"She will recover a future, and I will recover a past."

ALLEGRA HUSTON (DAUGHTER) AND ENRICA "RICKI" SOMA

San Lorenzo, on Beauchamp Place in London, was my mother's favorite restaurant long before it became the favored lunch spot of the famous. I will be early, and as I wait for her, I will see a few people I recognize. With my unsteady sense of facial recognition, I won't know at first whether these are friends, acquaintances, or just faces from movies and magazines. My mother, when she enters this bright, sunlit room, will be one of them. She will look as familiar to me as the royals and movie stars, and as much a stranger. I will recognize her only from photographs. I don't know the sound of my mother's voice or the music of her laugh. I don't know my mother's face in three dimensions. In the few memories I have of her, she is not looking at me. I see her from the side, driving a car, but it's her hand on the gearshift that has my attention. And again her hand, as we run for a train. In these memories, I can have been no more than four years old.

I have no sense of my mother's face in movement. Warm people have mobile expressions, changing from moment to moment—and from the love of the friends who survived her, I know she was warm.

But perhaps I will recognize what she smells like. Smell is, they say, the sense most closely associated with memory. As I sit at our table, nervously picking at a rosetta of bread, I will be hoping that her scent has been stored in some primitive part of my brain so that, when I stand up to embrace her, all sense of strangeness will dissolve. I'm fairly certain that she will be wearing Shalimar.

She has no photos by which to identify me. She will laugh when I explain that she recognized me because I look like my father in drag.

I know that my mother found the marks of age beautiful: I have a few of the objects she collected, things that are cracked and stained, faded and frayed. Will she find the lines and sags of my fifty-three-year-old face beautiful, or will they make her sad to see them? My father once told me that one of the rudest insults of age is seeing your children grow old.

Her own face, at thirty-nine, will be at the height of its extraordinary beauty. As a young woman, she looked sad and out of time, her face too dramatic for her years. In time, she grew into it; it no longer overwhelms her. It has acquired fun and lightness and kindness. At last, she is grounded.

My mother was born Enrica Soma, the daughter of Italian immigrants. Her father owned a restaurant in New York, Tony's, where he entertained customers by standing on his head and singing operatic arias. (My mother's scrapbook, which I have, contains an illustrated clipping from the *New York Times*.) When she was eighteen, she appeared on the cover of *Life* magazine only because she was so beautiful. The caption was "Young Ballerina"; she danced for Balanchine at the New York City Ballet and was already a soloist. I've often wondered why she didn't send me to ballet class; four wasn't too young to start. I will ask her.

That cover resulted in a train ticket to Hollywood, where she was placed in the back row of *Life*'s photo of the young starlets of 1949, hands crossed over her heart like a doleful Madonna, labeled, strangely, "Rick Soma." Center front, sitting cross-legged, is the only one of these hopefuls who made it: Marilyn Monroe. My mother never made a feature film. She married the director John Huston and gave birth to her first child at twenty, my brother Tony, and her second, my sister Anjelica, just after her twenty-second birthday. Did she regret the lost career that I believe she never really wanted? Did she wish she had stayed in New York and had kept dancing? I will ask her.

The name by which everyone knew her was Ricki: a unicorn's name. I have never met, or heard of, another Ricki. I thought, if I had a daughter, I would name her Enrica Luz, after her two grandmothers, but I would have called her Lulu. I would not have dared to call her Ricki, both because it would feel like sacrilege and because it would have been too heavy a burden for that notional little girl to bear.

My mother had, I think, grown out of wanting to please her tyrannically demanding father. She had, for the first time, embarked on a love affair with a man who was not more powerful and seen in the world than she is. Her glamorous, glittering husband had sucked out her energy and her talents, and after the children have been raised and the house restored and decorated, he had left her in his wake. Why had she hung on to the marriage? Because she was afraid of her father's explosive wrath? For the identity of "Mrs. Huston"? My mother lived at the intersection of bohemia and society; might divorce have exiled her from at least some of the places she wanted to be? I will ask her.

Her husband had fathered a child with another woman, and she had had a child with another man: me. This other man was married. Every man worth having was married then—and my mother had been brought up to look only at men worth having. My father was not her first married lover; indeed, John Huston was married when she met him. And there were others, once the marriage died. But my father was the one whose child she carried, and I know, from reading her letters to him, that this time she was not quite able to keep her yearning, her frustration, or her fury under control. Did she ever wish I would just disappear and never be born? I will ask her. I will not mind—not even a tiny bit—if she says yes. And I will see in her eyes if she is concealing the truth.

When they opened her safe-deposit box after her death, they found little tags on her most valuable jewelry, with my name and my sister's name on them. Did Mum have a presentiment that she would die? But then why didn't she make a will? I will tell her that I've been making wills since my early twenties, and I don't believe it's tempting fate. I will tell her that my son, her grandson, laughs at me when I say casually that I could get hit by a bus tomorrow. She will be relieved that he is nearly grown, that the pattern is broken: for she, too, lost her mother when she was four.

Having read my mother's letters in order to write my memoir, *Love Child*, I know how she thinks, how intensely she feels, what she finds funny, what tormented her. I brought her joy, but I brought her worry, too. Would this not-technically-illegitimate child carry the stigma that she'd manage to sidestep by not getting divorced? What terror must she have felt at the moment of her death, knowing that she would be leaving this fatherless child motherless, too? Everything about me was a risk, with my own happiness the stakes. My name—which means "happy"—was an amulet. She will want to know if it worked.

I will want to comfort her. Though for decades I felt like a problem, a misfit, adrift, I will tell her that I have weathered the turbulence and reached calmer waters. After all, I am now fifteen years older than she lived to be. Not yet forty, she was still caught in the tumult, suspended at the moment when the car crash snatched her away.

We will both order the same thing: prosciutto and figs, veal piccata with lemon risotto and spinach. We will be amused by how quickly we devour our food. I know this because my godmother, seeing how fast I eat, told me that my mother ate quickly, too. I cannot have learned it from her; it must be genetic.

It will be a rather uproarious lunch. Mum will find that I share her love of wordplay and silliness. We will laugh at all kinds of things: incongruities, idiosyncrasies, foibles—our own and those of people we love. I will catch her up on a number of her close friends and tell her about my own beloved friends. She will be amazed to hear how close I am to my biological father and my brother and sister on that side, and how loved I was by my legal father, her husband, who took me as his daughter when she died; and she will feel, if not exactly vindicated, at least relieved that her gamble paid off so spectacularly, impossibly well. We will talk about books and movies and music and places we love. We will linger over dessert—zabaglione—and cappuccinos. We will not want our time together to end.

So I will stretch the rules and, once we have hugged Mara and Lorenzo goodbye—for they, too, will have been resurrected for this lunch—I will teleport Mum to Taos, New Mexico, where I live. She loved people who carved their own path, so she will be happy to see that I have found a place in the world unconnected to either of my families: a majestic landscape and a culture with a complex depth of history. The two-foot-thick adobe walls of my house will remind her of Ireland, and the hundred-mile view to the west, across ranked horizons of extinct volcanoes, will remind her of the ocean.

I will sit down at the antique Mason & Hamlin piano that I have learned to play in the last five years, with its ivory keys and carved legs, and play her my favorite Chopin nocturne, dotted with mistakes as usual—but maybe with fewer than usual, because her presence will suffuse me and stop my mind from thinking, and I will be nothing but heart and fingers playing. I will describe to her the pleasure of learning a skill for my own enjoyment only, with no measure for judgment other than feeling myself get better. I will tell her that my sister has taken up pottery and sculpting in clay and show her the bowls Anjelica has given me. Mum will, maybe, get a glimmering of the future she will never reach, in which she might take up some similar pursuit, something in which—unlike in her ballet career—striving for perfection is an absurdity.

She will recover a future, and I will recover a past. I'm hoping that these fleeting hours with my mother will bring back the warm, intimate memories that my consciousness suppressed as too painful to keep. I never dared attempt to unbury them, not wanting to second-guess my own forgetting. But if they don't come, I won't mind. Now, once she has scattered again, I will know her scent, the ripples of her voice, the expressions of her face. I will know the color of her eyes, their depth, the way the light in them plays on her thoughts.

If you had asked me a few years ago to have lunch with my mother, I might not have said yes. I'm not sure I could have borne it: to hold her and have her ripped away from me a second time. But now I am content with the luck of my life: proud of the son I've raised, the books I've written, the house I designed, the pattern of my days. I feel lucky even that Mum died when she did—because if she had lived, I would not have the wealth of family she left me. And in her absence, I feel an identity with her that I would be unable to feel if I'd known her as a living woman, with personality and moods and grievances. I feel in a strange way as if I'm carrying on her life, which was so violently interrupted—as if I'm finishing it for her. She is my lodestone. She is also the unicorn I follow and will never catch, led always on by flashes of her beauty as she vanishes again and again into the mist.

Allegra Huston is the author of Love Child: A Memoir of Family Lost and Found *and the novel* Say My Name, *as well as articles for many publications in the US and UK. An editor for more than thirty years, she is also the founder of the publishing company Twice 5 Miles Guides: The Stuff Nobody Teaches You, for which she wrote* How to Work with a Writer *and co-wrote* How to Read for an Audience. *She lives in Taos, New Mexico. Please visit allegrahuston.com for details of books and workshops.*

23

LEE CLOW (COLLABORATOR, FRIEND)
AND STEVE JOBS

I'M LEE CLOW.
FORMER CREATIVE DIRECTOR OF CHIAT\DAY,
AND NOW
FOUNDER AND CHAIRMAN
OF THE MEDIA ARTS LAB
(THE ADVERTISING AGENCY CREATED
FOR STEVE JOB'S APPLE COMPUTER).

I KNEW STEVE SINCE 1980; WHEN WE FIRST MET
HE WAS TWENTY-FIVE.

I WORKED FOR STEVE FROM THE EARLY DAYS,
WHEN WE INTRODUCED
THE COMPUTER CALLED MACINTOSH,
TO STEVE'S RETURN TO APPLE IN 1997,
WHEN HE LITERALLY SAVED THE COMPANY.

AND WE WENT ON TO INTRODUCE
TECHNOLOGY THAT CHANGED
EVERYTHING.

INCLUDING LUNCH.

"LUNCH WITH STEVE JOBS"

WE'D SIT AT MY FAVORITE TABLE IN THE BACK OF CHAYA VENICE. WE'D HAVE SUSHI AND A BOTTLE OF SANTA MARGHERITA PINOT GRIGIO.

IT SURE WOULD BE GREAT TO SEE HIM AGAIN.

Lee Clow is Chairman, TBWA\Media Arts Lab and has been making "advertising" for more than fifty years. He started at Chiat\Day when there were ten people and two accounts and has been there ever since. He prefers to think of what we do as Media Art. No better example of Lee's impact in the industry than his thirty-year-plus partnership with Steve Jobs. They created the now famous work for the rebirth of Apple in 1997. It recognized those who "think different." And, during the past twenty years, Apple has changed everything. Since he began with Chiat\Day and its humble beginnings in a hotel in downtown Los Angeles, the agency has grown to be one of the ten largest global networks and is without dispute one of the most innovative and awarded agency networks in the world. Lee Clow is a member of the One Club Hall of Fame, the Art Directors Club Hall of Fame, and the Museum of Modern Art's Advertising Hall of Fame, and he has received the Clio's Lifetime Achievement Award. In 2013 Lee was made the third Lion of St. Mark at Cannes.

24

"You have malaria," I tell him in a low, comforting voice.
"You have a high fever. Look at my face.
Don't you recognize a Jones when you see one?"

KAYLIE JONES (DAUGHTER) AND JAMES JONES

I push aside the flap of the hospital tent, carrying a backpack over my shoulder, and I am hit with the smell of old blood and perspiration. The not-so-badly wounded soldiers are restless in sleep, those who can sleep. Some stare out vacantly, groaning from time to time. I walk slowly down the aisle between the cots. They're still wearing their filthy, stinking combat fatigues and boots, as if they're expecting to have to run for cover at any moment. They don't see me because I don't belong in their fever dreams, only in my father's.

I find him in the before-last cot on the left, lying back with his arms folded behind his head, one knee bent toward the ceiling. I recognize the pose before the young face that looks ancient and drawn under the head bandage. His slim, almost too-slight body is alien to me. He was a featherweight boxer in his regiment before the war, not broad-shouldered and muscular, as I remember him from later in life.

I crouch beside him, look into his feverish, startled eyes, and murmur, "I am your Athena, born whole from your mind. Don't be afraid."

"What the fuck—!" he cries, ready to defend himself, his hands flying out in fists from behind his head. He smells of sweat and old cigarettes, but the smell is familiar. As a little girl I would go to my parents' bedroom late at night, frightened by a nightmare, and hear my father mumbling urgently in his sleep, warning someone to *watch out!* He'd awaken with a start as soon as I stepped into the room, a sixth sense born of the war. I'd crawl up and snuggle in between my parents, and he smelled like this.

Now, I gently grasp his right hand, the closest. My touch seems to calm him, and he doesn't pull away. "You have malaria," I tell him in a low, comforting voice. "You have a high fever. Look at my face. Don't you recognize a Jones when you see one?"

"How did you—?" He carefully, gently, brings his left hand to his head and feels the bandage, wincing, blinking rapidly as if to clear his mind.

"You're having a fever dream. I'm old now. I'm fifty-eight. In my timeline, you've been dead for many years. Just try to think of it as one of those sci-fi stories you like to read. We call it SF now. Or speculative fiction."

"Spec . . . what in the fuck—" He looks closely at my face, inspecting every detail, and the fiery glow of fear in his eyes begins to dim. "Your eyes are just like my sister Mary Ann's."

"So are yours. I have your eyes and your chin. But I look a lot like my mother, too. When you meet her, you'll know right away."

Somewhere behind me a soldier shouts in his sleep, *"Move! Move, goddamn it, you son of a bitch!"*

"What . . . what's your name?" he asks with suspicion.

"Kaylie Ann Jones."

"I never heard that name before. How do you spell it?"

"It is my godmother's Hebrew name. You looked it up in a phonetic dictionary to find the correct spelling. K-A-Y-L-I-E."

His eyes go out of focus as he considers this, thinking hard. When he was thinking hard when I was a girl, his left eye would cross slightly, just like this.

"It smells awful in here. Let's go outside. I brought you a picnic lunch." I lift the backpack from the floor, so he can see it.

"Lunch? It's the middle of the goddamn night."

"It's lunchtime where I am."

He says uncertainly, "But . . . are you real?"

"I exist, just, not yet."

He slowly and with great effort pulls his legs over the side of the cot and sits up, hunching, getting his bearings. He lets go of my hand and reaches down to rub his ankle.

He sits there, thinking.

Finally, he sighs and pulls himself up to standing with the help of my arm, his knees still wobbly. He's limping quite severely, I notice, as we head toward the tent's back flap.

"Your twisted ankle from high school football is all messed up. You have torn ligaments, and your ankle is swollen to twice its size and you wrapped it. You don't want to tell them because it seems like so little, compared to the others." I nod back over my shoulder toward the cots filled with the not-so-badly wounded soldiers. The most seriously wounded have already been evacuated by air or hospital ship. The ones who are still here have been deemed fit to return to combat.

Outside there is a blackout, no lights, no fires, but the moon is in its last quarter and a tropic sky full of stars casts a silver glow over the shadowy landscape. The air is so thick and warm it feels like we're slogging through broth. The clearing, which is in the rear and relatively safe now, was once covered in tall grass and is surrounded by the black presence of mountains. Looming in the darkness are the even darker shapes of machines of war—Jeeps, machine guns, stacks of mortars—and soldiers moving about, holding their rifles at the ready, but they don't see us, for we are alone in this fever dream.

By the wheel of a parked Jeep I pull a small, tightly woven Navajo blanket out of the backpack and unfold it on the flattened grass. A little beauty is what he needs in this hellhole of churned-up earth and chewed-up trees and men. He sits down on the blanket and rests his back against the Jeep's wheel, and I drop cross-legged, facing him.

Out of my backpack comes the little Limoges lithophane candle-holder on its saucer, an anniversary gift from my late husband. I light the votive candle, and three-dimensional scenes of Paris magically appear as a dark bas-relief on the gold-lit porcelain dome—the Pont Alexandre III, the Opéra, the Seine with a barge, and Notre-Dame, almost the view from our house on Île Saint-Louis. He stares at the images, mystified.

"I never seen anything like that in my whole fuckin' life."

I hold it up and turn the globe slowly on its saucer. "This is where we're going to live, right here, in Paris, in a house on the quai overlooking the Seine." I give him the little golden light to hold, but his hand is shaking so badly the globe jiggles in its saucer and makes a clinking sound. He sets it down between us.

Mosquitoes loud and mean as fighter jets move in squadrons all around us. But they don't bother us. At the edge of the field lies the jungle, huge, thick, impenetrable. He stares out toward the thick canopy of alien trees, his face tight with pain. I know he's thinking about the Japanese soldier he killed in hand-to-hand combat just two days ago, in that very jungle. They were afraid to fire their weapons, afraid to alert other enemies, both.

"That Japanese soldier came at you with his bayonet while you were taking a shit. The Asian woman with the baby in the photo, she's not his wife. She's a prostitute from the Philippines. I had the writing translated by a professional. You know he would've killed you if you hadn't killed him—"

"He was starving to death! I could see his skeleton through his skin!" He looks sick, his face gray in the dim light. "He was just some kid, poor as shit, just like me." And suddenly my dad is blind with rage, his eyes filled with tears that refuse to fall.

"Look here, I brought you some of the delicacies you've read about in Hemingway." I pull out a baguette, still warm from the oven, and place it on the blanket, along with a dozen oysters from New Orleans laid out in a circle on a tray of ice, with a little silver container of vinegar and shallot mignonette in the middle; a whole square of Pont l'Évêque cheese and a little round Camembert from Normandy; a sauçisson sec from the Ardèche; a tin of Beluga caviar from the Caspian Sea; and a plate of American bacon, not too cooked, not too greasy, which is one of his favorite things in the world, and which, from the summer I turned ten until he died, three months before my seventeenth birthday, he could not eat because salt was bad for his congestive heart failure. And the pièce de résistance: a bottle of Château Margaux 1921—the year of his birth—and one stemmed crystal wineglass. I fish in a side pocket for my stout Swiss Army knife and open the corkscrew and uncork the wine. Then, with the short, razor-sharp blade I cut the bread into slices, and the sauçisson, and the cheese.

I pour the wine. He drinks the first glassful down greedily and I refill his glass to the brim.

"That's damn good. What about you?" he says. "Ain't you drinkin'?" His Midwest accent, which he was so proud of, which he never lost in all his years of fancy living among the literati, is stronger suddenly, and so familiar I feel a knot forming in my throat. I have forty-two years' worth of things to tell him. But if I'm going to follow the Prime Directive like in *Star Trek,* his favorite show, there is only so much he needs to know.

"I quit drinking. Twenty-six years ago. Booze almost killed me. Just like it's eventually going to kill you. I'm older now than you'll ever be."

He nods pensively. "Life ain't much worth living if you cain't drink." He says this with a certain bravado, a cockiness he was apparently famous for in his youth. It dispersed in middle age. The man I knew was kind, wise, patient, but still prone to losing his temper when irritated. When he first joined the army, they gave him an IQ test and his score was off the charts, so they suggested he apply to Officer Candidate School. He did not want to be an officer, and anyway, the upper echelon soon realized that he was not good officer material, as he questioned everything he was ordered to do and talked back to his superiors. By twenty-one, he has already somewhat learned to curtail this impulse, and he can fit in when he wants to, which isn't often. People still think he's cocky, but that's because half the time they can't understand what he's saying, or he's so mad at them for not understanding what he's saying that he tells them off. I know this both from his books and from listening to him argue with people when I was a kid.

"Eat the oysters first, before the ice melts. You're going to get hepatitis from an oyster in your forties and you'll never eat oysters again."

"I'm not gonna make it to forty," he says calmly. "I'm not gonna make it to twenty-two. Tomorrow I'm going back up to the line."

"Tomorrow you have to show the surgeon your ankle."

"I'm not leavin' my old outfit," he says, his voice suddenly hard. "Not for a fuckin' twisted ankle." He's pretty much demolishing the oysters, pouring the mignonette sauce onto them from the little container and slurping them down, tipping the shells toward his lips with dirty fingers. He doesn't like dirt or sand, never did.

I forgot the Ready-Wipes! Out they come from the backpack.

"Here, wash your hands and face. These are great!" I hand him the plastic packet of towelettes, opening them first because he won't have a clue. He inspects the packet, curious. He knows Kleenex, so he gets the general idea. He starts pulling out the towelettes, one after another, and rubs them against his face and hands. He has a week's worth of reddish-gold beard, which he's proud of. The beards mean combat experience.

"This is like Ivan's delirium in *The Brother's Karamazov*." He giggles, almost delightedly. The wine is helping. "When the Devil comes to visit him and tries to convince Ivan that he's real." He says Eye-vin.

"That's one of my favorite scenes in all of literature," I tell him.

"It's actually very funny, if you read a good translation. The Devil as a good-for-nothing hanger-on in threadbare fancy clothes. The genius is that he is so fully realized, clothes and all."

I'm trying to impress him, yes. I am. Reading was my father's escape in the prewar army at Schofield Barracks, but even as a small child, books were his only respite from his miserable life at home, a Bible-thumping mother and an alcoholic father who wasn't violent, only depressed and filled with guilt and remorse. *She* was the violent one. At four my father rode his tricycle across the parking lot to the public library in his hometown of Robinson, Illinois, and told the librarian he wanted to read books. By the time he was eight he'd read every book in the children's section. The librarian started to give him adult books, carefully culling them to avoid filling his young mind with images of sex and violence.

"Remember Vera Newlin from the library?" I ask him, smiling. "I met her. I went to Robinson. She was already very old."

He smiles with deep warmth at the memory of the woman who guided his young imagination. "She was tough as a goddamn Sherman tank, that Vera Newlin."

I scoop a little heap of caviar onto the knife blade and pile it on top of a thin slice of baguette. "Here, try this. Caviar from Russia."

"From Russia, huh?" He pops the whole thing in his mouth and barely chews before swallowing. I start to laugh.

"Caviar should be eaten more slowly," I inform him, as if I'm the parent and he's the child. "It costs a fucking fortune."

He holds out his empty wineglass. I refill it again. His hand is still shaking, but it's getting steadier.

"Here, try this Camembert. It goes great with the wine."

I spread some caviar on a sliver of bread for myself, relishing the taste, the great pops of flavor as the little balls explode in my mouth.

He picks up the bottle and inspects the label in the dim golden light of the globe. Two soldiers guarding the perimeter walk by, cupping their smokes in closed fists and talking in low voices. *Jap cocksuckers cut off their dicks and balls. . . .*

He listens, alert, suddenly pale and frightened.

"Château Margaux 1921," I say, drawing him back. "Think of it as a late twenty-first birthday present."

He chews the bread and Camembert thoughtfully. Then he reaches for the plate of bacon. "You're not really here, are you?" he says, his mouth full. "But this sure as shit tastes real. Gimme more of that there cheese. And more wine. Why din't you bring real booze? Like whiskey?"

Out of my magical backpack I whip out a bottle of White Label, which is what the Colonel drinks in *The Thin Red Line*. My dad downs the wine, then takes the whiskey bottle, nods approvingly at the label, turns the twist top with a satisfying crack, and upturns the bottle into his mouth, guzzling in a very undignified manner.

I cut a square of Pont l'Évêque and spread it on some bread and lift it to my mouth. This is my favorite stinky cheese in the world, but I have a hard time swallowing, as if something is stuck in my throat. He wipes his lips delicately with a towelette, scratches at his beard, and looks at me askance, with a wince. "You know what I was thinking about when you showed up? I was thinking about islands. And hills. Endless hills and islands and jungles, all the way to Japan. What's the chances of any of us making it till the end? It's all up to fuckin' chance. A lottery. No reason why. My mother used to beat me over the head with her Bible for playing with myself. I don't believe in God no more. Those that do, good for them. If it helps them, good. But in my opinion, there's no reason why the guy next to me got it full in the face and I just got a scratch."

"The reason why is that you're the one who's going to write about it."

"No one would believe it," he says with a grim, sullen laugh, shaking his head. "No one will want to know what it's really like." This is the nihilist in him, the one who really doesn't care if he lives or dies. This is why he drinks. Well, this, and because his dad the dentist became the town drunk and shot himself in the mouth and my father feels guilty about that, too. The other side of him is pure romantic. He believes in the heroic. And he'll make heroes out of twisted, flawed, ordinary, uncivilized men. These two sides of him will fight each other for the rest of his life.

"They called World War I *the war to end all wars*. Horseshit. The wars'll keep on comin'. The only thing that matters to me is the old outfit. I got to get back."

"It's not even going to be your old outfit anymore. It's already changing. Dead, wounded, transferred out. Replaced, by green recruits."

"Some of them are still up there," he says, his chin jutting out in defiance. "There's a rumor we're heading to New Georgia next." Then he adds, "It's easier being dead."

"That thought will always tug at you, but there will be so much goodness, too. So much light. All those places you've dreamed of seeing, you will see them. You're going to be a writer."

"It won't matter one goddamn bit," he growls.

"You're never going to think your writing matters one goddamn bit. You're never going to believe it matters, even while you're writing it all down. You won't be doing it for posterity."

"Yeah. Fuck posterity," he says morosely, swigging from the bottle.

"You're feeling sorry for yourself. Cut it out."

His head jerks back as if I've slapped him. This, he also used to say to me. I'm just giving him a taste of his own medicine.

"Got any smokes?" he asks.

"Lucky Strikes or Camels?"

"Camels."

I whip an unopened pack of Camels and a disposable lighter out of the backpack and hand them to him. He cups the flame and cigarette in his fists and lights up quickly. Puts the pack and the lighter in his front pocket and pats them, somehow reassured.

"You're still carrying that Japanese soldier's wallet in your pocket, too, aren't you? You're going to keep it for the rest of your life. You're going to pull it out and weep over it from time to time, looking at the pictures. You showed them to me once."

"I just cain't bring myself to throw it out," he says, as if this is a sign of weakness.

"You know how you believe that one day we're going to find other planets circling suns, other planets that could sustain life?"

"Everybody laughs at me for sayin' that."

"Well, astronomers are going to find the first exoplanets in 1992. Two of them, actually. They circle a pulsar star called PSR 1257+12."

"PSR 1257+12? Are you shittin' me?"

"And since then they've found over two thousand more. I know you don't believe in God. Certainly not the God your mother believed in. But doesn't this give you hope for mankind? That we don't know or understand the Order of Things but that it has to be way bigger than just us?"

"I'll be damned," he muses. "Is that really true?"

"It's really true. And the United States will be the first to land men to the moon. You woke us up in the middle of night to watch the lunar landing, and you cried."

He's sipping slowly now from the neck of the whiskey bottle, almost serene, slumping back against the Jeep's tire and running his left hand lazily over the zigzag pattern in the Navajo rug.

"I know this is all in my head and I'm making this shit up but

I'll be goddamned if this rug doesn't feel real. I'd love to have a rug like this."

"And you will. You had several in your office upstairs, in Paris. You have to survive."

I pull the skin off a slice of sauçisson sec and lay it on a piece of baguette with some Pont l'Évêque on top and hand it to him. The silvery light from the sky casts shadows on his face, accentuating the deep hollows of his cheeks and eyes. He looks like some twisted version of his older self. He looks like he did on the day he died. Until I saw his heart monitor flatline I had never believed for a moment that he would die. There was so much I'd never asked him, so much I didn't know, and had not cared to know, at sixteen.

Afterward, I started reading his novels. I started at the beginning and read through them all, trying to understand why he died and what I was supposed to do now.

"Even if they send me back," he concedes, "even *if* they send me back Stateside for surgery, they're just gonna reassign me to another outfit, probably send me to Europe for the fuckin' invasion."

"After you go AWOL Stateside for the third or fourth time, they're going to send you to an army psychiatrist. When the doctor asks you what's bothering you, you're going to laugh bitterly in his face. 'I'm done killing for you assholes.' That's what you're going to say. The psychiatrist's report says that you were mentally unstable."

This makes him laugh uproariously, the deep, guttural howl that I remember.

"You'll get an honorable discharge. And when your first book comes out, it's going to change the way people see the army. You're going to be famous."

"I don't give a shit about being famous." He lights another cigarette. "So tell me what I'm gonna write about."

"That's not my job. That's your job. But I can tell you this: your books are the ones the soldiers will read. When they get home all fucked up at the end of this, when it's all over and they go home and try to be normal and go back to work and get married and have kids, and when they lie there shaking and screaming in their sleep and contemplating killing themselves because they can't stand the thought that they survived and left their friends behind, one day their kids will ask them what it was like, they're going to hand them your books, and they're going to say, *This is what it was like.* There's no one else. You're the one. You have to live. The only way the old outfit is going to survive is through your books. You'll keep them alive forever."

The last thing in my backpack is a piece of paper, which I unfold and tilt toward the golden light of my little Paris lithophane from Limoges. I read a section aloud to him.

"If the home we never write to, and the oaths we never keep,
And all we know most distant and most dear,
Across the snoring barrack-room return to break our sleep,
Can you blame us if we soak ourselves in beer?
When the drunken comrade mutters and the great guard-lantern
gutters
And the horror of our fall is written plain,
Every secret, self-revealing on the aching white-washed ceiling,
Do you wonder that we drug ourselves from pain?
We're poor little lambs who've lost our way,
Baa! Baa! Baa!
We're little black sheep who've gone astray,
Baa—aa—aa!
Gentlemen-rankers out on the spree,
Damned from here to Eternity,
God ha' mercy on such as we,
Baa! Yah! Bah!"

"Kipling," he says gruffly. "What a bunch of phony horseshit. He was never in no army."

"My point exactly."

"Am I going to remember this?"

"No. This is a fever dream. But you damn well better remember that you have to get the fuck out."

"You swear like a buckass private, you know that?" he says with a twisted grin.

"That's because I'm a buckass private's daughter. Everything you taught me, every lesson that hurt like hell—like when you read me *Stuart Little* and cried at the end. I begged you to tell me Stuart finds the sparrow he's in love with, and you said, 'Probably not.' Why the hell did you have to say that? My whole sense of the world came from you, and sometimes I wish I didn't know."

"Didn't know what?"

The truth, of course. The shitty, ugly truth. "That Stuart Little may not find the sparrow, but he goes to look for her anyway."

This is the kind of heroism he believes in.

We sit for a while in a heavy but companionable silence. He has drunk half the bottle of whiskey, and his eyes are starting to close.

"On your feet, soldier," I say with a shaky smile. He would say this to me when I fell down roller-skating and skinned my knee.

I offer my hand to help him to his feet. He takes it, and rises, swaying slightly.

"Well," he says when we reach the hospital tent, "I'll be seeing you, I guess."

I nod, swallowing back tears. I remember so clearly the day I found him sitting at our dining room table in Paris with the Japanese soldier's wallet in his hands. I was quite young, because when he was sitting our heads were about level. Tears streamed down his face, and I had no words to help him. I laid my small hand on his wide shoulder and just stood beside him in silence until he turned his eyes to me. In that moment, our gazes locked, and in his eyes I saw his helpless sorrow, and I knew I would have given all I had in the world to comfort him.

Kaylie Jones is the author of five novels, including A Soldier's Daughter Never Cries, *adapted as a Merchant-Ivory film. Her memoir,* Lies My Mother Never Told Me, *was published by William Morrow. Kaylie chairs the James Jones First Novel Fellowship, a ten-thousand-dollar annual writing award, and teaches in two university MFA programs.*

25

"Baby, baby." He wipes my tears with the end of a balled-up tissue, like he did when I was little. "Precious bane. Don't cry. Your waffle will get salty."

RF JURJEVICS (NON-BINARY CHILD) AND JURIS JURJEVICS

We meet at the Highway Diner, my father and I.

The Highway Diner has not been the Highway Diner as we knew and loved it for over a decade now, but when I drive up, there it is. And there *he* is, standing on the minuscule front porch, right by the *Hartford Courant* box.

It's not quite been two weeks. My throat is closing. My heart is breaking. I'm running before I realize it. He opens his arms.

I can't speak, just embrace. He's all there, *right* there, smelling like the cedar blocks my stepmother tucked into his closet. Smelling like *him*.

"It's *you*!" he says, as though he's surprised.

"Shut up and hug me." I'm crying into his shoulder. There's no possible way I can let go.

"I'm going to hug you for the next century," I tell him.

"I guess I'll have to wear you into the restaurant, then."

This gets me to laugh. I let him go, slowly. "After you."

He walks over the threshold with an ease I haven't seen in I don't know how long. His legs move as fluidly as they did when I was a small child and we went walking, me high on his shoulders. He's buoyant, almost.

Inside, the Highway Diner is intact, as we left it years ago, before it closed. The old counter is back with its line of wobbly red stools; the

Formica tables are back, too, also red, their spider-vein cracks patched over with packing tape.

"Same old place," my father says.

I cannot say anything.

We sit at our favorite booth, the one directly under the window facing Route 7. I'm in shock at all of it—the stack of jam packets, the sticky menus, things I haven't seen in years. Even the old cigarette vending machine is there, right between the doors to the bathrooms.

Dad notices it, too.

"Your first felony," he says.

"Wait, what?"

"Your first felony." He points to the machine. "I was settling up the tab and I turn back around and you've got a pack of Parliaments in your little hands."

"I did not!"

"You did! At three years old, too. I never found out how you did it. You wouldn't tell me!"

I cross my arms. "You're lying."

"Okay, okay." He looks chagrined, but not really. "It was such a good story. I couldn't resist."

A server slides by, her long braid flicking over her shoulder. Before I can speak, my father catches her attention, says, "Two Belgian waffles, please, deluxe—one for me and one for my legal guardian over here."

"Still getting mileage out of that one, huh?" I tell him.

"Yup," he says, then sighs. "I haven't had a waffle in about . . . oh, twenty years or so." His expression is dreamy.

The server is back astoundingly fast. "Two deluxe," she says, lifting the plates from her tray. She places one plate in front of Dad, one in front of me. Belgian waffles, the Highway Diner staple. *Deluxe.*

Slathered in whipped cream, topped with strawberries. One little metal creamer of maple syrup on each plate.

It's like a magic trick, all of it—*his* magic trick. I'm staring and staring at him. He *can't* be gone; he's right here. He's always *been* right here.

"Dad." My voice breaks and I'm crying; maybe I never stopped, I don't know. My brain is a few steps behind me, hovering there. "Dad." I want to put my head on the table and wail.

"Baby, baby." He wipes my tears with the end of a balled-up tissue, like he did when I was little. "Precious bane. Don't cry. Your waffle will get salty." Leaning back, he makes a show of cutting into his. Melted whipped cream sinks into its little squares, mixing with the syrup.

"A diabetic's dream," I say to him, sniffling.

He stuffs a napkin into the front of his shirt. It's a favorite, a black tee with INNOCENT BYSTANDER in bold, capital letters—just his humor. I can't believe he's here. I can't believe he's *not* here. It's a strange, if not entirely unfamiliar, conundrum.

My father takes a bite of waffle big enough for a moose. "I don't have to worry about that *health* stuff anymore," he says, his mouth full. "*So there.*"

I watch him enjoying his waffle, without a hint of guilt or worry on his face.

"Do I have maple syrup in my beard?" he asks.

"No."

"Are you sure?"

"Yes."

My father makes a show of brushing his entire face with his napkin-bib, then lets it fall back into position to reveal a Cheshire Cat smile. Sight gags have always been his best gags, his method for easing me into relaxation—this time and all the thousands and thousands of times before it. He has always been so much better at being calm than I am, miraculously able to guide me through it.

As if he can read my thoughts—and hell, perhaps he *can* now—my father reaches across the table to uncurl my fingers from around my thumb; I've gripped them up tight without meaning to, my nervous tell.

"Dad?"

"Child?" He gives me a goofy smile, showing off his perfect top teeth, ones he bought himself years ago. Those teeth and my college tuition, on a book contract. A gift I can never repay.

"Did . . . Did it hurt?"

He's chewing another bite of waffle now. "Did what hurt?"

"When it happened."

"Oh—God, no." He makes a face, waving away the thought. "Not at all."

"You're not lying, right?"

"I'm not. It really didn't."

"Good."

Out the window, a semi flies by, tires ringing on the wet road.

"I always wondered what it was like to drive one of those," Dad says.

"Really? Me, too."

He looks at me, beaming that grin, the one that's half knowing, half baffled. "I guess it's in your genes," he says.

My genes. *He* is my genes. He's in my eyes, my hair, the set of my stance, the broadness of my shoulders. I have his wonky eyesight and his detached earlobes, his knack for rhythm, his crummy math skills. He taught me to use a camera. He taught me to flip the bird. He taught me to put on my socks, for god's sake.

"What am I going to do?" I ask him, in a small voice. "What am I going to do without you?"

He waves the thought away again. "What are you going to *do*?" he repeats. "You're going to go to work. You're going to pet your cats. You're going to love your pal—your partner. You're going to write your book. You're going to do your art." He says this last word with a pronounced imitation of a Long Island accent—"ahht."

He wants a laugh, but I can't oblige him—not now. "I mean, what am I going to do without *you*? I need you, Dad."

There's a huge slice of strawberry on his fork, loaded down with whipped cream. "No, you don't," he says, popping it into his mouth.

"Of course I do!"

He shakes his head. "You don't. Look at you! You are a grown person with a grown person's life. You're not the size of a bag of flour anymore."

"That doesn't matter." I'm near tears again. "I could be a bazillionaire with three penthouse apartments and a Rolex for every day of the week—I would still need you."

"Honey." He puts his hand on mine, gives it a small shake. "You are okay."

"Okay? Are you crazy? I'm the opposite of okay!" I push my plate of soggy waffle to one side.

Dad holds up his palms. "Agree to disagree?"

I don't answer him right away. "This is just . . . such a raw deal."

"I know."

"First Mom and now you. Like . . . I just . . ."

Neither of us speaks for a moment.

"You remember what I said to you a long time ago?" Dad says finally.

"You've said a lot of things to me all kinds of times ago."

"Fair, fair. But do you remember when I told you that you have a really amazing capacity to be happy? To be really, actually happy?"

I do remember; I tell him so.

"Well, it's true," he says. "It's something I always admired about your mother, too."

"But then why am I so fucking *miserable*, Dad?"

Instead of answering, my father nudges my plate until it is in front of me again. "No one can be miserable while eating a Belgian waffle," he says. "So, eat."

I stare at the waffle. "I'll never get to buy you a car."

"So what?"

"A red Pontiac. I wanted to get you a red Pontiac. Or at least a computer, and not some crap from eBay or a hand-me-down from the neighbor across the street."

"I don't need a red Pontiac. Or a computer."

I glare at him. "Well, not *now* you don't."

My father has one bite of waffle left. He spears it with his fork, then holds it out to me. "It's goo-ood," he says in a singsong.

I shake my head. "I wanted to, I don't know, get you *something*. I wanted to make you happy."

"You *do* make me happy," he says. "You always made me happy."

We've had conversations like this many times before; we both know the patter, for this last time, too.

"Even when I was a total jerk I made you happy?" I ask.

"*Especially* when you were a total jerk!"

"Even when I peed on the lawn?"

"*Especially* when you peed on the lawn!" He's laughing now. "I may have taught you to put on your socks, but *you* taught *me* a ton. Like 'I'm sorry, are you sorry?' And the Napoleon joke. Where does Napoleon keep his armies?"

"Where?" I ask dutifully.

My father throws up his arms. "In his sleevies!" he shouts. His favorite. Mine, too.

"*You* taught *me* that joke," I point out. "I most certainly did not."

"I guess that one's lost to history.

"Really. Don't worry about the Pontiac," he says. He covers my hands with his bigger ones. "Really, really. Just finish the revision for the agent. Type faster!"

I groan. "You'll never even get to see me publish a book, if I ever get there."

"You will."

"How do you know?"

"I know."

"But *how*?"

"I'm a fire chief."

I roll my eyes. That old line, from a book we read when I was little. I can't remember the title, and neither can he. Another thing lost to history.

"I miss you, Dad," I tell him.

He slides a jam packet under our hands. "It's strawberry," he whispers.

"I know. I saw."

"I love you, *milais*," he says. He has always called me this—*milais*, a standby term of endearment in his first language—Latvian, the language he's told me he still dreams in. *Lovable one; dearest.*

"I love you, too."

"I love you *more*."

"Do not."

"Do so!"

His eyes are bright now. Mine are full and spilling over. I let them. I'm crying and crying again, and this time I'm all caught up, I'm right there on time with myself, and I'm afraid the tears will never stop.

"Dad," I croak.

"Baby."

"Forever," I say. "I love you forever. Always and always."

"I love you forever *more!*"

I'm laughing through the tears. He holds both my hands. The sky outside the Highway Diner has gone dark. Above the trees, stars are out, just a few little dots. It's time. I know it, and my father knows it.

"Say goodnight, Gracie," my father instructs me.

"But I don't want to."

"I know."

"Can I think it instead?"

"Uh-huh," he says. "You can think it instead. Close your eyes."

I close them.

Goodnight, Gracie. Goodnight, Gracie.

I can feel his hands in mine. They're big and warm, as familiar as my own.

Goodnight, Gracie.

Goodnight, Dad.

Goodnight.

RF Jurjevics works in tech by day and does just about everything else possible by night. The decidedly master-of-none Jurjevics is a hobbyist woodworker, incorrigible doodler, and sometime journalist.

26

"Every time she said, 'When Ari did this' or 'Jack said that,' the way you or I might talk about our Jim or our Bob, it never failed to startle."

NANCY EVANS (BOSS) AND
JACQUELINE KENNEDY ONASSIS

Jackie and I walk the two blocks from our office at 666 Fifth Avenue to Prunelle, our go-to restaurant when it's just the two of us. "When the restaurant is filled at lunch," wrote the *New York Times*, "with expensively dressed patrons, most of them male, the noise level is high but cheerful." Mostly male is a good description of wherever we went. When we were trying to woo big-time names to become authors with us at Doubleday, we'd walk a few more blocks east to the Four Seasons. There, the original home of the power lunch, every table was filled with brand-name male media tycoons. Not one of them didn't swivel his head when Jackie O walked in. And Jackie did what she always did: kept her eyes straight ahead, ignoring the stares in her wake.

Funny, at Prunelle, with those expensively dressed male patrons, plain old businessmen, they didn't take much notice. If we were there on a Monday, they might not have even recognized her. On Mondays, she often came straight in from her house in New Jersey, with her hair pulled back. Without the Kenneth blowout, she didn't look like the Jackie O from all the photographs. Her work clothes were simple: pants and a top. Today she was wearing a shirt that I thought was fabulous. Valentino, maybe. "It's a Brooks Brothers boys' shirt," she said, "and I put in shoulder pads." Now there was a fashion tip. What she did always wear were her Schlumberger bracelets and earrings. Trying to find the one earring she took off when she made calls at the office was always a fun hunt.

The first time I had any association with Jackie was an item in the

New York Post that reported she'd ordered a copy of a book I'd written called *How to Get Happily Published*, with the snarky comment that she must need it to learn about publishing, now that she'd become an editor at Viking, after she returned from her Ari years. (Every time she said, "When Ari did this" or "Jack said that," the way you or I might talk about our Jim or our Bob, it never failed to startle.)

The next time was when I became President and Publisher of Doubleday, where Jackie was now an editor, and the first thing she said when she saw me, was: "Thank goodness! Now I don't have to keep doing all these coffee table books. I can do real books now. Can't I?"

You bet, was my answer. And we were off and running.

At lunch she asked, "You've heard of Joseph Campbell, haven't you?" She had just come from an editorial meeting where no one had heard of him, and she was very frustrated. I had in fact heard of Joseph Campbell because as luck would have it, I'd read Campbell's *The Hero with a Thousand Faces* in English class my senior year of high school. The book project under consideration was a series of conversations Bill Moyers was going to conduct with Campbell on PBS. I told Jackie I was in; let's go after it.

It turned out that we weren't the only ones who were interested in the book. There was going to be an auction, and we had to put forward our publishing plan. Here's where it became interesting. Traditionally a book is published as what is called a B-size book, a traditional-size hardcover. But what if . . . ? That night I pulled out my dog-eared copy of *Man and His Symbols* by Carl Jung, a big influence on Campbell. It's an oversize book with wide margins in which spot art appears, of mandalas and the archetypal imagery Jung referenced. I also brought in my copy of the *Whole Earth Catalog*.

Jackie and I sat on the floor of my office—the good news of women wearing pants. I opened the books on the floor. What if, to make Campbell's philosophy accessible, to move it out of academia and into the mainstream, we packaged it as an oversize paperback? If it was affordable and looked more like a book you didn't just read but you *used* like a handbook for living, we could maybe make it popular. And what if we dropped art in the margins, illustrating the mythology Campbell would undoubtedly refer to, so it wouldn't appear as a heavy tome of type? The number crunchers weren't pleased; adding pictures would increase the cost, and we'd lose money not putting it out as a hardcover. But, we argued, we'd sell more as a paperback.

Moyers was not sold on our idea, either. So we quickly made up sample pages, sent copies of the pages from Jung's *Man and His Symbols*, and then Jackie went to bat trying to convince Moyers.

The book became *The Power of Myth*, of "Follow your bliss" fame, which became a huge bestseller on the *New York Times* bestseller list for more than half a year. It was Jackie's and my first bestseller together.

Yes, it's true, Jackie had a breathy voice. More than once when Jackie and I would make a phone call to woo a prospective author, the author would think it was an impostor, doing an imitation of that trademark whispery voice of hers, and hang up. We'd call back and I'd explain it really was Jackie Onassis.

The only voice that was breathier was Michael Jackson's. He was at the height of his fame and ready to write his autobiography, and the only editor who was fit for the King of Pop was Jackie. So, the book was hers. Things were going smoothly; the manuscript was in, we were planning a five-hundred-thousand-copy print run, and then I got one of Michael's 2:00 a.m. calls. "Wouldn't it be nice if Jackie wrote an introduction to my book?" I said Jackie didn't normally do that kind of thing; she liked to keep a low profile. "But it would be nice, wouldn't it?" The next call, during office hours, was from Michael's lawyer: either Jackie writes an intro or the book is off.

Another lunch at Prunelle. The last thing she wanted to do was to write an introduction; I already knew that. And when she didn't want to do something, people were always trying to use her, she was firm. (When I pleaded with her to accommodate our German owners, who wanted a dinner with her, to trot out their show horse, so they could say, *When I had dinner with Jackie O*, the deal was when she put her handbag on the table we were out of there—and we were; we fled to her waiting car.) This lunch, she was wearing a Valentino sweater (I knew, because I had the same one; she'd sent me to her personal shopper at Bergdorf's; "You need to look the part," she said, when I first came on board, because I was young and probably wearing Ann Taylor). "Okay, here's the deal," I told her. "The intro can be three sentences, but it has to be something. And if you write it, you can do a couple of books, books that we know won't make a penny, any one of your dance or Russian books. Because you'll have earned that with the money this book will make." She submitted the shortest, most generic piece of prose— actually it was a tour de force of nothingness—that met the requirement, and not a word more. *Moonwalk* was our next #1 bestseller.

How do you give Jackie Onassis a raise? Answer: with great difficulty. Once she was on a roll, bringing in hit after hit, making big bucks for the company, I went to her office, a small office, by choice—she didn't want anything fancy because of who she was—and I said, "I'm giving you a raise. You're doing great, and your salary should reflect that." And she said, "I don't need it. Really, what I'm getting is fine." And I said, "It's not a matter of need; you deserve it." I don't think I gave her a speech about how this is how women get paid less—*Oh, you don't need it, you have a husband who works*—but it's what I thought. Her next paycheck reflected the raise.

This is Jackie, racing into my office, pitching *The French Woman's Bedroom*, which she was eager to publish: "*The Englishwoman's Bedroom* sold really well and Englishwomen don't even have sex. So just think what *The French Woman's Bedroom* will do!" She was smiling mischievously. And she was right.

Anyone who knew Jackie can tell you how funny she was. Her voice may have been small, but her laugh was big. In her box at the ballet one night, her partner Maurice Tempelsman leaned forward and said, "If you girls can't quiet down, go out into the hall." We were laughing, at what I don't remember, but I do remember we couldn't stop ourselves and people below were looking up with those how-dare-you, shut-up expressions, and when they saw it was Jackie, they swiveled back, and that made us laugh even more until we did what Maurice said and went out into the hallway, holding our sides, laughing like adolescents.

I think I'm supposed to tell you what we ate at lunch. I have no idea. We did eat, though. She ate. I mean, she didn't pick at her food like those wafer-thin women do. We had salads, salmon, sometimes double-the-appetizer-please as an entrée. We cleaned our plates. We didn't drink at lunch, though it was the era when the publishing crowd took two-hour, very liquid lunches. We did, in her beautiful library, after work, knock back a few drinks and chain-smoke, her legs curled up on the sofa, with her butler coming in periodically to empty the ashtray, leaving no evidence of this dirty little secret.

Even though she moved like a dancer and had not an ounce of fat (she did sit-ups every day and yoga every afternoon—"I've gained one inch in height," she told me) and talked like a little girl, she was no faint flower. She had mastered a way of keeping her eyes on the middle distance so she could walk the city without making eye contact. Still, I felt protective when people came up to her, sometimes sticking their faces within an inch of her nose. "You're Jackie Onassis, aren't you?" "No," she'd say, and we would keep on walking, with a small giggle, once we got past them. Walking up Fifth Avenue one day to her apartment, she said, "Keep your head down, keep walking, there's a photographer up in the tree," and—I couldn't help looking—in fact there was a photographer planted up in the tree, and I did as she said, which she had learned to do her whole life, to keep walking like the world wasn't watching her, like she was normal.

"After Jack died," she told me one afternoon, "I had to look perfect when I went out; I didn't want people feeling sorry for me." Which may be why one of my favorite images of her was at my daughter's birthday party, when I hadn't gotten the memo that a Carvel ice-cream cake is supposed to be out for a couple of hours before you serve it. Twenty little heathens were beating the table with their forks, shouting, "Cake! Cake! Cake!" I pressed the microwave for all it was worth, but the cake was still hard as a rock. "Do you have a chef's knife?" said Jackie, striding into the kitchen. She grabbed the knife and hacked that cake into chunks to serve to those little children. And when the guests were gone, Jackie and I and her granddaughter Rose and my daughter went up to my bedroom where I had those step things you use for exercise, and Jackie built a bridge off my bed and piled pillows at the end. The girls walked the gangplank, jumping into the pillows, over and over. "You know that's the best thing about having grandchildren; I get to do all the things I didn't do with Caroline and John."

It was her partner Maurice who, one night when we were at dinner at the Russian Tea Room, said, "If Jackie could only take one thing to heaven with her, it would be a toss-up between her books and her horses." I like to think she has both.

Nancy Evans is a media veteran and entrepreneur. In addition to being the President and Publisher of Doubleday and the Editor-in-Chief of Time Inc.'s Book-of-the-Month Club, she founded Family Life *magazine, which she published in partnership with Wenner Media, and co-founded* iVillage, *the internet pioneer credited with introducing women to the web. Nancy has written two* New York Times *bestsellers, as well as articles for numerous publications, and she was the co-host of PBS's* First Edition, *a national show where she interviewed authors like Toni Morrison, Raymond Carver, and Joseph Heller. You can find her at www.nancyevans.media.*

27

"Could you make a poem out of that?"

HILMA WOLITZER (CLOSE FRIEND) AND MAXINE KUMIN

We weren't ladies who lunch,
except once when you came
down from the horse farm to
see a painting of a horse.
Dear country mouse, your city
cousin would like to meet with
you again and talk of horses
and paintings and villanelles.
Is there a poem in any of that?
Let us dine together once more,
gorging on berries you canned,
downing them out of season for no
reason at all but pleasure.
Max, you lived free and died,
and I am still on the eighteenth floor
of life, wanting to continue
my conversation with you.
Could you make a poem out of that?
I guess you could. You made a poem
from the winking of a mare's vulva, and
from the deaths of a woodchuck family,
garden pests you killed yourself.
The table is laid but you will not come.
Dreamy pragmatist, you knew there is only
this earthly heaven. Never mind. I'll sit here
with your book for company.
There will surely be poetry in that.

Hilma Wolitzer's novels include An Available Man *and* The Doctor's Daughter. *Her poems have appeared in* Ploughshares, New Letters, *the* Southampton Review, *and* Prairie Schooner. *She has taught in several university writing programs. Among her honors are grants from the Guggenheim Foundation and the National Endowment for the Arts and an Award in Literature from the American Academy of Arts and Letters.*

28

"He finally says, 'I have to get going soon.'
'Why?' I ask.
"That's the deal.'"

CATHY LADMAN (DAUGHTER)
AND LEO LADMAN

I'm really nervous. It feels like I'm going on a date—which is especially creepy because I'm having lunch with my father.

I haven't seen him since his death eleven years ago, and I want to look nice. What should I wear? Well, my bell-bottoms better not drag on the floor!

Let me explain: In the sixties, it was the style to wear your giant bell-bottoms, "bells," dragging on the ground. You didn't actually hem them if you wanted cool bells. Eventually, a ripped and tattered ring of fabric would fall off, and a natural hem would form. And then you had yourself a fucking cool pair of jeans.

Now, my dad had not liked teenagers. He owned a bowling alley, and he hated when they hung out there, "up to no good," spending no money. He found them "arrogant." That's what he always said. "They're *arrogant!*" And to him, long bell-bottoms were "arrogant."

So, whenever he was home before I left for school, he would make me stand on the top step of the six steps to the bedroom level of our house and he would inspect my bells. I would try to hold them up by squeezing my thighs together. Sometimes that worked. And sometimes it didn't. If he saw that my pants touched the floor, I had to change into others. Ugh.

Constant scrutiny. Not fond memories.

But he and I gradually, slowly, painfully, came to a pretty good place in our relationship. So, why am I so nervous?

Well, I've never had lunch with a dead person. There's that.

This is My Dad. *That's* why I'm so nervous. He'd always been strikingly critical. When I see him, I know he'll appraise me immediately. He'll look me up and down and give me a grade. Nothing gets by him. He'll find the *one* thing that's out of place. And that's how I feel right now. Out of place.

Oh, Jesus, this is silly. We're past that. Am *I* past it?

I'm sixty-one years old, I've had a successful career doing what I love—even though . . .

But, at this point, our relationship is certainly at a place where we're on equal footing. At least, we could be if *I* would only assume that. Don't go in there looking for validation, Cathy. Validate yourself. Know who you are. Remember that. Things have changed, and work has slowed down quite a bit. Still, I am what is known, to some, as a legend in stand-up comedy. It's so silly to hear that. When someone says that to me, I think, "*Really?* Have you seen my calendar? There's lots of blanks in there." I try to prove to people that I'm not all that. Why do I always do that?

See, that's what's making me nervous—what Dad is going to say about the fact that I'm not working enough and not earning enough. Money has always been very important to him. And, I guess, to me, too. I've inherited the legacy.

Now, what to wear. It's a nice place, the old-world Italian setting he chose, but anything goes, really. I'd love to wear jeans, but maybe I'll wear something nicer. Lightweight wool pants, maybe. Am I doing that for me or for him? If I'm being honest, for him. However, I am probably going to have some pasta, and I don't need constricting jeans reminding me of what I ate and lighting a fuse under my anorexia. Sure, I'm in recovery, but it's always a slender thread I hang by.

We're going to Café Continental, of course. That's where we always went for occasions. My dad used to go there with his stock club. They spent some money they'd made, or money they hadn't. And then our family started going there for celebrations. The waiters were all Italian; the food was great. They called Dad "Mr. Leo." He loved the personal attention. I guess he and I are alike in that way.

I'm on time. I walk in. It's not busy yet. It's dark and cozy. It feels good to be here. Nostalgic. I spot Dad with his back is to me. I figure it's okay to sneak up on him because, if I startle him, what can possibly happen to him now? I put my hands on his shoulders.

"Hi, Dad!"

"Ah! Cathy! Look at you!"

He stands up, with no effort, and we share a really long hug. Extra long. When we pull apart, I see that his eyes are welling up just like mine. We laugh to cover the tsunami of emotion, hug again, briefly, and take each other in.

"You look so good, Cathy! You know, you really turned out great," he says to me, gently clocking me on the chin. We're seated in a booth.

I smile. "You, too, Dad. You look good. You look the same. No, you look better."

"You smell the same, too," he says. "Same perfume?"

"Yeah. I never thought you noticed that."

"I notice everything," he says, wagging a finger at me.

I laugh. "Oh, yeah. Yeah, you do."

"You want to order something to drink?"

"Yes. Yes, I do," I say, smiling.

My dad waves the waiter over.

"Yes, Mr. Leo." There it is. Leo Ladman is in his zone.

"Antonio, you remember my daughter, my youngest? Cathy, Antonio."

"Hi, Antonio! It's nice to see you!"

"Hello, Miss Cathy!"

I order a glass of Cabernet, Leo asks for a Scotch, and he speaks first.

"So, how is everyone at home? Catch me up."

I'm surprised at this question. Family was never something that my dad wanted to talk about. He was more interested in money, business. And animals. He loved animals.

So, we talk about my family, some work highlights. We finally have to stop to decide what we're going to have to eat when Antonio comes over for the second time to take our order. We get some of the old favorites: Baked Clams Oreganata. Dad has Veal Française; I order Eggplant Rollatini.

There's a small bit of silence, and I break it.

"I was nervous coming here today."

"Me, too!" my dad says.

"I wasn't sure— What? *You* were nervous? What about?" I say.

"Hey, I haven't seen anyone in eleven years. I didn't know what to expect. I didn't know if you'd be happy to see me."

"Really? Wow, Dad, I am *so* happy to see you."

"I thought maybe you'd have . . . some residual problems with me."

"Well . . . yeah. But I'm still happy to see you."

"So, you do have issues."

Another surprise. My dad is talking about *feelings*?

A few moments of silence before I speak.

"Dad, everyone's got issues." A beat of silence, while I form my thoughts and words. "I think the hardest thing for me was how critical you always were, how strict. You were scary."

"I didn't mean to be," he says. Somewhat sheepishly, I detect.

"There was a reason I went away to college when I was sixteen. I had no freedom at home. I couldn't socialize. I couldn't dress the way I wanted to. That's a big part of self-expression, especially at that age: personal style. I was constantly scrutinized. It was hard for me. And you were terrifying."

"How so?"

"You yelled, you hit, you controlled. Both you and Mommy were very controlling, in different ways." I stop. "I'm sorry. I don't mean to dump on you as soon as you rise from the dead."

We both laugh. Then we both begin stuffing our mouths with the delicious bread that's been put before us.

"I mean, there were great things about you, too. Your sense of humor, your intelligence, your good taste, your love of animals. Those have all informed who I am, to a great degree. But the tough and judgmental guy that you were made me choose a guy who's similar, and that's been a challenge."

"I love Tom," my dad says.

"I love him, too, but he's negative and critical, and I don't love that about him. And I wonder if I was drawn to that in some weird, pathological way. It's also possible that I didn't realize that about him until later. Who knows?"

Then I ask him, "What about you? What do you want to say to me?"

My dad thinks. "That I'd like more bread?"

"Ha-ha! You never had a problem saying that! Seriously. What?"

"I guess I wish that you knew how terrific you are. How talented and kind and polite. What a good person you are. You never seemed secure. You were always second-guessing yourself. I see that I contributed to that."

I'm touched.

"I never felt good enough for you, Dad. I never felt successful enough. And now I'm struggling to make a living, and I feel so ashamed."

I start to tear up again. Dad hands me his clean handkerchief.

"Oh, I don't want to ruin it."

"Don't worry. They do laundry where I live."

I laugh.

"Let me tell you something," my dad says as Antonio sets our drinks before us. "I put a lot of stake in money when I was alive. I wonder if I'd lived past eighty-seven if I would have had the chance to learn that it wasn't as important as I made it out to be. But in the past eleven years—and I can't tell you how, it's strange—I don't really know how, but I've learned that it was a mistake. And I'm so sorry that I caused you to be anxious or to not feel good about yourself, based on whether or not you were earning. You have proven yourself many times over, Cathy. You're an exceptional person. Don't let the money and the career run you. *You* can run it."

Well, now I'm bawling. I use the handkerchief, my napkin, the tablecloth, and my sleeve. Dad's hand is on my shoulder.

"Have a sip of that wine. A gulp." He takes a swig of his Scotch.

I do. I feel better.

I take a deep breath. My nervousness had all been for nothing. Nowhere in sight was the stern, judgmental disciplinarian I'd been skittish about breaking bread with. Instead, it seems as though my dad has finally grown up. It's so hard to raise parents.

"I miss you," I tell him. "Even more so now."

"I miss you, too," he says.

We hold hands. We understand.

"Be careful! Very hot plates!" Antonio says, placing our food in front of us.

"Oh, this looks great!"

"*Buon appetito!*"

"Oh, Antonio," my dad says.

"Yes, Mr. Leo?"

I answer. "More bread, please."

My dad and I smile at each other.

Draining his glass, he says, "I might have a second drink."

We eat with real enthusiasm, Dad tastes mine and loves it; I tell him I don't eat veal, when he offers me a taste. That's something he never did before: share his meal.

Who *is* this person?

All in all, we sit for more than three hours. He finally says, "I have to get going soon."

"Why?" I ask.

"That's the deal."

We order dessert, which is not normal for me, but today I won't do my ridiculous calorie counting. Well, I am counting, but I don't give a fuck.

We finally have to pay the check. My dad grabs it.

He looks at the check. It reads, "For Mr. Leo and his daughter Cathy. The pleasure of Café Continental." Wow.

We thank everyone and say goodbye, that we hope to see them again soon.

"I want to see you go," I say to my dad.

"No. I need to walk out alone."

"Why?"

He shrugs. "Also part of the deal."

We hug, a very long hug, even longer than the first one.

"I'm so glad we had this time, Dad. I hope we can do it again."

"Me, too. And even if we can't, it was so good, wasn't it?"

I nod.

"Give my love to everyone in your family. And don't tell JoAnn or Leslie or Mommy that we met. It will only make them feel bad."

"Okay, Dad. I understand. I love you."

"I love you, too."

I watch him walk out the door and out of view. He has the same jaunty walk he'd always had. It seems like he's very comfortable in his own skin.

I turn around. I'm happy and so sad. Antonio comes over to me and puts his arm around my shoulder. He hands me a box of cannoli.

"For your family," he says.

I walk outside. It's very sunny out. I look up at the sky, shielding my eyes, as if I'm going to see my dad. I laugh to myself. Silly.

I decide to walk into the bookstore next to the restaurant. I find myself in the DVD stacks. Dad and I loved movies, loved watching them together. I stop, and my mouth drops open.

There is a poster of Fernando Rey in *The French Connection*. Everyone always said he looked so much like my dad. He did. He does.

Hi, Dad. Bye, Dad.

One of the country's top comedians, Cathy Ladman has appeared on The Tonight Show *nine times and a myriad of other late-night shows. She's had her own HBO and Showtime specials. She was awarded the American Comedy Award for Best Female Stand-Up Comic. Her film credits include* Charlie Wilson's War, The Aristocrats, *and* White Oleander. *Many people remember her from her role in* Don't Tell Mom the Babysitter's Dead. *Her TV credits include* I'm Dying Up Here, Modern Family, How to Get Away with Murder, Scandal, Mad Men, Curb Your Enthusiasm, *and* Everybody Loves Raymond.

29

"It's answers I'm after, not him."

CAROLINE LEAVITT (DAUGHTER)
AND HENRY LEAVITT

I arrive at the restaurant first. I don't know if my father's going to show because he's dead and because he hasn't ever come to see me when he said he would when he was alive. The lunch was his idea, the details on a cream-colored invitation sent through snail mail requesting a meeting. It's a nice place, one I am surprised my father chose or even knew about, because my father is tight and he would have been happy going to Joe & Nemo's, the hot dog place he took my mom to on their first date. This place has four shiny stars and a menu full of fish, steaks, pastas, and fine wines. The tables are far enough away from one another so no one can hear us. There's even a maître d' in a penguin suit who seats me at the table, a good one, by the window, far from the bathroom and kitchen.

I hope he's not going to be wearing those awful ice-cream-colored pants he favors, those big shirts. I don't know how the dead change, but I wonder if he'll be fat the way he used to be so that he has to cram himself into the seats and even then, he might be so larger than life, (ha, that sounds funny), he spills out over the armrests.

I don't know how I feel about seeing him. I rustle in my seat and play with the linen napkin. I know I won't cry because I really cried enough when he was alive. I won't hug him or even touch him, but I remember he smells like tobacco because he's always poking Q-tips into his pipe and his skin is clammy. If he's the same as he was alive, he'll probably yell at me but, as always, not tell me for what. Maybe he will punish me with silence or kick a chair over and leave it to me to apologize to the staff in this fancy place.

It's answers I'm after, not him.

He walks in, and I'm stunned by how young he looks, or maybe it's just because I've grown old. He's actually wearing a suit, and it's a little baggy on him, and I wonder how he lost so much weight. Maybe death does that to you. Maybe the food's not so good there. He's wearing a black tie on a white shirt, which seems appropriate. I can see the comb marks raked across his gray hair. He smiles and squints, his hazel eyes blink, just like mine, but he doesn't hug me or kiss me or say anything sweet. Instead, he sits down opposite me and puts his napkin in his lap and reaches for the menu, not looking at me.

"I found them after you died," I tell him, and he looks up at me. "Found what?" he says. He turns the pages of his menu, frowning.

"The potato chips in your coat pocket. The candy bar wrappers in your jacket." Before he died, my father was on a restricted diet, dangerously obese with blood pressure so dramatically high it could win an Oscar, while I was always swizzle-stick skinny. He was supposed to take pills for it. My mother put him on a diet. He ignored both of them.

"I liked them," he said. "I wasn't going to deny myself."

"I found them," I say again, louder now, and this time, as if the staff knows exactly what we want, a steak and potato appears for him, a vegan pasta made of zucchini and cashew ricotta for me. "You like that?" he says, shaking his head. He starts salting his steak so heavily it has a coating. "Hey, don't you give me that look. I'm dead," he says. "I can eat whatever I want. You and your mother. All this about food, for Christ's sake."

I remember my mother cooking him lean meats, plain chicken, giving him fake butter or no butter. Instead she chose olive oil because it was supposed to be good for you. She didn't love him, never had, but had married him on the rebound, carrying a torch for the man she had really loved for most of her life. But every night, she cooked for him and we all had dinner together. The day he died, she took out a meat loaf, a new recipe that was leaner, cleaner, and she cried, "This was his dinner."

I swallow hard. "My letters," I tell him. "I found them, too."

In high school, when I had my first boyfriend, my first kiss at seventeen with a bad boy so glorious I could have inhaled him like a drug, my father came out in boxer shorts and bare chest and big belly, and while my boyfriend blinked at him in astonishment, my father yelled at me. "Where have you been?" he shouted. I gently shoved my boyfriend out the door, his kiss still on my mouth, and told him I'd see him the next day and the next day and forever after. "You will never see that boy again!" my father screamed. He threatened to drive me to school and pick me up to make sure he knew where I was, to put a monitor around my ankle, and then my mother came in and looked exhausted by all of it. "Henry," she said. "Henry." She took his arm and led him back to bed.

Every morning, I called the summer camp where I worked and coughed into the phone and told them I had bronchitis. "Gee, it's going on so long," the director said. "Get better soon because the kids are asking for you." I didn't care about the money. Then I took all the side streets and walked forty-five minutes to my boyfriend's house and up to his small blue bedroom, his rumpled bed, his lean lick of a body, the way he loved, loved, loved me. Once, there was a sleepover at the camp and I lied and we slept out on an abandoned ski slope all night long. I came home with forty-five mosquito bites on my feet, but to me, they were badges of honor.

But back then, I worried that my parents knew. I felt my father watching me, threatening. My mother would snap at me, too, but only because she didn't want to deal with my father. I couldn't deal with the stress, with what might happen if my father found out I was sleeping with my boyfriend. "Let's run away to California," I begged my boyfriend. He smoothed my hair. "We can't," he said.

I began crying all the time. In my room, at school, with my boy-friend, who now couldn't deal with the consuming suck of my sorrow, plus he was a hormone-fueled seventeen-year-old, amazed by all the girls who wanted him, who brought him books of poems, who put their hands on his hips. Girls who didn't have terrifying fathers. Of course, he broke it off with me.

I had a nervous breakdown, or at least I thought I did. I began crying more, so much, I even worried myself. "Now, you just stop this," my mother said, and I cried harder.

"I think I need to see a doctor," I told my parents. "You talk to us," my father told me. "No daughter of mine is seeing a shrink." My mom took me to a social worker, because it sounded less ominous, but my father refused to go with us, and the social worker told her, "I want to see the whole family here." I wanted to throw my arms about him. I wanted him to be my father. He was hope.

But when we left the room, my mother said. "Your father will never agree to this. Let's just forget coming here again. It's no use."

Now, I pick at my fake ricotta cream. It's silky on my tongue. "Why did you do that with my first boyfriend?" I ask him.

"I didn't like that boy. He wasn't Jewish."

"But I loved him. I loved him. And I was only seventeen. I wasn't going to marry him."

"I'm your father, and you listen to me."

"No," I say. "I don't listen. I didn't listen." I tell him that I had kept seeing my boyfriend, even after we had broken it off, off and on, for three years afterward, sneaking away. I told him I saw him in college, that we are still friends. That I slept with him over and over for years until I got out of college. I wait for his shock. He shrugs.

"I'm dead. What do I care?" he says.

"I'm your daughter. That's why you care."

I ask him what it's like being dead, and he shrugs. "I have no real use for it," he says. "It's one big stinkeroo. Just like life was."

"I don't think that," I tell him. I tell him how I married young and then divorced. I told him how I had become engaged and my fiancé had died two weeks before our wedding. I told him about Jeff, my husband, how before we had kids, we sat down and decided to do everything the opposite of how I had been raised.

My father pushes the steak away. "Who the hell do you think you are?" he asks.

"Why weren't you a good father?"

"Don't give me any of that," he says. "Ever think it was you?" I feel as if he slapped me.

I remember a summer, when I was sixteen and I wanted to go home from the Cape because I hated the beach, the sting of the salty air, the way the sand breaded me like a cutlet. I hated being away from my boyfriend, and my father told me I had to stay with him and my mom at the ocean. I had lashed out. "Why?" I asked. And when he said, "Because I'm your father," I said, "Oh, really? Who is my best friend? What is my favorite class in school? What books do I read? Some father." And then I took my things and slapped out of the cottage. And as I left, my mother cried, "Don't leave me alone with him." I saw her face, pleading, like I was the only hope she had left.

My father now puts down his fork. "Your mother didn't love me. I knew that," he says. "But if I didn't have you, then I had nothing. You had to stay. For me and to prove something to your mom."

I had run from the cabin and walked along the beach. I had no idea which direction the train station was, and I had no money, but I had my thumb, and people hitched back then. I was young and pretty, and I was wearing a tank top and shorts to show off my long browned legs. I could get a ride. I could fend for myself.

He came for me in the car, crying. I had never seen my father cry. "Get in," he begged, his voice knotted with grief, and I did. He started talking almost immediately, more than he ever had told me. He said he hated his own father, who wouldn't pay for him to go to law school or med school even though he had the money, how he was never loved, not even by his mother or his brothers. He was sobbing so hard I put an arm around him, even though I didn't want to. He was gulping tears, and I said I would go back to the cottage with him, and when we did, the first thing I saw was my mother's face. Her disappointment that I was back. "If you weren't here, I would have divorced him," she said. I heard the longing in her voice, the surprise that she couldn't get what she had wanted.

"Did you ever love me?" I ask my father now. I don't remember being taken anywhere by him. I don't remember hearing *I love you, I'm proud of you.* He never told me I was pretty or smart or fun to be around. Instead he called me "an animal" when I burped or farted. He looked at me with disgust.

"Of course I loved you," my father says. "What did you think?" I think how girls who grow up without fathers don't know how to have relationships with men. I think of my friend Judy, who was a daddy's girl, and how her father always hugged me when he saw me. He always asked about my classes, my family. Once, he bought Judy a baby blue cashmere sweater, and he must have seen the yearning in my face, because he bought one for me, too. My parents made me return it. "We're not taking charity," my mother said. Judy's father never returned the sweater, and every time I was over at their house, I wore it, even in the summer.

I used to dream that Judy's father would adopt me and my parents would let him. "Bye," they'd say with a wave. "Have a fun life."

This is what I remember. One time he took me on a roller coaster. I screamed the whole time.

When I was a little girl, I had bad dreams. I would sleep beside my mom, comforted, and one day she came to me and said, "Your father is hurt that you sleep beside me, but not beside him." I was six years old and terrified. I had to sleep in my father's bed, separated from my mom's by an end table. I was careful not to touch him, not to let him touch me. In the morning, he got out of bed naked, and I stared at his penis. He saw me and snapped, "Aren't you ashamed of yourself for looking?" In kindergarten, I drew paper dolls of my family, everyone naked, my father with a long sock-shape between his legs that touched his knees. The teacher called my mother. "She has a big imagination," my mother said.

I never would sleep with him again.

"The letters," I say again. My father beckons the waiter for more water. Months before he died I felt confused. My father never called me at college. Never wrote me. So I wrote him. Two long letters that I watercolored designs on the edges. I don't know why, but I wrote that I loved him. I told him about my life, my boyfriends, my dreams, as if it might change things. It was a totally pretend letter, but I thought it might make him really see me.

But when he died, I found the letters in his dresser, still sealed. He had never even bothered to open either one of them. "Why not?" I ask, and now I'm practically crying. "Why did you keep them if you weren't going to read them? Why the fuck not?"

"Watch your filthy mouth," he says.

We're finishing our meal, or rather he is. I haven't been able to eat. "Do you miss me?" I ask, and I know my voice is a plea.

He calls for the waiter, the check.

I reach for the bill, and my father takes it from me. "I earn good money," I tell him. "I'm a novelist."

"And I'm your father and I'm paying."

He tips the waitress the exact right amount because he was an accountant, and then he stands up. "It was nice seeing you," he says, and I want to hurl myself on him, sobbing, Nice? Nice? What does "nice" mean? Don't they teach you things in the afterlife? Why didn't you love me, why wasn't I enough for you? Why did you have to repeat the pattern your dad did with you? I want to call him a bastard, to tell him good, I'm glad you're leaving. Go, go. I want to say that maybe we have horrible people in our lives to show us who we never want to be. I want him to say he loves me now, that he's sorry for how he was, that he regrets everything, especially keeping me silenced so I couldn't ever tell him how I was hurting.

Instead, he waves and steps out into the blinding light. "See you," he says, and I don't know what that means. I wait until I cannot see him anymore, until it seems like just another day, another restaurant. I remind myself that my husband, Jeff, and I had never ever thought to hit our son Max, had never raised our voices or even snapped at him. We had never chased our son around with a belt. We had never denigrated him or told him to shut up or mocked what he said or kept him from friends. I remind myself that Jeff is affectionate and silly and kind and devoted. My father never changed.

But I did.

I motion the waitress and order chocolate cake. I eat it slowly, savoring the sweet, and then I find my cell and text both Max and Jeff. I love you, I say. I just wanted you to know.

Caroline Leavitt is the New York Times *bestselling author of* Pictures of You, Is This Tomorrow, Cruel Beautiful World, *and eight other novels. A book critic for the* San Francisco Chronicle *and* People, *she teaches writing online at Stanford and the Writers' Program at UCLA Extension, as well as working with private clients. Her work has appeared in the* New York Times, New York *magazine,* Real Simple, *and more, and she was the recipient of a New York Foundation for the Arts Grant, as well as being a finalist in the Sundance Screenwriters Lab and the Nickelodeon Fellowships. Reach her at www.carolineleavitt.com.*

30

"You look great for a dead guy!"

ELIZABETH MAILER (DAUGHTER)
AND NORMAN MAILER

On November 10, 2018, eleven years after my father's death, Dad and I meet at Elephant & Castle, on Eleventh Street and Greenwich Avenue, in the West Village. It's one of my favorite haunts.

As I enter the restaurant, I am hugged by its nurturing ambiance: an intimate, warm eatery—long and narrow like a railroad apartment. With cherrywood tables, chairs, floors, and walls. The all-wooden interior gives one that sense of hunkering down inside a treehouse on a cold autumn afternoon. On each end of the restaurant, a great, big white ceramic elephant holds court on a white-tiled window seat with floor-to-ceiling windows looking out onto Greenwich Avenue on one end of the restaurant and out onto West Eleventh on the other. I've always chuckled at the irony of the name, Elephant & Castle: as my own big person vs. the diminutive size of this eatery makes me feel more like an elephant in a teapot than an elephant in a castle.

I arrive right on the dot of 1:30, as instructed.

The place is bustling and the tables are mostly full. I look around to see if Dad is already there. He is sitting at the table opposite the espresso machine and coffee station, with the black-framed antique ink print of Freud hanging just above him.

It takes me about five seconds to spot him; and when I find him, I do a double-take. I expected to see an older man at the table; but instead, Dad has manifest as his younger self.

I race down the narrow aisle between the tables. I rush to greet him—so eager that I almost trip on the leg of someone else's chair. Dad jumps up from the table to meet me halfway. We throw our arms around each other. Ah, there's that bear hug I have missed so much. So invigorating and reassuring. His shirt smells faintly of cigarette smoke. (He smoked back in the early sixties.) I sit down opposite him.

"Wonderful to see you, darling! You look terrific."

Okay, I'll take "terrific," I think to myself. "Terrific" sure beats the time he called me "a handsome woman" when I was in my twenties. At the time, I was mortified. I mean, what young woman in her twenties wants to be called *handsome*?

"And you look great for a dead guy!" I say.

He smiles. "How did you expect me to look?"

We sit. "Well, I expected to see an old man sitting here! Because right before you died, you looked ancient!"

He laughs. "Gee, thanks, kid."

Weirdly, Dad appears today the way he looked when he was in his early forties. But without the boozy, scary, volatile demeanor he had back then. This time, he is sane, calm, and sweet.

He is handsome in his own way: five-eight with a husky physique, short, dark-brown curly hair, a strong chin, and Paul Newman eyes. He is wearing blue jeans and a navy-blue T-shirt under an orange-and-brown-checkered, tweed jacket, with sable-brown suede elbow patches. This is the jacket he wore often when I was about three years old.

"I hope you'll enjoy the lunch here, Dad."

"Well, seeing that so many of you in the family eat here so often, I've always wondered what all the fuss was about." Dad grins. "I never joined you for lunch in all those years because I could not interrupt my workday."

"Well, I'm glad you made it this time," I say.

Mozart, Bach, and Haydn is the favorite background classical music here at Elephant & Castle. But today, appropriately, it is Vivaldi's *Four Seasons* (the "Spring" and "Summer" movements). The latter is what was played as the actors come onstage at the start of my father's play adaptation of *The Deer Park*, which was performed at the West Village Theater de Lys in the mid-1960s.

"So, Dad, tell me, what on earth is it like in the Hereafter?" I ask.

"Well, it's essentially a blank slate. It's tabula rasa. It's very individual. It mirrors the nature of our own personal perceptions and beliefs."

"Since you died, your granddaughter Christina has been wondering if you've been hangin' out with Hemingway at a bar in the astral realm," I say.

"Oh, yes! You can tell her that she is absolutely correct! And tell her I also hang out with Dostoyevsky, Karl Marx, and Picasso!" He laughs.

Just then, our waiter, Luis, appears at our table and fills our water glasses. He is a smart, congenial man in his early forties, from Ecuador. He has known me, my sisters and brothers, my cousin, and my aunt for many years. I introduce him to Dad, who chats with him in Spanish. Luis takes our order and heads for the kitchen.

"Dad, tell me more. What do you do with yourself, once you die and pass into eternity?"

"Well, from a timeless perspective—because there is no linear time in other dimensions—you have an opportunity, right after death, to review your whole life: You examine all the joys and all the sorrows;

the triumphs and the failures; the gifts and the deficits; that which was settled and unsettled; completed and unfinished. You *feel* all the pain and suffering you ever caused anybody at any point in your life. And when you are ready, you embark on a ritual for purification. Like the ghost of Hamlet's father, I chose to walk, for what felt like endless miles, along corridors of cleansing white fire—to transmute the psychic stain of my own iniquities."

After so profound a mini dissertation on the afterlife, there was something very comical about the juxtaposition of purification rituals and today's soup at Elephant & Castle: a black French lentil soup with andouille sausage and butternut squash, thyme and bay leaf. Gary, the chef, has managed to coax deep flavor from these simple ingredients. Over the years, Dad used to come up with his own soup concoctions in the kitchen of his Brooklyn Heights apartment. Inspired by his service in the army as short-order cook in the mess hall, he threw into the soup pot everything he could get his hands on.

"Well, enough about me and my soul!" Dad laughs. "How are you?"

"You know, Dad, I'm in a really good place. I've worked very hard on myself for the last thirty-five years—to face my demons, to face myself, to grow and to heal. I've opened my heart to love and abundance. I am committed to my truth."

"Well, that is a mighty powerful declaration, my dear. I'm very moved by that," Dad says.

Luis brings us our soup, and we both dive right in. Suddenly I'm starving.

"Wow, Bets, this is extraordinary! I'm so happy for you! You've worked so hard over the years and you deserve all of it."

In my enthusiasm at seeing Dad again, a spoonful of soup misses my mouth; and bits of butternut squash and lentils land on the front of my red chiffon button-down blouse. I wipe up the spill with my napkin.

Following our soup, our entrées arrive. I'm having the guacamole burger on a brioche bun, with Stilton cheddar, sliced tomato, red onion, and pickle. E&C's burger is to die for. The burger pairs well with a cup of E&C's house coffee with half-and-half. A medium Peruvian roast, rich but smooth with caramel notes and no smokiness (which I hate).

Luis graciously handles Dad's special order of tuna salad—hold the guacamole—on top of an iceberg wedge with sliced tomatoes and rye bread with butter pats on the side. E&C's tuna salad is prepared with chopped onion, celery, capers, housemade mayo, and a schmear of guacamole on lightly toasted seven-grain.

Our lunch today reminds me of the many meals Dad, Norris, my siblings, and I relished at our favorite restaurants over the many years. There was so much going on in our lives all the time. But no matter what upheaval or crisis we faced as a family, when we all went out to dinner—for sushi at Tanpopo, or Veal Parmigiana at Nicola, or grilled swordfish at Pepe's, Dad was at his best. We all came alive in his presence; all was right with our world, and we could forget our troubles.

Dessert arrives. Pecan pie for Dad and Indian pudding for me. I take a big forkful of his pecan pie. It's a little bit of heaven. Meanwhile, E&C's Indian pudding takes me back to a week-long school trip I took with my classmates to a farm in Otis, Massachusetts, in the fall of my fourth-grade year—when we were learning all about Colonial times. We learned how to make Indian pudding, how to milk cows, how to weave on a loom, and how to write on the bark of pine trees. Now, the pudding, served with freshly whipped cream, is comfort food at its best. I am warm inside and full of nostalgia.

"Dad, speaking of the Hereafter, do you ever see Mom there?"

"Yes, I see her all the time. We get along famously!" he says, winking at me.

"I found an old diary of Mom's, going back fifty-nine years ago. I want to read you an excerpt."

"I'd love to hear it," Dad says while chewing.

I pull from my bag a tablet of unlined paper, with the Woolworth's logo on the cardboard cover. The corners of the pages are yellowed with age. I open the tablet where I bookmarked it with a Post-it note, and I read the following out loud to Dad:

> Saturday night, November 19, 1960
>
> Tonight, Norman took me and the girls out for a little spin in the Chevy. We drove up as far as the Palisades (about an hour north of the city); and then headed back down to our apartment on West 94th.
>
> We had decided after all not to host a cocktail party tonight at our place. It would have been a big party and so unwieldy, right before Thanksgiving, and all.
>
> I'm just glad we had a quiet evening instead.
>
> It's just what we needed.
>
> Sunday morning, November 20, 1960.[1]
>
> This morning, Norman and I were up before the girls. He and I were cuddling on the couch, having our coffee. We were talking about my painting class with Hans Hoffmann. And Norman was excited about getting started on his next book.
>
> Suddenly, I put my finger to my lips. "Shhh! Listen, Darling!" I said to Norman.
>
> He and I were quiet for a minute. Then we both faintly heard the sweet voices and laughter of our two little girls, playing together down the hall.
>
> "Well, I guess the girls are awake! Let's go see what

---

[1]   In the wee hours of Sunday, November 20, 1960, my father stabbed my mother with a pen knife at a cocktail party they were hosting at their Upper West Side apartment. My version (in this piece) of events on that date represents my fantasy of how things might have been, had the incident never occurred.

they're up to!" Norman said, smiling. This moment brings all the mellow sweetness of a leisurely Sunday morning.

Then we head to the kitchen to make banana pancakes on the griddle, with melted butter and Log Cabin maple syrup.

I finish reading the diary entry. I set down the tablet and look up at Dad. He has tears in his eyes.

Our empty dessert plates are cleared, and lunch is about over.

I don't want this lunch with Dad to end.

I don't want to say goodbye.

Dad takes care of the check with cash. We put on our coats and walk outside. It's already after 4:00 p.m. It is that magical hour when shadows are purple and the autumn sunlight of a late afternoon turns everything golden.

Dad gives me his great big bear hug. I'm guessing that this is the last time I'll be seeing him for a good long while.

"Ah, Bets, my Bets . . . I see in you the best of me and the best of your mother. I'm so proud of who you are."

Dad hails a yellow cab and gets in.

I'm all choked up.

He rolls down his window and gives me that Bogie "Here's lookin' at you, kid" look.

The cab makes a left onto Seventh Avenue and heads south. Like something out of a 1960s *Jetsons* cartoon, the whole cab (with Dad and driver inside) lifts up several feet and hovers high above the street, then it suddenly accelerates upward and disappears into thin air.

Elizabeth Mailer has published nonfiction pieces in Provincetown Arts Magazine *and the* Mailer Review. *She is currently writing a memoir about her relationship with her father. Also in progress: a darkly comic novel about a middle-aged woman's sexual odyssey. Elizabeth holds a BA degree in English from Princeton University (1981). She lives in New York City with her husband, Frank; their daughter, Christina; and their cat, Shea.*

31

*"Mom, do you mind not picking a fight with this waitress? I know her.
I come to this place a lot and she's always been very nice."*

MERRILL MARKOE (DAUGHTER)
AND RONNY MARKOE

*Afternoon. Fade in on a mini-mall in the San Fernando Valley. In the mid-
dle of a line of identical nineties-style storefronts sits a very pedestrian-
looking hole-in-the-wall Chinese restaurant, with a panoramic view
of the large parking lot. Inside, the walls are decorated with dozens of
inexpensively framed and signed head shots of occasionally recognizable
B-level actors, like Tom Arnold. At an upholstered red vinyl booth on the
left-hand side of the room sits a slightly agitated middle-aged woman
named* MERRILL, *who has tidied herself up as much as she could, in a
freshly ironed blouse and a new sports coat. She appears to be waiting
for someone she wants to impress. There are no other customers.*

*As the front door opens, a bell rings, heralding the arrival of a woman
in her sixties, sporting an imperious Bette Davis–level take-no-prisoners
air of grandiosity. Her makeup, her dark lipstick, and her dark eyebrow
pencil are perfect. Her short, fashionable strawberry-blond hair is freshly
combed. She is dressed in a pair of beige stay-pressed slacks, a polyester
print blouse with a bow, an expensive watch, and her signature large
diamond engagement/wedding ring, which she unconsciously turns as
she eyes this humble restaurant with displeasure.*

Then she raises her eyebrows and waves when she sees her daughter
MERRILL *seated at a booth, signaling to her.*

MERRILL *rises, and the two women hug briefly before they both sit down.*

MERRILL

MOM! It's overwhelming to see you again. I can't believe you made it all the way back here from the Great Beyond! You look so much better than you did the last time I saw you.

RONNY

On my deathbed? Talk about damning with faint praise.

MERRILL

What I meant was you look wonderful. Apparently death agrees with you.

RONNY

Well, that's because they stop you in your tracks when you die. I'd always heard that they let you revert to your favorite age or era. Complete and total bullshit.

MERRILL

Can you believe it's been twenty-five years since we saw each other last?

RONNY

Unfortunately, I can. I couldn't help but notice how much older you look than when I saw you last. And you've put on some weight. Which is to be expected. It's de rigeur as one gets older.

MERRILL

Can you believe you and I are almost the same age now? Wow. That's weird.

RONNY

I'd have come back sooner but I never got the feeling you were particularly *interested* in a reunion. I've heard how you talk about me.

MERRILL

You can eavesdrop on me in the Great Beyond?

RONNY

Of course, though that's not the word I would have chosen. Let's just say that when the curtains rustle in your house, it's probably me being unable to stifle an exasperated sigh.

MERRILL

So I'm still pissing you off, even in the afterlife? I didn't think it worked that way. I read somewhere that once you walk into the light, you're engulfed in such an all-knowing wave of love and forgiveness, all petty concerns are utterly transformed.

RONNY

Whose religious garbage have you been reading?

A WAITRESS *comes to the table with two glasses of water and a plate containing two small complimentary eggrolls.*

WAITRESS

These are special spring rolls for you. Ready to order?

MERRILL

I think we need another minute.

RONNY

This is a very meager amount of eggrolls.

WAITRESS (*not understanding*)

Okay. I give you time.

The WAITRESS *leaves.*

MERRILL

Mom, do you mind not picking a fight with this waitress? I know her. I come to this place a lot, and she's always been very nice.

RONNY

They bring out a ridiculously skimpy portion like this, but *I'm* the one causing a problem? Am I not entitled to my opinion?

MERRILL

Never mind. It's fine. Let's get back to our discussion. So it's not true that after you die, you get a chance to review your life and gain unlimited perspective and insight that you can use when you choose to be reborn?

RONNY

There are those who do that. Frankly, it never interested me.

MERRILL

Hmm. Because gaining perspective was one of the things I wanted to talk to you about. How I understand you better now. How I've gotten past blaming *you* for all the . . .

RONNY

Come again?

MERRILL

I no longer blame you for all the fights that we . . .

RONNY

Oh, that's rich. *You've* stopped BLAMING *me*? (*long exasper-ated sigh*) How stupid was I to believe that you summoned me back to offer an apology?

MERRILL

I kind of did. I mean, I was hoping to show you how much work I've done on myself. A lot of your behavior was incom-prehensible to me when I was younger. Of course it didn't help that you refused to ever explain yourself to me.

RONNY

Me EXPLAIN myself to *you*? I'm your *mother*. What in God's name would you imagine I needed to explain?

WAITRESS (*returns*)

You ready to order now?

MERRILL

Okay! Mom? You know what you want?

RONNY (*looks at menu*)

You said this food was Chinese? I don't see Chow Mein. Or Chop Suey.

MERRILL

Chinese food has evolved a little since you shuffled off your mortal coil. But I think you'll like this new version. They've really added some unusual recipes.

RONNY (*to* WAITRESS, *suspiciously*)

This fish: Is it fresh? Or fresh frozen?

WAITRESS

Neither one. It's *mock* fish.

MERRILL

The menu is vegan.

RONNY

Do you mean vegetarian? Which this most certainly is *not* because right here, under specials, it says Mongolian Beef.

WAITRESS

Its mock beef.

MERRILL

Let's get that. Andy and I love it.

RONNY

That's the most ridiculous thing I've ever heard. Who would order such a thing?

MERRILL (*to* WAITRESS)

I think we need just a couple more minutes.

RONNY

Who is Andy?

MERRILL

The guy I've been with for seventeen years,

RONNY

"Been with." As in "not married to"? So in other words, you are still making choices simply to spite me?

MERRILL

You know, sometimes I worry about that. . . . Mom, I'm just curious. When you decided to make this trip, what were you hoping I'd apologize for?

RONNY

Ha. You're joking. Where to begin? Should we start with that direct and purposeful attack on everything your father and I held dear: those shoes you wore to your high school graduation?

MERRILL

You can't still be angry about those shoes! They were my regular school shoes that I wore every day. You couldn't have traversed time and space to talk about my choice of shoes.

RONNY

So much for your claim of gaining perspective.

MERRILL

But isn't it a little shortsighted and humorless for you to remain angry at a decision about footwear made by your sixteen-year-old kid? Who, by the way, had already gotten early acceptance into college?

RONNY

They looked disgusting with that pink taffeta dress I picked out for you to wear.

MERRILL

I hated that dress. Why was it was *your* job to pick out *my* clothes for *MY graduation*?

RONNY

That wasn't YOUR graduation. That was OUR graduation. Who do you think paid for all those years of your schooling?

MERRILL

I can't believe we're still talking about this. I told you at the time I didn't want to wear that dress because I spent all my high school years creating a very specific badass image. And then at the last minute, when the whole class is getting together to say goodbye, you try to force a makeover on me by demanding that I dress in pink taffeta? I know that's not a mature decision, but I was a kid! Plus, why did it even matter? All anyone was going to see was the cap and gown.

RONNY

Those shoes were far from invisible. They were an embarrassment to me and to your father, who was in complete agreement with me.

MERRILL

So why are you still so upset? You won. You and Dad didn't even show up. AND it was FIFTY YEARS AGO.

RONNY

I'd forgotten how impossible it is to talk to you. You never did give a good goddamn about anything I had to say.

MERRILL

That's wrong, Mom. I still quote you regularly.

RONNY

I've heard those quotes you use, which I think you make up half the time. You think I don't know you're trying to make me sound ridiculous?

MERRILL

Those quotes are real. I know because I always ran into my room and wrote them down right after you said them.

RONNY

So say YOU.

MERRILL

You don't remember when I let you read a script I wrote the night before I moved to LA to try to find work as a writer . . . and you looked me in the eye and said, "I don't happen to care for it, but I pray I'm wrong"?

RONNY

Would you have wanted me to be less than honest?

MERRILL

Couldn't "tactful" have been on the table as an option?

RONNY

I can't imagine why you would repeat that comment since it only makes *you* look bad. I mean, if your own mother, who wants only the best for you, thinks your work isn't up to snuff, how good can it be?

WAITRESS (*returns to the table*)

Now you ready to order?

MERRILL (*to* WAITRESS)

We'll split an order of mock Mongolian Beef. I think you'll really like it, Mom. And I promise it won't kill you. But if it does . . . you're already dead! Win-win! Ha-ha! Get it?

RONNY

I fail to see the humor in that.

MERRILL

And also can you bring me a bottle of your Chinese beer? Mom, do you want anything to drink?

RONNY

What would they have that might possibly interest me?

WAITRESS

Okay, I'll get your order.

RONNY

This is all really a moot point. My appetite is completely gone. I don't know why I thought this would work out. I give up. Again.

RONNY *pushes back her chair and rises. She picks up her purse and heaves a final exasperated sigh.*

RONNY

I certainly hope it gives you pleasure knowing you've been able to make me miserable even after my death.

And then POOF. RONNY *disappears.*

MERRILL *sits quietly, chewing her lip for a beat. Then the* WAITRESS *reappears and places a steaming plate of mock Mongolian Beef on the table, along with a bottle of Chinese beer for* MERRILL, *who drinks it down in one long, continuous swallow as the lights fade down.*

Merrill Markoe is a five-time Emmy Award–winning humorist and filmmaker who has also published nine books and written for a ton of publications. For more information, check her website at www.merrillmarkoe.com. Her most recent book is called The Indignities of Being a Woman *and can be found on Audible.com.*

32

*"H. L. Mencken wrote, 'A legend is a lie that has attained
the dignity of age.' H. L. Mencken was right."*

BOB BALABAN (ACQUAINTANCE)
AND GROUCHO MARX

If I could take absolutely anyone to an imaginary lunch, it would have to be Groucho Marx. And I would take him to Lindy's. No question. That is, if Groucho were still alive. And if Lindy's still existed. The famous delicatessen opened in 1921 and closed on February 27, 2018. Groucho opened in 1890 and closed on August 19, 1977, five years after I last spoke to him.

Lindy's was known for its artery-clogging cheesecake and mile-high pastrami sandwiches. But their most amazing specialty wasn't on the menu, and they never ran out of it: a seemingly endless supply of insulting waiters. Their witty invective casually aimed at the givers of the occasional ungenerous tip or the slightest complaint about the cold coffee would have bankrupted any other restaurant quicker than a salmonella outbreak. Instead, it made Lindy's one of the most popular places in town. It was the reason you went there in the first place.

Which is exactly why I wish I could have taken Groucho there. Groucho was the human equivalent of the restaurant. He never appeared to give a damn about anything or anybody. His repartee was as cutting and as effortless as the Lindy's waiters' retorts. And his lack of the need to be adored, or even liked, created the opposite effect in his many fans. It certainly did in me.

When I was a little kid, I watched Groucho's TV quiz show, *You Bet Your Life*, religiously. I liked the part when the fake bird flew in on a wire and gave out the prize for the secret word of the day. But what really made the show such a "do not miss" for me was Groucho and the cranky, unpredictable, and unrepressed put-downs he ad-libbed in front of millions of people every week.

Groucho simply uttered whatever popped into his head. You could practically see the thought bubble forming above him as he spoke. The contestants weren't faking their responses, either. They really were embarrassed. And amused. And sometimes even a little mad. The effect was subtle but unforgettable.

Years later I was at a party and ran into a hardworking, not hugely successful actress I knew named Erin Fleming. She casually introduced me to her date—an old man with thick black glasses . . . and an unmistakable moustache. I don't remember exactly where or when the encounter took place. But I'll never forget what it felt like to experience Groucho in the flesh. And hear the voice I'd first heard when I was in my single digits.

Groucho was clearly crazy about Erin. Why not? He was eighty, frail, and decidedly lonely. His particular brand of misanthropy may have endeared him to audiences, but it didn't exactly make for close personal relationships. Erin was charming, gorgeous, and probably, I decided, infatuated with his fame, money, and exalted position in the show business pantheon. But she also seemed—to me, anyway—to have a real affection for the man. His family would come to heartily disagree. But that's another story.

I pretended not to be awestruck when he shook my hand, but I practically dropped my drink when Erin breezily asked me if it would be all right if Groucho gave me a call sometime. And then, like *Brigadoon*, they both disappeared into the night, and I was left standing alone wondering what the hell had just happened.

Much to my surprise, the great Groucho called me a few days later to ask if I would be willing to replace him at an event he had agreed to host the following week. I was still trying to wrap my brain around the unimaginable concept of me replacing Groucho Marx at anything when Erin got on the phone to confirm the request: Groucho had indeed agreed to host an event at the esteemed Hillcrest Country Club and then realized he wasn't up to it. For reasons I will never comprehend, she has told Groucho I would be the perfect replacement, and he deeply hopes I will be able make it.

I take a deep breath.

I want to scream, "Ask George Burns. Ask Milton Berle. I'm sure Morty Gunty would be happy to do it," but I carefully explain to Erin that I am hardly qualified to replace the most revered comic genius in the world at anything. And even if I were, when the audience hears an unknown character actor like me is replacing Groucho, they will throw bricks at me.

She seems so genuinely crushed by my response that I tell her I will think about it, hang up the phone, spend twenty-four hours feeling horribly guilty, wait another twenty-four hours to make it look as though I am seriously considering it, and then call Erin back to say I can't do it. I have suddenly booked a commercial in Toronto. And that's the last I ever see or hear from either one of them.

The entire Balaban/Groucho "experience" lasted less than a week and occupied a scant ten minutes. And yet the event occupies a much larger seat in the balcony of my brain than it has any right to. How many times do we get to meet one of our heroes in the flesh? And how many of those times do they ask us to help them out of a jam?

I have been mulling over this brief and perplexing encounter for decades. In the litany of regrets I recite to myself when it's late at night and I'm sitting in an airport waiting for a much-delayed flight, Groucho never fails to make a brief appearance.

It would be a relief to have my imaginary lunch with Groucho. I'd get to ask him about his friendships with T. S. Eliot and Carl Sandburg. Did they think it was funny when he insulted them? Did he take them to Lindy's? How did they meet in the first place? Did they all belong to the same temple group?

We'd talk about Margaret Dumont and whether or not she really didn't know the movies they did together were comedies. Or whether Bob Hope really kept Groucho waiting for an hour when he first appeared on Hope's radio program and Groucho got so mad that he needled Hope mercilessly and was so funny that he ended up landing his own insult-filled quiz show that lasted for thirteen years?

I'd finally get a chance to tell Groucho that the theatres in Chicago where he and his brothers performed their vaudeville act were built by my family after they fled Russia at the turn of the last century and ended up in America. I would tell Groucho that his mom, Minnie, had been pals with my grandmother Gussie. I'd ask if he remembers what my grandmother was like. I've always wanted to know more about her.

I'd reminisce with Groucho about the time I auditioned for a voice-over for Chico's daughter Maxine Marx, a successful casting director, and we talked about the old days in Chicago. She told me about the time she was standing backstage with George S. Kaufman, watching her dad and his brothers perform one of Kaufman's new plays, when Kaufman suddenly pointed at the stage and whispered excitedly to Maxine, "My God, my God! They just said one of my lines!"

I'd really like to know if Groucho ended up hosting that Hillcrest event or if he managed to find some braver soul than I to take the bullet for him.

H. L. Mencken wrote, "A legend is a lie that has attained the dignity of age." H. L. Mencken was right. The lesson I learned from my decades-old encounter still resonates. Legends don't necessarily seem like legends when they hold still long enough for you to get a good look at them.

In person, my legend couldn't have been less funny, special, or memorable if he tried. In fact, he bore an uncanny resemblance to a good third of the adult male population of the building I grew up on Chicago's North Side. They, too, came equipped with cigars, bushy eyebrows, and a heavy dose of sarcasm.

And yet it's precisely that unquantifiable, illusive dissonance between the legend and the person behind it that so tantalizes us.

There will be no surprises at my imaginary Lindy's lunch. And no disappointments. The matzoh balls will be hard as rocks. The chicken soup as cold as ice. The waiters will, of course, refuse to even acknowledge Groucho's presence until he puts out his ever-present cigar. They'll grunt disapprovingly when he orders his beloved banana shortcake. And when the check finally arrives after an unconscionably long wait, Groucho will have conveniently forgotten his wallet, aim his perfectly timed shrug in my direction, and say more with his eternally ironic smile and half-raised eyebrows than a thousand well-chosen words ever could.

Bob Balaban has been an actor for more than a hundred years. He sometimes directs and produces. Previous literary endeavors include a bestselling series of children's books called McGrowl *and a memoir about the making of* Close Encounters of the Third Kind *called* Spielberg, Truffaut, and Me. *He currently resides in Bridgehampton, New York, where he's contemplating what to do with the next hundred years.*

33

"Going into a restaurant, opening a menu, perusing it,
and ordering whatever the body could digest was
always a wonder to my brother and me."

MALACHY McCOURT (BROTHER)
AND FRANK McCOURT

Well, wouldn't you know it, my brother Frank visited me last night. He just wriggles his way into my dreams sometimes, after I partake of certain spicy foods late at night, or doze off, reading something just too bloody boring. Last night I was guilty on both counts, which was practically an invitation for Frank to come and visit. Still, just how he creeps in, I'll never know.

May I tell you about the dream? In it, it was lunchtime and present were Terry Moran, Pat Mulligan, Sean Carberry, and myself, Malachy McCourt. Someone suggested we ought to do this lunch on a regular basis. Then came the whens and the when nots. One can't do it on Monday, other can't do it on Wednesday, and so on. I said let's do it every first Friday because though we were all collapsed Catholics, we knew that the church said if you went to Mass and received communion for nine first Fridays you were assured of a priest when your death was nigh. I proposed that if you did nine of our Fridays, you would not die without a bartender in attendance. The motion was carried, and thus the First Friday Club came into existence in March 1973.

There is still a vestige of it in existence.

With me the only founder still attending.

Until he retired from teaching at Stuyvesant High School, my brother Frank could not attend, but he did start after retirement. And a very great addition he was, too. Over the years, our venue was

Eamonn Doran's Saloon on Second Avenue, and we were often graced with some saintly celebrated folk like Pete Hamill, Jimmy Breslin, Dennis Smith, James T. Farrell, William Kennedy, the various Irish ambassadors and consuls. It was a largely Irish male gang until Mary Higgins Clark, Mary Karr, Mary Tierney, Marcia Rock, and Mary Breasted Smyth founded a rival group calling themselves the Legion of Mary. Catholics will know this one.

They assembled on the opposite side of Eamonn's and would have nothing to do with our crowd. One time the writer Peggy Noonan outraged the women by insisting on sitting with the men. She, of course, is a Republican.

There was an element of the Algonquin Round Table in our gatherings as the wit flowed as freely as the Guinness and savage sarcasm was not unknown.

It was at a First Friday that the following exchange took place between my brother Frank and my friend Mary Breasted Smyth.

Mary: What are you doing now that you are retired, Frank?

Frank: I am getting the miserable childhood down on paper. Finding the voice was elusive, but now it's coming along.

Mary: May I have a look, as I know an agent or two?

Frank: Certainly! I have about a hundred pages!

Mary: Let's go.

Now, I can't vouch for the veracity of this story, but I heard Mary took Frank's pages to an agent, who glanced at it and tossed it back to her with the comment that he did not think anyone would be interested in a book written by an unknown teacher about a miserable childhood in an obscure town in Ireland.

Mary took it to another agent, Molly Friedrich, who leapt on it and hand-carried it to Nan Graham at Scribner, and not for the first time, the First Friday lunch club gave birth to a book.

As I said, I don't know for certain that that was the sequence, but true or not, it does illustrate the triumph of great writing over stupidity and cupidity.

And I became Frank McCourt's brother, and he was never again Malachy McCourt's brother. Even in my dream, he had a rapscallion's twinkle in his eye, and in conversation there was, as usual, the quips, rejoinders, and comebacks that Frank was noted for, particularly as people could never get past his deadpan delivery. In the dream, he was so vivid, so real, so close to me, he could easily have kicked my grizzled, doddery, superannuated arse.

There were many times over the years that we broke bread, commiserated, laughed, remembered.

It was as a result of imitating our Limerick teachers, neighbors, and clergy at various mealtimes. Frank said we should write it all up as a play; we did, and thus the play *A Couple of Blaguards* was born and is still being performed.

We no longer said grace before meals anymore, which was mandatory in the old days.

> *Bless us, O Lord,*
> *In these thy gifts*
> *Which of thy bounty*
> *We are bound to receive*
> *Through Christ our Lord*
> *Amen*

We did joke about having on the table that which was missing when we were children, namely *food*. Frank said we had had a balanced diet, a liquid and a solid, namely tea and bread. Sometimes in childhood we got to share an egg. You have no idea how carefully the mother was watched as she sliced a hard-boiled egg into four equal pieces for us. Likewise, bread was also sliced with surgeon-like precision, and crumbs were quickly grabbed and scooped up into the gob.

Going into a restaurant, opening a menu, perusing it, and ordering whatever the body could digest was always a wonder to my brother and me. When the two of us lunched, it was at a diner near Stuyvesant High School, while Frank was still teaching there. Between riotous chuckles and mostly salty anecdotes and reminiscences, we would happily stuff burgers into our gobs (Frank's was always bunless; he had that gluten nonsense), and plates heaped high with lumpy, leaden mashed potatoes. My drink of choice was tea, while Frank was known to toss back a beer or two.

I never tired of his company. My brother was one of the most eloquent human beings ever to have been born. He could hold forth on a huge variety of subjects with humor, satire, and exaltation of language and clever speech. He was not interested in proper English, nor was he always grammatically correct, though he taught English and felt that colorful speech was important.

It's possible that he was the only high school teacher in New York City who never went to high school and did not have a high school diploma.

Generally speaking, we had no agenda when we met. When he was living with his first wife—the War Department, as I dubbed her—his life was more miserable than our childhood. There were no cell phones in those days but she always managed to track Frank down, and the waiters would have to take long, abusive messages before they came and got him to the phone. She disliked me, so he could never admit he was meeting me, but she always knew and berated him for wasting his time with me, or else she couldn't find the dust pan, or something else like did he mail the ConEd bill, or where's the toothpaste and other nasty, pointless forms of lunchus interruptus.

We did chat about the doings of the two younger McCourts, Mike and Alphie, what they were not doing right, getting involved in ill-advised ventures, with some solemn older-brother headshaking. Then there was our mother, Angela, still here on holiday, after twenty years, having weight problems and smoking, which she eventually stopped, but not early enough to avoid that dastardly emphysema.

Then the subjects were our children and their doings and undoings.

Frank's only child, his daughter, Maggie, absconded and joined a loony group of aimless young people meandering around the United States following a band, and they called themselves Dead Heads. A more appropriate appellation was never invented. It was a terrible insult to actual dead people, however, as there is more life in those dead folk.

But there they go yelping, screaming, gyrating, and boasting about the number of times they have seen the Grateful Dead onstage, still not knowing the amount of money they have been conned out of.

I had five offspring to discuss, two from a previous legal entanglement; two with Diana, my always present beloved; and one stepchild who is severely autistic. There were enough of them to cause various concerns, but none of them were off in cuckoo pursuit, flinging money at a disguised capitalistic enterprise known as rock.

To my relief, Frank took a permanent leave of absence from his awful alliance with the War Department but leaped into another alliance with a woman who put the powder into her nose rather than on it. That did not last too long. Then he met the light of his life, Ellen, married again, and lived happily ever after. She encouraged him to write, unlike the War Department, who disparaged him at every turn. Finally, with Ellen, *Angela's Ashes* emerged.

My last breaking of bread with brother Frank was at his bedside in the hospice, the marvelous visiting nurse service in New York City.

He had that Irish skin that welcomes melanoma, which hit him on the knee and rampaged through his body, finally landing in the brain and depriving him of hearing, so we had to write down every word to him. And this is the part that creeps into every dream that Frank sneaks into. One day he was having soup and I was into a tuna sandwich when Alphie's wife, Lynn, arrived, clumping noisily on the two canes she had to use. Frank saw her and said loudly: *It was very quiet in here until you arrived*, the usual Frank sort of welcome, though he couldn't even hear the clumping of her canes. We laughed, of course.

Then he asked Lynn: *When would you like to die?*

Lynn wrote: *January seems like a good month.*

Frank: *Why January?*

Lynn wrote: *I would have gotten all my Christmas gifts.*

I wrote: *When would you like to die?*

Frank: *February!*

I wrote: *The ground is frozen, making it hard to dig graves.*

Frank: *Let the Israelis do it.*

We all laughed. I don't even know what he meant—I suppose that they were rugged, strapping, and unflagging—but it sounded funny. That was indeed the last laugh and the last lunch. We were sitting in the little living room adjacent to the bedroom when Frank slipped into a coma, chatting quietly, when we heard a very loud sigh and that was Frank letting go of his last breath. It was July 19, 2009, at 3:03 p.m. That was the end of my dear brother Frank McCourt but the beginning of his frequent nightly forays into my deepest, darkest sleep. A place where he is always most welcome.

Malachy McCourt is or has been an actor, a saloon keeper, a gubernatorial candidate, and an author/writer husband to his wife, Diana, for fifty-four years, father to five, grandfather to eight. His most recent book is Death Need Not Be Fatal.

34

*"I miss her ceaselessly. And in the rare moments when I forget
to miss her, it's simply because I'm not paying attention."*

RICK MOODY (BROTHER)
AND MEREDITH MOODY

QUESTIONNAIRE

1. *Name*
   Rick Moody

2. *Occupation*
   Writer

3. *Who would you choose to have lunch with?*
   My sister, Meredith.

4. *Describe your past relationship with this person.*
   My sister was: a complex person, capable of being short-tempered,
   self-destructive, sad; my sister was: incredibly short, barely over
   five feet, with a mischievous smile and bottled-blond locks; my
   sister was: notable for her exuberant and sunny personality, always
   up for a party, or a concert, or a beer, or a long hang at the beach.

My sister's death was sudden, out of the blue, and came far too early. I miss her ceaselessly. And in the rare moments when I forget to miss her, it's simply because I'm not paying attention. The rest of my family misses her in a similar way. She was binding agent, the adhesive, the lover par excellence, and we never were as tightly knit as when she walked among us.

The loss of my sister changed the way my adulthood turned out. It made me a less trusting person, and it blasted away whatever spiritual core I had at the time. And yet: I experienced a fair amount of success and accomplishment after my sister's death, and often I have wished that she had been here so that I could have shared it with her and had her perspective on it. Her love and support were things I counted on, and I wish I could talk to her from where I am now about all that has happened since her death. The good and bad, the poignant and funny.

5. *What was her name?*
Meredith Moody

6. *Did she have a profession?*
Photographer, retail salesperson, mother of two.

7. *When/at what age did she die?*
November 1, 1995. Aged thirty-seven. By reason of cardiac arrest.

8. *Where would you meet for lunch? At home? At a restaurant?*
Fishers Island Country Club Snack Bar, Fishers Island, NY, 06390. From 1975 onward, my family summered on Fishers Island, a ridiculous, overwrought, and patrician fantasyland of the WASPy elites of the Northeast, all of them dressed in lime-green shorts and Lacoste with sockless penny loafers. A dreadful place, really. Annihilating and grim. I regret ever having set foot there. But it's where we spent our summers with my father, and so the legends

and stories of the place are numberless, among Moodys. (For example, once we went on a fishing trip, caught nothing, as per usual, but actually managed to catch a lobster trap around the propeller of the boat. We dragged it home and ate the lobsters instead.) Fishers Island was so important to my sister that we scattered her ashes there. The snack bar at the "big club," as it was known in those days, was hard to love. It was staffed up by college students on weed and foreign exchange students who had no idea what they had gotten themselves into, which was some modern-day equivalent of indentured servitude. The fare was hamburgers and fries, although you can get a salad and a soup there now. The main reason to eat at the "big club" was that the snack bar was right on a beach. Or: the main reason to eat there was that they had a really amazing ice-cream dessert called a "gold brick," in which the ice cream (usually vanilla) was encased in a chitinous layer of hardened exo-chocolate, a sort of reinforced chocolate exterior. There was also malt involved, and chocolate syrup. The gold brick must have been in the six-hundred-calorie range. A whole childhood was spent eating these confections no matter what else was going on. I think it would be great for my sister and me to have just one more gold brick together.

9. *Would you show up alone?*
I'm sure everyone in my family would like to come to this luncheon, but for the purposes of this questionnaire I'm going to be selfish and say that I'm going by myself.

10. *What emotions do you imagine would be felt on both sides at first seeing each other?*
Here's what we know about popular culture: we know that in popular culture, the dead family members or deceased honored friends of protagonists invariably come back. They are always resurrected

with wisdom from the other side just before a high school dance, or out in front of a baseball stadium, etc. If you watch enough movies, if you drink in enough of this slightly watery popular culture, you could be forgiven for thinking this was inevitable, that your dead sister would return from the other side and give you a hug, the boatman tarrying just behind her. Nevertheless, I have waited now twenty-two years for my sister to come back, other than fleetingly in dreams, to talk again in the easy way of the old times, with her rapturous laughter, and her bounteous care and concern for her parents, siblings, and children. Why, I have often wondered, do I not get to experience this thing that so many people in less fortunate circumstances than mine, namely the somewhat impoverished protagonists of not-very-good films and television programs, do? Why do I still wander around with this ache, as if there is no mitigating force in the universe? My feeling at these moments has often been of envy. Envy of those characters in films, and irritation that death and its finality have been so unrelentingly final in my own life. To see my sister again, for a lunch, even if it were just a snack-bar luncheon, our feet were covered in sand, the sunburn was acute, and it was low tide, and there was no surf to speak of, even under these circumstances, to see her again would be the greatest. If we could just talk through a few things, I would feel so much better about going on with the grief and loss.

11. *Would you embrace?*
   Definitely.

12. *What would you both order?*
   I think she would probably eat something sensible. You can get a lobster roll there, at the snack bar, which is not sensible at all. It's expensive. I doubt she would get a lobster roll. She might

have grilled cheese, but more likely a salad, and some fries, and a Diet Coke, maybe. While I would have a salad, maybe a corn chowder if available, and some fries. Maybe we'd order a lobster roll in honor of others of our family and pick at it occasionally. And then we'd eat some kind of ice cream afterward. Probably a gold brick.

13. *What would the general mood at the table be?*
Celebration, but colored with the circumstances of our separation twenty-two years ago, and recognition of the wound that this inflicted on her parents and her children, though without blaming her for what was an act of God. I think it would be worth letting her know how much we missed her, how wrecked we were, and what happened to her children since then. That they turned out great, that they are sturdy adults, but that there have been many ups and downs getting there, as is often the case. That all of life is a wobbly parabolic curve, arcing in the direction of grace, and after her death, our own arc has bent toward the type of warmth that she excelled at.

14. *Would you raise questions/issues you'd never expressed while this person was alive?*
I would tell her that I had been concerned about her drinking, and that when she told me, six months or a year before her death, that she was thinking of doing something about her drinking, I didn't bug her about it, because that is not my way—nobody ever got sober for their sibling—but that I had been worried about some of the decisions she'd made in the later years of her life, and I thought maybe she could have eased the journey a bit if she had pursued sobriety. I would have liked to see the responsible adult she was already becoming without the alcohol.

15. *Would there be laughing? Crying?*
    Hard to imagine otherwise.

16. *Bringing this person up-to-date on your life in the interim, how would they respond?*

    In a way, it would be more interesting for her to bring me up on her life, by pulling aside the curtain that separates where I am now from where she is. Maybe she could shed light on all of that. To what degree do the dead attend to the travails of the living? Or do they ignore the entire business? Is the self a complete self after the terrestrial period, or is it more a bit of dust in the infinite, a bit of energy (neither created nor destroyed) that unites with the first purpose of the universe? Is consciousness and the linearity of time a thing that is perceptible from a post-biological perspective? And what about ecstasy? Is her ecstasy in the afterlife, an ecstasy that is experiential in the same way that one might experience it in daily life, or is it different? Is the end of bodily decay and the concerns of the body enough for ecstasy to flourish, or does ecstasy require a creator and/or a religious or spiritual space, and/or a decaying body to be activated?

    I would bring this stuff up because it's embarrassing to talk about oneself all the time. I don't want my sister on this day to spend all her time listening to my own tales. True, it would be funny to tell her about my all-over-the-place personal life, and how I eventually married the last girlfriend she met of mine, had a child with her and then separated, and then got remarried, had another kid, etc. She, who argued that I would never have a family, might be amused. But more important than a catalog of life events would be the simple joy of being in the company of someone so long gone, and so missed, and for me that joy best expresses itself in wanting to listen. Once my sister asked me what it felt like to make up a short story, and I remember really getting into the minutiae of that question for far longer than was necessary. Like many moments with my sister that I could pursue differently now, in which I more concentrated on feeling lucky about having her around, I feel like I ought to have listened then and I would like to listen now.

17. *Would recriminations be expressed?*
No.

18. *How long would lunch last?*
You are asking about time itself. Does time intrude in a luncheon simply because I, one of the participants, am a time-based creature? Or might it be otherwise because my sister, coming from some other obscurely understood space, outside of time, or from nonlinear, non-Euclidean time, doesn't need a duration for her meal? Maybe the luncheon doesn't have a duration because my sister's effect on things is such as to create a rupture as far as duration goes. In which case the luncheon appears to go on forever, and indeed feels like it goes on forever; is unfolding like a lifetime is unfolding or maybe more, even as it does end at a certain point, perhaps when my sister, having exhausted whatever legacy of feelings are required for her energy to rematerialize, begins to vanish before my eyes, with a solemn or playful or solemn and playful wave, after which time reappears somehow. It's just a thought.

19. *How would you say goodbye? Tearfully, with relief, with exhaustion?*
Intimacy, and especially the open and honest exchange of feelings among family members, is exhausting. And so one longs for the end of family intimacy, even as one craves it, requires it, in the

instants after it goes away. These things are inseparable, the relief, the exhaustion, the longing for the kindness of one's family. The goodbye is not worth prolonging.

20. *Who would pay?*
We'd charge it to my dad's account at the country club.

21. *Would the lunch resonate in your mind for very long?*
Definitely.

22. *Would there be things you wish you had said?*
I would leave it all on the table.

23. *In summing up, how was the lunch?*
In a way, the exercise of imagining such a lunch rubs in the pain. Even now, I have to recognize again that no such lunch is going to happen, and that is the way of it, until my time is short here, too. That means the lunch, as a fictional exercise, was great, and funny, but it also means that the exercise makes clear how consistently family members no longer living make themselves felt in life, in a ghostly, almost imperceptible way. They really are the absence that is present. They really are a manifestation of the passage of time while nonetheless outside of time. I miss my sister, that is, and you can't bring her back, and nor can I, and the memory of her is a place where she is stuck, and I am, too.

Rick Moody is the author of six novels—including The Ice Storm *and, most recently,* Hotels of North America—*three collections of stories, a memoir, and a volume of essays on music. He writes about music online regularly at the* Rumpus, *and also writes the column "Rick Moody, Life Coach" at Lit Hub. He's at work on a new memoir.*

35

"I plan to swear a lot at our lunch."

DAHLIA LITHWICK (ACQUAINTANCE) AND PAUL NEWMAN

Lunch would happen, of course, at a long table in the dining hall, at the original Hole in the Wall Gang Camp in Ashford, Connecticut. It's a massive red building at the heart of the camp Newman founded in 1988, for seriously ill children. He wanted the camp to have a Wild West theme; wanted sick kids to have a non-hospital place to, in his words, "raise a little hell." Our lunch would happen with the campers piled next to him on the long benches—some from this world, who survived their cancer and sickle cell anemia, and a few from the world currently housing Paul Newman; kids still loud, still bald, but no longer in pain.

He would just materialize into his old laughing self, on the bench across from me, and reach for the Newman's Own salad dressing—ubiquitous on the camp tables, along with the pasta sauce and the lemonade—and make a joke about how it's healthier now than it was in the nineties . . .

The first time I met Paul Newman, my co-author, Larry Berger, and I were trying to scrape money together to write a book about the Hole in the Wall Gang Camp, and it was 1990. I was just a few months out of college, Larry and I had been doing creative writing with the campers over the summers, it all seemed like a good book idea—kids, poems, illness, campfires—and a board member from the camp wrangled a dinner to find us some funding, and there, suddenly materialized at the dinner, was Paul Newman. The first time I saw him he was in the kitchen of the host of that dinner, making his own salad dressing from scratch.

Newman (and nobody called him anything but "Newman" in my experience) wrote a check to fund the first stage of the book project on the spot. Later, he wrote the foreword to the book, something he did painstakingly and with tremendous care, because he kept saying he wasn't a good writer, except he really was. He wrote the chapter by listening, listening, listening and then creating something deeper than mere sparkly words. I just watched and learned as he wrote that foreword like he made vinaigrette; like he was inventing the form for the first time.

Newman later helped us promote the book, with a TV hit and radio interviews and lots of time with reporters who wanted to talk about movies and not his camp or his campers.

I worked at Newman's camp for four summers. At camp, none of the children knew who Paul Newman was when he visited, which is, I suspect, why he visited so often. I worked on the book for a year. One time I picked him up to visit a sick camper in the hospital and he wouldn't let me drive because, he said, I drove like a Canadian, trying to ingratiate myself to the mystifying world of high-speed vehicles. Newman was, after all, a seasoned race car driver. I was twenty-two and in possession at that time of my brother's sweet red Toyota MR2 and drove politely and carefully, eager to let anyone pass and merge as needed. The way I drove that car made Newman so very sad for me. This is a memory I have managed to repress.

When Newman died, the obituary I wrote for *Slate* was mostly about how for him, Hollywood fame was purely transactional: He seemed to have used everything he'd ever achieved as a celebrity as a lever to do good things for others. He cared more about kids, and the environment, and addiction, and healthy food, and peace, and dialogue, than some of the people who actually did that work professionally. And in this modern world of the celebrity-millionaire-activist-philanthropist, we forget how much he invented that form as well. Long before it was understood that every actor had a cause and a platform, he had both. And I have no memory of grandiosity. I think he just tended to think, "Hey, I can make some calls, and good people will fall in," and good people always fell in. He tended to view all of it—the money, the success, the adulation—as a freakish accident that required paying forward. The philanthropy felt like a means of material unburdening, not an imposition of morality on an immoral world.

I'd open my miracle lunch by asking him how he'd managed to raise money for good causes with minimal fanfare and zero ego. I would glug down camp lemonade (Newman's) and ignore the small floating bug in it and ask how someone so enormous had led such a contained life. People would follow Newman on any new philanthropic venture because he was always convinced it would be easy. If there was a glitch in any plan, he'd find a workaround that would also save the wildlife and also foster international discourse. All the humanitarian and ecological benefits that followed in the slipstream of his ventures were just more happy accidents. He believed he had simply been lucky, and he shrugged off the possibility that he had earned a thing by hard work. Or something called talent. And that, too, is a rarity, in the modern age of celebrity-philanthropist. I would ask him how he'd come to feel so lucky, despite personal tragedies, so lucky that the world handed him luck.

One time Newman called me very early in the morning to talk about the foreword for the book. At this point I had been on camp staff for four years, and he woke me from a deep, drooling sleep. I swore like a trucker before I realized it was really Paul Newman on the phone. Eventually, I also repressed this hideous memory. He loved that story. I plan to swear *a lot* at our lunch.

Here's the thing I haven't yet communicated: I only actually hung out with the man perhaps ten to fifteen times, but he was always ducking out from whatever people expected him to be, and always smiling at it. When I think about our lunch now, years after he is gone, in my head, I am mostly just grieving aloud at him about how everything he and I had believed about the world is upside down now. I am so famished for the optimism and belief that the world is capable of repair that I learned from him, that I would lunch on an IV drip of hope alone. In my head I am desperate to understand how the worldview I learned at his camp and his charities—that you make lemonade and pasta sauce, then give the money away, and the world gets better—went so thoroughly upside down in two decades.

The detailed lunches I recall with Newman happened at the dining hall in the Hole in the Wall Gang Camp. He'd slide in quietly at a long table full of kids who were, in some cases, terribly ill, and he'd just be a guy with white hair they'd never heard of. He'd engage the kid sitting next to him in a lengthy conversation, usually about the food or fishing. The staff would try not to break out in flop sweats. I would for sure expect to have a whole bunch of kids in wigs and prosthetic arms at this lunch. That would make it hard to talk. But he'd be happier. I think wherever he is, the kids he built a home for at his camps are whole.

Another thing about Newman? He'd come to camp and grab a few kids and take them out on a perfectly safe boat on a fully stocked lake and they would fish and the counselors would be frantic because they were all out there so long baking in the sun, and maybe a kid missed his meds, but they'd all come back laughing, and the kid would be better and happier all summer, and Newman would go back to the real world. Often the kid had no idea who the guy on the boat even was. But you always suspected Newman believed camp was actually the real world for these kids. I think that was why he loved it there. I mostly want to ask him whether the place he is now is more like camp or more like Hollywood. I'm fairly certain there are long tables with ranch dressing and lemonade and very little silicone or Instagram.

So that's where I'd have my lunch with Newman. At a long table filled with singing campers. Probably just pasta, cookies, and lemonade. Nothing intentional or fussy, for sure. I guess if I brought salad there would be salad dressing. He'd have his dark glasses on, and the baseball cap. You do get used to the eyes, but it takes a while.

I would keep talking on and on about injustice and poverty, and I suspect he'd find me boring with all my agita. He'd talk to the kid on his left. I would remember to thank him for teaching me about living an authentic life, separate from what the world needs me to be. I would tell him that virtually everything I now know about using a huge public platform to ask others to be active repairers of the world, I learned from him alone. Mostly, I think I would want to thank him for letting me see in my early twenties that marrying the absolute love of my life and doting on my children is an authentically and deeply lived life; that living a relatively small life but doing meaningful things is much more important than fame.

And when I can stop talking, I want him to persuade me again of his weird and elusive philosophy—the inversion of what psychologists call the fundamental attribution error—his abiding belief that people are all basically pretty good, and they all mostly just want to do good, and that errors and frailties aren't character so much as quirks. I want him to remind me that we all have more in common than we ever supposed. I want him to tell me again that there is no global problem that can't be fixed if a bunch of people allow themselves to believe in solutions.

I would say something about how this country needs genuine moral wisdom and leadership now more than ever, and he would laugh at me and say he has neither. I would say once again that he always seemed more kid than grown-up to me, except that he got things done so quietly, effectively, without fanfare, that I think he was, in secret, the only grown-up I saw for a long time. I am ravenous for humility in public life, and he was the last, best version of that I ever knew.

I have been planning this lunch with Paul Newman for more than a year. I think it would break his heart, knowing what this country has done to the kids—especially the poor kids—he thought about all the time. Perhaps because he always seemed to live his life so close to the seam of childhood, he would be the person most apt to understand that a whole generation of American children are being poisoned and polluted not just by toxic air and water but by filthy ideas about race and religion and violence that we believed we had left behind in the 1950s. He would be the one to ask what is really happening to this cohort of children raised in this moment of mass public shame and bullying and Twitter-terror. I like to think that he would have an answer or at least know who to call for the answer, by the time we set down our forks.

Maybe because the two qualities I most prized in this man were his optimism and his capacity to listen, I actually hate the idea of telling him what we've done to the world he unspooled for me, right out of college. I can't even imagine reporting what his beloved country has done to American childhood. This makes me hope that he doesn't show up for lunch. But oh, I hope he does.

Dahlia Lithwick is a senior editor at Slate, *and in that capacity, she writes the "Supreme Court Dispatches" and "Jurisprudence" columns. Her work has appeared in the* New York Times, Harper's, The New Yorker, *the* Washington Post, *and* Commentary, *among other places. She won a 2013 National Magazine Award for her columns on the Affordable Care Act. She has been twice awarded an Online Journalism Award for her legal commentary and was the first online journalist invited to be on the Reporters Committee for the Freedom of the Press. Ms. Lithwick has testified before Congress about access to justice in the era of the Roberts court. She has appeared on CNN, ABC, and* The Colbert Report *and is a frequent guest on* The Rachel Maddow Show. *Ms. Lithwick earned her BA from Yale University and her JD from Stanford University.*

36

"Come on, my Kate. Let's have a pissy lunch, shall we?"

KATE O'TOOLE (DAUGHTER)
AND PETER O'TOOLE

Strangely enough, I had been invited to have lunch with my father, my dead father, in London, where we used to live. The instructions were to pick him up in a minicab from his creaking Georgian house near Hampstead Heath.

My father died many times *before* he died, of course. I was at his bedside when he drew his final breath, but mostly I watched him die on-screen. As a ten-year-old in Venezuela during the filming of *Murphy's War*, I learned how to make fake blood from cochineal beetles for Daddy's "wounds." When I saw the results of my handiwork up on a big screen in the cinema, the trickery of it delighted me. It's safe to say that at a tender age I well knew the difference between reality and make-believe.

I'm not so sure my father did. He inhabited his roles so completely they became entwined with his DNA, where reality and shape-shifting became indistinguishable. It wasn't a case of my having to live with a different personality whenever Dad was playing a different part; it was nothing that exotic. It was the more ordinary fact of his relaxed, off-duty self being inaccessible while his mind was absorbed in his work to the exclusion of all else. For that reason we're going to enjoy our last lunch together while gloriously unemployed, as actors often are.

A long lunch with my funny, affectionate father was usually a late-ish affair to begin with and very late indeed to finish. It was known to us as a "pissy lunch." Peter was appalled by the concept of a working lunch, looked askance at people who spoke of "breakfast meetings" and pronounced the odious word "brunch" with as much withering disdain as his tongue could extract from each unfortunate consonant.

This being the special occasion of his temporary resurrection, we shall enjoy luncheon at Rules, the oldest restaurant in London. One of his and my favourite rooms to dine in, Rules sits in Covent Garden, in the heart of Peter's spiritual home, his cherished West End theatreland. The stews of Soho are within walking distance for a jar or seven afterward.

It's the first week in November, the month my ailing father faded from my sight. The poor man was still alive until December, technically speaking, but not really. The life spark was absent long before he breathed his last. I like to think it was the thought of Christmas that finished him off entirely.

Happily, with characteristically superb timing, the real anniversary of his passing coincides with the very best time of year to eat at Rules. The menu is strictly seasonal, coming into its own during autumn. A preponderance of furred and feathered game is on offer, accompanied by a casual warning that "gamebirds may contain lead shot." We're agreed the possibility of great balls of lead crashing into our gnashers halfway through lunch beats the more modern hazard, "traces of nuts." The food here is unashamedly red-blooded and hearty, the star attractions sourced from carefuly managed herds and flocks reared on private English estates in time-honored, traditional ways now known as sustainable.

While he was still alive, I'd typically arrive over from Ireland and make myself at home in Dad's large, light-filled sitting room while he busied himself upstairs, preparing to be seen in public. When he did make an entrance, he was always impeccably well-dressed and ready for action in one of his exquisitely cut bespoke suits, of which he owned dozens. Mr. O'Toole never went shopping for clothes; he only went to fittings for clothes. When ready, handmade shirts, shoes, and suits would be delivered in sturdy cardboard boxes so large I used to hide inside them and wait for my chance to jump out and give an unsuspecting grown-up a heart attack. Daddy's appearance would be heralded by the unmistakable sound of his eager footsteps leaping down the stairs two at a time before the heavy sitting room door would swing wide open and a tall, pale figure would stand in the doorway, rooted to the ground, crackling with energy and beaming with delight at the sight of me. I'll beam back at the sight of him.

For lunch Daddy would be wearing something not too dark, perhaps a suit of pale green Irish wool with a fine ivory silk shirt and a perfectly chosen waistcoat with a heavy jacquard silk weave. Pinned to his lapel, the discreet, pea-size, green-and-white-striped rosette signifying his title as a Commandeur of France's Légion d'Honneur, Ordre des Arts et des Lettres. At his neck, a psychedelic silk scarf from the ladies' department at Hermès, worn as a loosely knotted cravat. This is Peter's casual daytime look. As usual he'll be wearing well-kept Lobb's brogues of the softest, most supple leather. The ensemble is topped off with a beaten-up old felt hat that gives Peter the raffish air of being the bookmaker's son that he was.

After the mutual beaming, I'll receive a shower of featherlight kisses on the crown of my head and a bear hug that makes me aware of how fragile his ribs feel. Always a delicate creature, it's extraordinary that he, the least robust looking of his friends and colleagues, should have lived to bury every single one of them, from Robert Shaw to Richard Burton and many, many more. Too many; how solitary he must have been as they all left the party long before he did.

After hugs, kisses, grins, and fussing with heavy overcoats, there'll be an enthusiastic cry of, "Come on, my Kate. Let's have a pissy lunch, shall we?"

Into the waiting minicab we get. Peter never sat in the back; he liked to ride up front so he could see where he was going while giving terrible directions to the driver. He scorned GPS systems as being useless devices for idiots and insisted they be switched off, with the result that no one, including him, could ever know where on earth he was leading us. The peculiar directions had something to do with how he knew a secret, lateral-minded route into the West End that avoided all traffic at any time of the day or night. Perhaps that was true when he first came to London as a drama student in the fifties, but never since then, I shouldn't think. Nowadays we have things like one-way systems and bus lanes to contend with; I have zero confidence that he knows what they are. Having no sense of direction myself, though, I have no contribution to make and am happy for him to take control. Inevitably we soon come to a complete standstill, mired in heavy traffic and roadworks. Outraged that his clever plan has been thwarted Dad will shout over his shoulder to me, "Camden fucking council are at it again, baby! Look at the state of these roads; it's like living in downtown fucking Lagos!"

Eventually the odyssey ends just as we're about to die of traffic fumes and thirst. We arrive at our destination in Maiden Lane and enter the faded Edwardian plush that is Rules.

The maîtresse d', Josie, is a stout, cheerful, down-to-earth Yorkshire woman who adores Peter, not like a film star but like a son. More bear hugs, more gentle kisses on the head. Josie leads us to our usual table; we settle into a red velvet banquette and take in our surroundings. Dark wooden partitions, etched glass, gas lamps, great carved swords, antlers, old playbills, bronze racing figures, taxidermy, a bust of Shakespeare. The aged décor and cozy atmosphere suit our tastes for the unfashionably welcoming and comfortable.

It's quieter nowadays, but Rules was once *the* place to be, the Sardi's of its time. Like my father, it's had a rich and colorful part to play in London's theatrical history. In its heyday, the place was positively ablaze with the glittering scandals of its A-list clientele, led in large part by Edward VII. When he was still Prince of Wales, Edward had a private room upstairs where he used to tryst with the actress Lily Langtry. The staircase to their chamber is narrow and rickety, its carpet worn thin, its walls lined with ancient menus. I like to stop and imagine Charles Dickens, once a regular customer, trying to decide what to eat, an oyster the size of a dinner plate or perhaps some pease pudding and saveloy.

Like all good friends of similar minds, our conversations flowed freely; today's is no exception. We have a tsunami of stories to exchange and topics to catch up on. We'll discuss what we're reading, or thinking about, our love lives, current political events, and how things are treating us in general. Naturallly, Dad wants to know what's been going on in the world since he died. I'll tell him that the weird hotel guy we had drinks with in New York years ago is now the president of the United States; that'll render him speechless for a minute or two. I won't have the heart to tell him about Syria, a country he knew well and was extremely fond of. News of its desperate plight would wound him deeply.

I'd prefer to tell him about things that'll make him smile, such as the memorial I held for him at the Old Vic Theatre, told through my frazzled eyes as the exhausted producer of the event.

We order the house pale ale served in pewter tankards and survey the menu. As a child it struck me as odd that the fare includes both venison and deer. I remember asking my father what the difference between them was and him explaining, "Deer is Bambi's mother, and venison is *Monarch of the Glen*." I'll order the wild boar today; I like how it's similar to steak but with a delicious hint of rasher about it. Daddy will have his favorite dishes, lobster bisque and Dover sole. His choice of seafood notwithstanding, we both prefer red wine to white and order a rich Merlot; one bottle each should see us through to dessert.

Given that he's been dead, I'll be compelled to quiz Dad upon the existence, or not, of the afterlife. I'm sure his considered and entertaining opinion on the matter will clear up any questions to my satisfaction. We'll expand upon the themes of deaths, friends' funerals, fondly remembered memorials, and the like. I could go for hours on the subject of his wake alone. He'd especially like the part where his old black cat jumped into the open wicker coffin to be beside his human. To amuse him I'll add that perhaps it was only because cats, like children, just like being inside boxes.

After port and Stilton for dessert we'll thank Josie for her long-standing hospitality, wrap up warm against the November chill, and step out into Covent Garden where I want to show Daddy something I know will please him greatly. Late-afternoon sunlight is setting low over the damp, gray cobbled streets. We link elbows and amble the short distance to the Actors' Church, St. Paul's. We take our time, our shadows lengthening as we stop to remark on points of interest along the way. We pass through the nighttime world of grand old theatres and their stage-door alleys, twinkling pubs, and secret gambling dens. We stand under the portico of the church, in the spot where Bernard

Shaw places Eliza Doolittle's flower stall. We look up to admire the gorgeous lines of Inigo Jones's elegant creation before entering its sacred space. Neither of us are religious, but this is a very special place of worship. The Actors' Church is where the great and good of our profession lie buried or are commemorated in plaques that line the interior walls from top to bottom. We enter and absorb the tangible presence of this great tribe of performers, Peter's true brethren. One can see familiar names placed side by side as if talking to each other across the generations, wanting to be together. After he died I inquired about having a modest wooden plaque erected there in my father's honor. This was readily agreed to, partly because of his stature in the profession and partly because he'd already had a funeral there once before, during the filming of *Venus*. It would have been churlish not to let him have a real ceremony there as well. As Dad heads farther into the darkness of the silent, candlelit church, I whisper to him that I managed to secure top billing for him by placing the plaque stage left of the altar, not down the back end of the pews like Vivien Leigh. Billing is everything, after all, even in death. Daddy chuckles and nods in agreement; then I bring him to the place I chose beside Jack Hawkins, one of his dearest friends ever. My pulse had quickened when I first saw the space on the wall next to Jack's name. The Hawkins and O'Toole families had been very close in the sixties. Jack appears alongside my father in *Lawrence of Arabia*, where he gives a memorable turn as General Allenby, playing him to British Bulldog perfection. Sadly, he died forty years before my father did. Without hesitation I knew this was the perfect place to leave Peter.

It's almost completely dark in the recesses of the church now; it's time for Daddy to slip away and join the ghosts of all those great actors who've gone before him. We won't move on to continue our pissy lunch in Soho as we used to do, bar-hopping and running into reprobates. *"We'll never get home now, baby, phone the house and tell them we've been captured by banditos!"* He'll take his leave of me, quietly. Saying goodbye isn't necessary; we both know he's already vanished into the velvet blackness of the church's wings. He'll be in the best of good company, here with his comrades. In a way it feels as though I've been through this before. Whenever my father died or was hurt on-screen, I flinched. Knowing it was only make-believe in no way diminished the truth always at the heart of his acting, truth that simply couldn't be denied. It pained me to see him play dead. When the time came for the real thing, I found the practice of having already experienced it a few times was something of a blessing; I, too, was ready for us to part. Having said that, the vacuum left after losing the most hilarious person I've ever known is perfectly horrid. Whatever about the grief of losing our loved ones, for me the absolute worst is when the funny people die. Every time it happens it feels as if an endangered species is closer to extinction. There's a vast silence where my best laughs used to be.

On the plus side, film stars really are immortal. Anytime I want to hear Peter O'Toole's voice or see Peter O'Toole dance, or fly a plane, or fall in love, all I have to do is press *play.*

I'll skip watching the death scenes, though. Enough is enough.

Kate O'Toole is an Irish actress. Her credits include John Huston's The Dead, The Tudors, *and* Titanic: Blood and Steel. *She was nominated Best Actress at the Irish Times Irish Theatre Awards in Terry Johnson's* Dead Funny *and won Best Actress at the UK TMA Awards in Edward Albee's* Three Tall Women. *She is board chair of Ireland's Oscar-accredited film festival, the Galway Film Fleadh. She lives in Connemara with her three donkeys, Jesus, Mary, and Joseph.*

37

"So, today, I write a new song about a lunch with Prince. The song title is . . . 'A Royal Lunch.'"

TAJA SEVELLE (PROTÉGÉE, CLOSE FRIEND) AND PRINCE

Detailed plans with Prince are not announced. They unwind within the moment, with ease. To the outliers of his mind, the "wheres" and "whens" may seem to unfold as a series of clues, rather than scheduled details. To me, it's normal.

This lunch is no exception. . . .

I am riding the short ride between the Viceroy L'Ermitage, where I am staying, and the Beverly Hills Hotel, the Polo Lounge—our lunch destination. On the ride, I recall first meeting him, in 1984. We were on the second level of First Avenue, the famed nightclub in Minneapolis. He asked me my name, and after my reply, I teasingly asked him for his name. As though I didn't know. He laughed. My hair was big, like Angela Davis's. I was just starting out. My get-up: gray leggings; pink, ribbed, sleeveless tee; shiny gray pumps. His get-up: Cool. He was cool, like the essence of the word. Our encounter felt natural. It was the beginning of a thirty-year-plus friendship. Of playing pool, walking by the lake, basketball, meals, long conversations, creative plans, songwriting discussions, jam sessions and recording, performing, movies, nightclubs, parties, roped-off corners, and circles with a circus of people surrounding us and asking me for my autograph before they even knew me—just because I was with . . . Prince. And, it was the beginning of my recording career.

All of this runs through my mind for some reason, as I'm perched in the back of a black Rolls, traveling west on Burton Way headed to our lunch. I am forever thankful that Prince gave me my first record deal. He told me a few years later that he had given me more creative freedom than he'd given any artist he'd signed at that time. I had purchased a small recording studio right after I signed the deal, and I began writing songs for my debut record. "Love Is Contagious" was the first real song that I had ever written. Prince heard it and was originally considering it for his next movie. But the song stayed with my debut album. I moved from Minneapolis to Los Angeles to record my first album. Shortly before the record was released, Prince weighed in on which song would be the first single: "'Love Is Contagious.' We'll put that one out first," he proclaimed. It charted Top 7 in Europe, and in many cities around the US it went Top 5 on the R&B stations. I flew to London in the spring of 1988 and performed "Love Is Contagious" at the Royal Albert Hall. I fell in love with London. Life was a ball.

I was off to the races.

Now, riding up North Rexford, I'm off to create another fantastic memory with Prince—another lunch that will inevitably be fabulous. After my lucrative seven-year deal with Prince had ended, he and I found out a few years later that we shared even more in common than we had known. We had read many of the same books, about spirituality, metaphysical concepts, humanitarian interests, and so on and so forth. Our conversations became deeper and more meaningful. I signed two more record deals, and soon I started a 501(c)(3) called Urban Farming. The organization began by planting community gardens of free food for people in need. Prince became a huge supporter. He loved the cause, the gardens, and the healthy principles. It was another shared passion—helping others. I know that we will discuss strategies at this lunch . . . ideas of how to help the world. Ideas that would really come to life—not just evaporate in a sea of good intentions.

On North Crescent Drive, as the car draws closer to the Beverly

Hills Hotel, the song "Try to Remember" runs through my mind. The part that says, "Try to remember the kind of September, when you were a tender and callow fellow . . ." It's the kind of lyric that captures the part of life that's tough to capture. Prince is *uncapturable.* He is the live wire of creation. He rides it with fervor. His life depended on it because he *knew* that riding the creative wave was life itself. And it is best served on a forward motion. No looking backward.

Thus, "Try to Remember" would not strike his fancy. Simply because, "No dwelling allowed." He knows that creation is an onward march. He does not allow talks about how great those high school years were. I can relate. So, in this lunch, there is no dwelling allowed. Or Prince will leave and I will, too.

The driver crosses Sunset Boulevard and turns into the hotel. Moments later, I float up the famous Beverly Hills Hotel wide red carpet, under the long black-and-white canopy, framed with tropical foliage and stunning flowers. I enter the majestic lobby. No care of the day or the hour. I think about the trait of time suspension that both Prince and I carry. Only *now* is relevant. What are we creating *now*? Well, now I am creating a lunch with Prince. I would rather that our lunch today be a collage of meals that we've shared, all wrought together within a new, fantasy lunch which has been granted to me, like a new song. So, today, I write a new song about a lunch with Prince. The song title is . . . "A Royal Lunch." As follows:

Meals in private settings, always. Restaurants shut down for us. Always.

Yesterday lunch at Paisley Park. Today . . . the B. H. Polo Lounge b4 Brunei Sharia law.

Front desk, secret code, "Here to see Strong Heart."

I'm ushered forward.

I walk through the green and white, polite, and silent.

I disappear behind that magic light. Secret room.

This is where the big decisions are made.

I take some, but not much notice of my surroundings. Moments with Prince are edged with fabled, secluded wonder and magic, and they are the only enchanted surroundings worth taking in . . . quite simply, nothing compares. It's a cocoon of dance and dazzle, brilliance and wit, creative, storybook fun. It's the "Tomorrowland" that we're all supposed to have.

Spring water is poured. Silver rows of sparkling cutlery. Bespoke menu. Formal with ease. The waiter silently travels about the room, almost invisible.

Prince is the consummate host. He is wearing a black, silk, custom-designed Jasmine Di Milo tuxedo jacket, looking fine as usual. Cool as usual. He politely gestures to the waiter—we're ready to order—his hands clothed in the triple fluted silk, diagonal cuffs, with prominent matching flutes on the pockets. It's the moon—to see him again. Every time, it's the moon.

"Is that broth vegan?" Details. He's looking out.

"Yes," the waiter replies. Prince gives him the okay. We both order salad, soup, and water with shaved twists of lemon. A simple and easy start. The waiter exits.

Prince turns to me. "I like how you live the way you want," he says. "You're free."

I state the obvious. "So are you."

"Okay, good point." He laughs. Then he gets serious. "Let's talk about Urban Farming. Where does Urban Farming go next? What's the next level?" he asks. He's on a mission. He jumps right in. "How about a community center? I want to buy a building and make one. You and Kathy will find a building in North Minneapolis." He's refer-ring to Kathy Adams, who had been working with him for years. A sweetheart of a soul.

"I love it! That's a great idea!" I answer enthusiastically. I am in a really light, happy way. This is the stuff on which I thrive: bringing dreams to life as soon as they're imagined.

"We'll put a garden beside it," he declares.

"Oh, *yes*! And we can teach about the guiding principles," I contribute, and I am gleeful.

"Like honesty. Love. A supportive place," he adds. He is also in a happy way.

"Yes. But . . . not preachy." I made a subtle reference.

"I agree." He understands. "I want you to run it . . . ," he adds.

I pause.

"I'd love to but . . . I'm fully loaded with the charge of Urban Farming right now, and I've not put my singing on the back burner forever . . . and besides, winter's no fun unless you're playing in it." I'm torn in that moment, because I would love to run it, and I know he really wants me to.

"We can change the weather anytime we want. That's just a plane ride." He opens up the world. An enticing offer.

Our waiter returns. Serves. Attention to detail.

We begin to eat.

"Do you like your salad?"

"Yes!" I am resolute, thoroughly enjoying my customized request: baby field greens with thinly sliced roasted Portobello mushroom, avocado, palm hearts, and pine nuts. "The palm hearts are delicious."

He smiles. I ask, "How is yours?" He has ordered a similar salad, without the Portobello mushroom.

"Almost as good as watching you enjoy yours . . ." He flashes me that look—the kind, playful one that melts the world.

"Do you remember the Lewis brothers?" I wonder out loud.

He reacts with a slight move back from the table and a laugh.

"Pierre?"

"Yes! And Andre."

"You knew them?" He's surprised.

"I worked with them when I first started out with Morris Wilson. Morris said he used to change your diapers."

He laughs. "Is that what he said?"

"Yes he did." I giggle.

"They are all really great musicians," he comments.

"Yes. Excellent. But Pierre really only got down when there was a fine girl in the club. No girl, you can't really tell how brilliant he is, but let a girl walk in . . . and he's up on the piano bench playing behind his back, doing tricks, all fluent," I say, laughing as I recounted the times in Minneapolis when I was just starting out, singing in saxophonist Morris Wilson's four jazz bands and one R&B band. The Lewis Brothers were in all of them. They were all well-known musicians in Minneapolis back in the day. And Pierre and Andre had bass and piano on lock.

Prince is rolling. We're both cracking up, in a real bellow.

That was our "Try to Remember."

Now.

We immediately land back on the now.

More food arrives. Somehow, he placed an order for us that I didn't know about. When? Artisan vegan burgers. Mine is smothered with vegan smoked Gouda with a hint of orange. How did he know? It's ambrosia in my mouth.

"What are we doing to create love?" He gets right to the point. He is a seasoned angel by now. I realize that I am now in the part where I've been granted my fantasy lunch. The room feels suddenly more elegant and ethereal. I'm in a bit of a daze. A lovely daze. A thought runs through my mind, one that I would give to a seraph. It rolls off my tongue: "I sometimes have to keep reminding myself to focus only on what I want." My remark is more of a question than a reveal.

"Why is that hard?" The inquiry is lobbed back.

"Well . . . you're in a storied place, for *real*, now . . . so, can you relate to my struggle here on earth?"

"Why do I need to relate to it? Why do *you* need to relate to it? You don't even have to think about struggle. Think only about where you're creating love." He passes me that gem, along with the pink sea salt, for my side order of sliced organic beefsteak tomatoes that unexpectedly taste like celestial candy—as though they were just freshly plucked from an Italian Garden of Eden.

"Yes . . . 'Think only on good things'. . . That's the real point, right?" I agree.

"Of course. That's all that matters because that is *God*. So that is the *only* focal point," he states, with a firm belief.

"Redirect my thoughts," I share, as I raise my glass and slowly sip my lemon water.

"Don't even get to that place where you have to redirect them. Don't even let that happen. And then pretty soon, it's not a struggle." He is steadfast. He continues. "But you know that really well. You've been free since I met you." His words are purposeful deposits of wealth. He is so kind to me. He always has been, and I tell him so. He tells me that he appreciates hearing that.

"And, by the way, thank you for reminding me," I say.

"Reminding you of what?" he asks.

"That I've always been free . . . ," I reply.

"You don't need me to remind you." He laughs. "You wrote it. 'Love Is Contagious,'" he decrees, in sync with the timing of dessert. Where did the server come from? Proficiently silent, he places silver plates of heavenly vegan strawberry cheesecake on the white linen. The sweet is topped with cloud-wisps of homemade coconut whipped cream.

Divine.

After the last bite . . . it's time. A quiet mutual understanding passes between us that our lunch is coming to an end. We push back from the table. Our forks are situated upward on our plates and placed along knives in the ten and four o'clock positions. Proper etiquette for the completion of a Royal Lunch.

"Now that the meal is over, I'll be gone like the wind . . . but never really gone." He flashes me that supremely fetching doe-eyed look again, along with his disarming smile. He always *was* enchanting—a charming, true Prince.

I'm a bit sad.

It's too soon . . . the finale. Much too soon.

But no dwelling.

So, instead, I say: "Thank you for this lovely lunch." We stand and share a hug. I whisper, "You know I love you always . . . Strong Heart." I smile, my eyes moist but bright.

"I love you, too, Good Heart." He gifts me with that extraordinary look once more.

It's been a blessed friendship.

And he's flying. And so am I, as we exit the Polo Lounge, floating past the décor of green and white and wood and stares, as royalty wafts through the moment . . . with ease.

Taja Sevelle was offered her first record deal from Prince in the same week that she was accepted into the Berklee College of Music. Opting for the record deal, she recorded two CDs for Paisley Park/Warner/Reprise and subsequently recorded with Sony 550. She has written songs with several legends including Burt Bacharach, Thom Bell, and Nile Rodgers. Taja founded the global nonprofit organization Urban Farming. Her work with Urban Farming has been featured on The Ellen DeGeneres Show, CNN, Fox, *Good Morning America, the BBC, and NPR, among numerous others. Taja is an inventor and an author. Her most recent book,* From the Root: A Memoir and a Philosophy for Balance in Our World, *was released in 2019. In 2017, Taja's song "Little Diva" spent eight weeks on the Billboard Dance Club Charts, reaching Top 30. For more about Taja, go to www.tajasevelle.com.*

38

"I love you now and then, baby girl."

RAIN PRYOR (DAUGHTER)
AND RICHARD PRYOR

My lunch with Dad takes place at the Hamburger Hamlet on Sunset. Well, it used to be there. It was my favorite lunch place with either my dad or grandpa.

It's lunch hour in Los Angeles, and Dad and I decide to hit up our favorite burger spot. It's a weekday afternoon, and the joint is bustling with Hollywood executive types and real estate brokers. You won't find many celebrities there since most want to be seen down in Beverly Hills at the Ivy. This place is for the confident money-makers, and it's noisy. You can make out bits of conversations by the ones with the most boisterous voices. I guess they're the real dealmakers.

We are seated right away, because after all, Dad is Dad and I am me. The hostess in her crisp burgundy-and-black outfit seats us at our favorite booth near the windows. We enjoy people watching. Here, the noise seems to fade as if someone has control of the volume. It's now muffled tones with clinking china in the background.

Our window booth gives enough light to a gorgeous amber hue that settles on us both. Dad is looking healthy and has that radiant Pryor smile. There is no sign that he ever was sick with multiple sclerosis, or sadness. I smile back, just because this lunch means the world to me.

We begin our conversation with the usual small talk. Dad looking at me intently, "So how's it feeling being a grown-up?"

"It's actually pretty great, Dad, other than the politics. How's it wherever you are?"

The waiter arrives and takes our order. We order our usual. Cheeseburgers well done, crispy French fries, and Cokes.

Dad says, "You still eat like a teenage boy."

"They have this stuff where you are?" He doesn't answer that. "So, what's it like there?"

He chuckles. "You had to go there, didn't you?" I nod. "It's interesting looking at all this shit here, realizing how fucked-up people really are. You think, I lived in a serious asshole time, and didn't wind up in prison." We laugh.

I show him pictures and videos of my now ten-year-old daughter, and he says, "Shit, she has that Pryor gene. Damn, you in trouble, baby. She knows things. Ya know what I mean?" He's right. My daughter, Lotus, is like a hyperaware, deep, precocious kid who makes grown-ups uncomfortable. Kinda like her mama. Me.

Our food arrives, and between bites and sips, I tell him about my now amazing life and how I wish I knew then what I know now: that happiness takes patience and there is no rush to the finish line.

I find myself staring at Dad and secretly hoping our lunch and moment together will never end. I miss him.

Dad picks up the check, "Let me get this one. With the way shit's going, I'd like to treat my baby to lunch. I'm proud of you, Rain. You keep turning shit into lemonade and muthafuckas into your ass kissers. Ya done good. Now, don't mess it up. Be better than me and your mom. Tell Shelley I'm sorry I was an asshole."

We smile our Pryor smiles, reaching across the table to hold hands. He feels ethereal. "Daddy Dude, I love you."

"I love you now and then, baby girl."

As our hands separate, he vanishes, I look out the window of Hamburger Hamlet onto the Sunset Strip, smiling because I got to have lunch with my Daddy Dude, and he was at peace.

Rain Pryor is an actress, writer, baker, mother, and wife. Pryor is the creator of Fried Chicken and Latkes, *an award-winning solo show, a hilarious and heart-wrenching story of growing up black and Jewish in a politically incorrect era. Her father was comic genius Richard Pryor, and her mother a Jewish go-go dancer turned astronomer. Discover how Pryor finds her identity in both worlds and works to change ours. Directed by Eve Brandstein,* Fried Chicken and Latkes *is currently in series development with Norman Lear, Olive Bridge, and MGM, where Pryor is a writer and executive producer.*

39

"My father who arts in heaven."

CHRISTOPHER RAUSCHENBERG (SON) AND ROBERT RAUSCHENBERG

When Erica asked me to write about an imagined lunch with my mostly deceased father,[1] I knew it would have to be in his kitchen on Lafayette Street. Everything happened in that kitchen, even though it was just a small part of his five-story New York building.

For this lunch, I wouldn't have any agenda of unfinished business or scores to settle with him or anything like that. My father and I loved each other, were excited about each other's work, and told each other so. This is a great gift that many of the others in this book may be seeking at their lunches.

Lunchtime is the very beginning of the day for both my father and me; we're both serious night owls. My father was a great cook and

---

[1]   I say "mostly deceased" because the whole purpose of the Robert Rauschenberg Foundation is really to minimize the amount that he is gone. We have his Captiva studio full of excited artists making collaborations, experiments, and beautiful artworks; we have his philanthropy chugging along merrily helping interesting, good things happen; we are sending his work out into the world where it's still inciting curiosities and blowing minds.

was an early foodie. Though he loved to cook, this lunch would be simple. Plenty of different cheeses and an array of various crackers. The TV would be on, roaring away as usual. He always had the TV on as a second kind of window, the same way you wouldn't be comfortable in a room that didn't have a normal window. For him, this TV window was not something that one controlled; he didn't ever change the channel. It was there to let the culture roll into the room and be part of his large understanding of the world. For those of us who don't normally watch TV, it was very distracting, but not for him. He could follow multiple simultaneous conversations in the room, plus whatever was happening on the TV, plus whatever sounds were coming in through the window, all at once. He was a great juggler of sensory input in his life, as in his art.

Many years ago, Bob and my mom both came to the opening of a show of my photography at the Portland Art Museum. After the opening, we were hanging out in Bob's hotel room when he asked Mom with a very serious expression, "Where do you think we go when we die?" Without a moment's hesitation, she said, "To the studio!" He was very happy with that answer. Consequently, the first question that I would ask at this imaginary lunch is "Was she right? When you died, did you go to the studio, and what have you been up to in that studio for the last nine years?"[2]

When my wife Janet and I visited Bob down in Captiva, I always loved to go with him in the evenings to his studio and watch him make work. Since he was an artist who was driven by his gigantic curiosity—who loved to make work of every possible kind out of every possible material—I can't begin to imagine what materials he would get his hands on in heaven and what he would do with them. Actually,

---

[2] For starters, I would expect him to be jamming on the "prepared harp" with John Cage and others.

I'm not confident that I could imagine it even after he described it to me, but I'd sure like to try.

My second question would be about which other people he is interacting with up there. When I imagine him in this heaven that I don't believe in, of course I know that he would be drinking (ambrosia, perhaps? At our lunch he's drinking white wine with ice cubes), carousing, and collaborating with his close friends who have also died. That goes without saying. He won't have stopped there, though. (For example, his dance piece *Pelican*, with Bob in a big round parachute and roller skates, certainly has room for Leonardo to join the dance in his flying machine.)

When Bob was near the end of his life, he said, "I'm not afraid of dying, but I don't want to miss anything." The best part of Erica's imagined lunch scenario is the implication that, rather than missing things, he is instead getting to explore a new world with new rules to break and new previously unimagined combinations, collaborations, and conversations to revel in.

My father, in his youth, wanted to be a minister until he found out that his mother's church didn't allow dancing. That was an immediate deal-breaker for him. Some people don't believe that animals can go to heaven, but that would be another deal-breaker. Bob's dogs would have to be there for sure, as well as his turtle, Rocky. Rocky didn't like the beautiful nature in Florida when Bob moved down to Captiva.[3] That makes me a bit worried about whether Rocky might be too much of a city turtle for heaven, but she would have to be crawling under the kitchen table at our lunch, trying to bite our feet a little, to remind us to set down a nice big piece of watermelon on the floor for her.

---

[3] She disgustedly shook the sand off her feet and put her head against a cinderblock until Bob gave in and sent her back up to New York, where she had her beloved wood floors and radiators and her favorite rectangle of sun.

Once we'd stuffed ourselves with cheese and crackers, I'd get down to business for a few minutes. Bob had so many philanthropic interests that his Foundation has to take them in rotation, a couple at a time. I'd ask him what issues we should choose to shine our "moving spotlight" on next.

Our artists-in-residence often report seeing Bob still lurking around in his Captiva studios and houses, customarily clad in his white shirt, with the sleeves rolled up, and matching painter's pants, but I wouldn't ask him about that. If he wants to discreetly check out what's going on there, that's more than fine with me.

If we have time, before our miraculous lunch is over, I'd want to ask him about his depiction of God in *The Happy Apocalypse*. This was a rood screen that the Catholic Church commissioned him to make for their new Padre Pio Liturgical Hall—they asked him to depict the Apocalypse but to not make it look too depressing. As its central image, Bob depicted God as a huge satellite dish enveloping the whole earth. When the finished work was presented to the Pope for his approval, in 1999, the Pope could not accept this depiction of the Lord, but I'd want to know what God himself thought of it.

Christopher Rauschenberg is the President of the Robert Rauschenberg Foundation, is the board chair and a co-founder of the nonprofit Blue Sky Gallery, and is an active artist photographer who has had 117 solo shows in eighteen countries. His work is held in the collections of eleven major museums.

40

"Just because a guy does tai chi, he can't enjoy a steak?"

ROBERT CHALMERS (APPREHENSIVE ACQUAINTANCE) AND LOU REED

A table in the otherwise deserted restaurant named Where the Light Gets In (recently acclaimed as the best in the UK by The Guardian*) in Stockport, Greater Manchester. The establishment opens to the public at 7:00 p.m. It is mid-afternoon. Where the Light Gets In offers a menu at a minimum of £100; diners have no choice in what they are offered.* LOU REED *arrives, fifteen minutes late, wearing the kind of somber leather outfit he adopted at the end of his life.*

LR (*in his customary, deeply sarcastic monotone*)
"I take it that you wrote that obituary?"

Which one?

"The one full of snide innuendo, dead metaphors, and obituarist's code. 'When he approached people on the sidewalk, the street would invariably be crossed by those who did not know him, and occasionally by people who did.'"

How do you know about—

"'He did not suffer fools gladly.' Oh, *please*."

Well, you didn't.

"Who does suffer fools gladly? What, was I supposed to walk around carrying a placard that read 'Assholes Welcome'? I mean, there would be risks to such behavior."

Such as?

"Attracting the company of people like you."

So you remember the last time we met?

(*Withering look*) "Oh yes. How could I forget?"

A young WAITRESS *arrives and delivers two small plates of avocado salad.*

LR (*poking at the dish with his fork*)
"Is there *cream* in this?"

WAITRESS (*nervous*)
"Just a little."

LR
"Yeah. Right. 'Just a little pregnant.'" (*Pushes the salad aside*) (*To me*) "Why have you brought me here? Where are we?"

Stockport. Greater Manchester. The Guardian *says this is the best—*

"Screw the *Guardian*. My idea of abject hell is to follow the advice of an English journalist. And didn't Friedrich Engels describe Stockport as 'a hole'? Though actually (*mean glare*) this place looks like it might belong to some failed stockbroker in the Village. You know the places I like. That I *liked*. The Kitchen on West Nineteenth. John's on Bleecker. Wallsé. Stockport. Jesus."

WAITRESS (*approaches with a bottle of white wine and pours two very small glasses*)
"*Cuvée Pollux*, from the *Jura*. It is stored for six years under yeast."

LR

"Oh really. And what is this, a sample?" (*raises the glass to his nose and inhales*) "I'm getting honey, toast, peach, pear, mandarin, and scheming hipster greed."

WAITRESS *offers to fill his glass more.*

LR

"No. I'm not . . . I'm not supposed to drink."

WAITRESS (*arrives with another small plate*)
"Diced ox-heart, in quince and pine oil."

LR

"You English are to fine cuisine what Burkina Faso is to space explor—" (*tastes a small amount*) "Actually that really isn't bad." (*To me*) "You could have chosen to bring anyone here today, right?"

Yes.

"Your late father. Or your mother, Joan?"

Yes.

"So why pick on me?" (LR *attacks the ox-heart with gusto*)

I thought you were a vegetarian.

"No. Just because a guy does tai chi, he can't enjoy a steak? Why pick on me?"

Because . . . a friend once said to me: "You know: I would hate to be a journalist, because it would mean meeting people whose work I really admired, and they would treat me like a dick."

"Your friend got that right. Who was that?"

Vivian Stanshall.

"A very great artist."

When you and I last collided, the meeting lasted three minutes, forty-seven seconds. That's shorter than most of your songs.

"Hardly my fault."

Yes it was. You were late.

LR (*mimicking Mancunian accent*)
"Oh. *You were late.* I am so sorry. And before I arrived, as I recall, you sat down with my personal assistant Jake . . ."

I didn't know he was your assistant. I thought he was some record company guy. So when he said: "Be careful what you say to Mr. Reed. Some American journalists have been asking inappropriate questions," I said . . .

"You said: 'Oh. You mean like, "Where's Rachel?"'?"

It was a joke.

"A joke. You were talking about somebody . . . how should I describe Rachel . . ."

Transvestite?

"Transsexual. The transsexual I was in love with and lived with for three years, to the horror of my friends and family. You think that's a *joke*?"

When you finally showed up and went off into a huddle with Jake in that side room at the Mayfair Hotel, I am assuming he informed you of that exchange.

"Oh yes. He informed me, okay. In some detail. And I said to him: nothing surprises me about the British. So when you said, after three minutes—"

Three minutes of monosyllabic rudeness.

"When you said, after three minutes, that 'if you do not enjoy doing interviews, here's an idea, Lou: don't do them,' I got up."

And left in a peevish swirl of leather.

"I wasn't peeved. I didn't swirl. I was angry."

You still angry now?

"Now? No." (REED, *who has been eyeing the white wine, swallows the contents of the glass in one go.*) "No. I am not angry now. Because now I have gained . . . perspective. So what are you hoping for this time?"

To know what made you the way you were in life.

"What way was I?"

Sullen. Moody. Aggressive. Contemptuous of people.

"What kind of people?"

People who loved and admired your work. People like me.

"It was the only way of achieving what I wanted and had never had."

A punch in the mouth?

"No." (*much more serious*) "Control." (*Waves away the* WAITRESS, *who has arrived with plates of beef marinated in Crozes Hermitages.*) "Control. I need . . . I needed, control."

Over?

"Control over what food I ate and when. Control over people attacking me for qualities I had that were a source of mockery."

Such as?

"Being different. Being a faggot. You are aware that my father, Sidney, took me to an institution in Rockland County where they placed a wooden probe down my throat that was supposed to stop you swallowing your tongue, but in my case made me vomit. You are aware that they strapped electrodes to my temples in order to 'negate homosexual urges'? You want to fuck a kid up, that's not a bad way to set out. Can you imagine the guilt?"

Were there things that you were rightly guilty of?

"Later, yes. Pride. Arrogance. Sloth. Anger. A lot of anger. A *lot*."

You seem different.

"I am. Very."

Have you forgiven me?

"Yes."

Why?

(*Absolutely serious and almost kindly in tone*) "I can't . . . I am not at liberty to answer that, Robert."

The owner of Where the Light Gets In, Sam Buckley, who is also an accomplished string player and session musician, approaches, carrying two brandy cocktails made with the juice of citrus fruits he has marinated for eighteen months.

SB

"Mr Reed . . . I love your work."

LR (*sipping cocktail*)

"Thank you."

SB

"I am a musician, too."

LR (*with a flicker of old mischief*)

"Oh, *really*. Would you go up to Jesus and say, 'You know: I, too, have suffered at the hands of my enemies?'" (*Pause*) "Forgive me. What I mean is: stick with the ox-heart and the fruit juice. You're very good at that."

SB *leaves.*

LR (*to me*)

"I think—I know—I became imprisoned by the image I had created of myself."

You mean you felt compelled to be, to borrow a noun frequently applied to you, a cunt? As I recall, you told an old lady on a phone in a show in Massachusetts that "I am so glad people of your age die of cancer."

"Yes, well . . . what goes around. It was my way of dealing with the world. It's very hard . . . you brought up the subject of Rachel when we met that day. . . ."

Where is Rachel?

"Rachel . . . Tommy Humphreys . . . is dead. Do you know what someone wrote about Rachel? The person that I loved? 'Bearded, grotesque, abject. She looks like something that might have grovelingly scampered in when Lou opened the door to get the milk.' That was Lester Bangs."

Why take that seriously?

"Well I don't, not now."

Which of your songs do you remember with affection?

"None of them."

"Perfect Day"?

"Perfect crap."

I remember you publicly denying that song was about heroin.

"I did deny it, yes. Of course it's about heroin. It's more about heroin than 'Heroin.' What song do you like best?"

"I'll Be Your Mirror."

(*Uncharacteristic glance of grudging respect*) "Well that . . .
all of those songs seem hugely insignificant to me now, but
that song—yes . . . it was imbued with certain qualities that
I tried to disguise in my life off-stage."

Such as?

"Compassion. Kindness. Empathy. Vulnerability. I was a very
vulnerable person."

Was your life a tragedy?

"In some respects. My relationship with my parents. The
fact that . . . what I really loved was literature. I felt inferior
because I didn't go to an Ivy League school, Harvard or Yale."
(*Steely look*) "I had the intelligence for that."

I don't doubt it.

"Yeah, and I worked in a business where people assumed
you to be an idiot."

People?

"Journalists. That's why I humiliated them. That's why I
sought to humiliate you. Ninety-nine percent of the time
I was dealing with people I believed were far less smart than I
was. Of course, going to the schools I went to, I had the great
good fortune to meet Delmore Schwartz. And later Hubert
Selby. And Burroughs. Wonderful writers. And I wanted to
be a wonderful writer."

You were. I mean . . . apart from things like "Hudson River Wind Meditations."

"Possibly not my finest hour. What I mean is that I would have loved to achieve on a more orthodox stage. In the library, not on the dance floor. That's one crucial reason I was an addict. It is not true that all addicts are interesting. Even if I think that me, Cale, and Dylan—each one of us drug addicts—were interesting. But it is true that all addicts are compensating for not being what they want to be."

You mean a poet and novelist?

"Yeah. And a straight guy with a black Trans-Am and a love for baseball and a dog and a wife called Sheila."

You were drinking again at the end. John Cale called your life "a slow suicide."

"Well, John *is* Welsh. And a melancholic. He might equally have said that I lived by reprieve."

Anyhow, you had the dog.

"Lola-Belle? Well, she was Laurie's, really. You know, I loved Laurie very deeply. She was the love of my life. Even if I don't know how happy I made her emotionally. My nature is . . . was . . . my nature."

The WAITRESS *arrives with the check.*

Are drugs evil?

LR (*unhesitatingly*)
"Yes. I mean . . . I believe so, yes."

How did you know about Engels describing Stockport a hole? How did you know the name of my mother? And about the obituary? Do we live again? Are we judged?

"Delmore Schwartz—another addict—once wrote a piece called 'In Dreams Begin Responsibilities.' And so I cannot respond to your questions because we . . . I . . . am not . . ."

Permitted?

Silence.

Anyhow, whatever the nature of the afterlife, I notice you managed to show up late again.

LR
"I promise that, next time we meet, punctuality will not be an issue. Next time, Robert, we will inhabit the same dimension."

Robert Chalmers was born in Manchester, UK, and was described by Hunter S Thompson as "the suavest man in England" and "a twisted Limey freak." As a journalist for the Observer, *the* Independent, *and GQ, he has won awards that include Interviewer of the Year and Writer of the Year. His relationship with Lou Reed, before they met, had been similar to that of any other devoted fan: occasional fleeting contact of no significance. When he did finally encounter him . . . the experience reminded him of what somebody said about another famous curmudgeon: "When it comes to this artist, there are two kinds of people: people who like him, and people who have met him."*

41

When you die, that's it. The lights shut off, and there is no more.
—Oliver Sacks, first night of Passover, 2015

ADRIEN G. LESSER (COUSIN)
AND OLIVER SACKS

Those words have lived in my head since the last time I saw Oliver Sacks, my family's beloved superstar cousin, at his last annual Seder. It was the fiftieth Passover that the renowned neurologist had spent with us. There was an assemblage of relatives as well as dear friends, some of whom he had not seen in years. His face lit up as he went from one to another, hugging each in turn. There was also an overwhelming sense of sorrow. Oliver had recently been diagnosed with terminal cancer. Five months later, he was dead.

Oliver's broadly read *New York Times* op-ed piece bravely informed the world that he was dying. It was to be the first of several articles in which he addressed the emotional and physical process of facing down his own mortality. It was a heroic effort. Today, I want to know if it's true that, as he always insisted, there is no afterlife. Given the unexpected chance to see Oliver again, I've invited him to have lunch with me at 12:30 at Russ & Daughters Café, a Lower East Side offshoot of the famed smoked fish appetizing store (where I believe they called Oliver the "King of White Fish").

Both Oliver and I believed that when you're dead, you're dead. It's the final act. The curtain falls on a hushed audience, and thereafter there is nothingness.

I have known Oliver all my life, yet I rarely had the chance to sit down and talk with him alone, so understandably, I am nervous. I'm now nineteen, a college girl, but as a child, I found his presence lovable yet intimidating. He would tell me about ferns or cephalopods, two of his great passions. But there was never a lot of back-and-forth. When he wasn't with a patient, Oliver preferred talking to listening. Today, I'd determined that our conversation would be different. It wouldn't be as specialized as plants or creatures of the sea. I suddenly remembered Oliver's laughter: childlike, almost giggly, but effusive. A welcome surprise in such a serious fellow. I hoped that somehow I would make him laugh today. But given his unshakable belief in no afterlife, would he even show? My watch told me it was already 1:00. To keep the solicitous waiters at bay and to claim legitimacy for hogging my table, I ordered a Dr. Brown's Diet Black Cherry Soda, which arrived in a huge frosted glass. I imagined Oliver striding in, wearing his familiar khaki Columbia sportswear safari suit, replete with matching pants. An intriguing instance of *Out of Africa* meets Sutton Place. His glasses, wire-rimmed and round, would be perched on his nose as always. And his posture would be ramrod straight, unless his bad back was bothering him.

A waiter comes to my table, and I assure him that the second person in my party would be here soon. I glance over the menu and automatically know what Oliver is going to order, though in truth I can't decide between herring or sable. Then, a large lox and whitefish platter makes its way to a nearby table, and I can only think about how much Oliver will enjoy devouring that meal with his customary brio. There are many stories of him sitting at my bubby's table finishing whatever was left of brisket and gefilte fish. He was also known to eat her entire fruit centerpiece every now and then or clear out the contents of her refrigerator. I check my watch and realize it's now 1:15, and I know Oliver had always frowned upon anyone's tardiness.

I very much want to talk with Oliver to learn the truth about death and dying from his unique—and now dead—perspective. A lot of people don't want to discuss the subject, but in his research of many of the great neurological unknowns, Oliver was almost eager. He saw people whose lives had been compromised by disease, few of which had cures. He was a doctor and knew very well what was happening to him. I suppose that's what also made him so open about death, the fact that he spent his life studying major question marks. Perhaps for him, death was just another example.

As I sit at the table waiting for Oliver, I get teary. I never imagined I would cry at our lunch or show very much emotion at all. I try to pull myself together in anticipation of his imminent arrival. I glance over at a table of six, with an older gentleman sitting at the head of it. It was the same table that had ordered the large fish platter, and I think once again about Oliver sitting at the head of our Seder table every year. Many more people were alive then than there are now, and all of a sudden, flashes of their faces go off in my head. I can hear us all taking our turn reading from the Haggadah. Oliver's beautiful British accent always made the passages sound profound, while his stutter humanized him.

Is there still a chance that he might show up? If not, I will never be able to tell him about my exciting summer working for my congresswoman, nor will I be able to tell him about my first year of college. Oliver was a beloved neurologist, author, human, but to me, he was the leader of the Seder. He was the man who gave me, when I was a seven-year-old, Helen Keller's four-hundred-page autobiography. He was the man who showed up at everything carrying a seat cushion. He was the man who sat me down three months before he died and told me to disregard any advice from my college counselor and just go for it. He was family, and while I have lots of family left, the first seventeen years of my life were uniquely special in large part because of him.

At 1:30, I finally realize that Oliver isn't coming. A deep wave of sadness washes over me. Now I will never be able to ask him anything, ever. I will only have the times I spent with him when he was alive and what I imagine he might have said in response to my questions about what comes after death. Maybe he would say, "It wasn't what I expected, *Adrienne*," pronouncing my name the way the French do. What I suspect he would say is, "Nothing. Absolutely nothing."

Utterly deflated, I summon the waiter and pay the check for my soda. Then I watch as he clears the neighboring table where the huge lox and whitefish platter had been. Oliver isn't coming. Of course he's not coming. He never was.

Adrien Gardner Lesser is a born-and-bred second-generation Manhattanite. She has worked in the district office of Congresswoman Carolyn B. Maloney, as well as at Trixie Films, a documentary filmmaking company. She is currently a political science major at Wheaton College in Norton, Massachusetts.

42

"I'll be thinking about that as I approach the gray porch.
If anyone can break through this time barrier and make
this meeting possible, it's my father."

ANNE SERLING (DAUGHTER)
AND ROD SERLING

We will meet in July when summer's finally taken root, defeated winter and the daylilies wave orange in triumph.

We've chosen noon. Exactly noon. But we'll both be early. I'm certain of that.

The reunion will be in upstate New York overlooking Cayuga Lake, where, after a sharp right turn, down a sun-dappled drive, our red cottage suddenly comes into view and the world behind vanishes. Built in the 1880s by my great-great grandfather on my mother's side, and though long gone, he's still there in a photograph down the hall, looking on through a dusty frame as three generations skip by.

My father loved that old lakeside cabin stuck in time, with its wavy glassed windows, three small bedrooms, the dirt path down to the water, and the fact that it was only an hour to Binghamton, where he grew up. Driving by his childhood home was a pilgrimage he took for years. "I'll be back soon," he'd say, and my sister and I would watch him go, his paratrooper bracelet glinting in the sun when he waved goodbye.

These trips, transporting himself backward, were not confined to those annual drives. He did that in his writing, too. In an interview my father said, "While walking on a set at MGM . . . I was suddenly hit by the similarity of it to my hometown . . . it struck me that all of us have a deep longing to go back. It was this simple incident that led to the script 'Walking Distance'—the one where Gig Young plays a tired businessman who, while driving upstate to get away from the city, stops at a gas station that's within walking distance of 'Homewood,' his hometown, his past."

I'll be thinking about that as I approach the gray porch. If anyone can break through this time barrier and make this meeting possible, it's my father. I just need to focus, concentrate, and stay attuned to each and every sound. I strain to hear him. Somewhere a dog barks, a branch breaks, *Dad?!*

But it's not him, and I can barely sit still. I've imagined, rehearsed this day for four decades. What if there's not enough time? What if we don't know each other? I get up. Pace. Look up at the cloudless sky. Listen down the drive. Finally I sit down, settling on the top step, the one I danced on as a child, where we planned our dog shows, played jacks, Go Fish, where my father last left his shoes.

He hadn't known he would not be back, that he was leaving, that his body was succumbing to years of smoking; a war he could not outrun, the death of his own father (to whom he never had the chance to say goodbye), and a demanding writing profession, where maybe some days he felt there were no more words.

I glance out at the empty yard, remembering him there so clearly: blue shorts, bare-chested, barefooted, sipping Cokes, smoking menthol Parliament cigarettes, roaring with laughter in that old striped hammock (that will eventually break beneath him) listening to tapes of Jewish comedians; Mel Brooks echoing through the canopy of trees: *"I've been accused of vulgarity, that's bullshit."* I think about how sometimes my father would rock that hammock with a stick and fall asleep, relaxed, away from the insanity of Los Angeles, the ceaseless ring of the phone . . . forgetting for a while the world and all its cracks—his glasses sliding down his nose as he dozed.

Closing my eyes, I feel the warm July wind pass across my face, down my arms and from somewhere, finally, I hear whistling, footsteps, down the graveled drive. I jolt my head around—a figure appears closer, closer, closer; it's him.

DAD!!!

Immune to the ravages of years he never lived—he's still fifty, not ninety-three—and so he's running. And I'm running. One of those agonizing movie moments where everything slows. Hurry! Hurry! Hurry! We almost knock each other over right there on the summer lawn. He holds my face. Calls me by one of the millions of nicknames I haven't heard for years. "Nanny!" He's looking at me looking back. "You're all grown up and lovely," he says.

"So are you, Dad!" We laugh. I tell him, "You're still so tan!"

He looks like he did the last time I saw him. Not on the eighth floor of that hospital, curled beneath a white sheet. Before that, when we were at that diner in Santa Monica, doing our annual routine, where, across the table, he'd tick off the days until summer on his fingers.

"See, Bunny," he'd say, "only three more months. January will whiz right by, and February doesn't count."

"Why not?"

"Too short."

It was always the identical silly dialogue—and we never tired of it.

We'll make our way to the porch. We're holding hands. Turning, he'll choose the old rocking chair, once green, where he used to sit. I sense he's thinking about that as he runs his hands along the wicker sides.

We both speak at once.

He's sorry, he says. "We never had a proper goodbye. The last thing I said to you was, 'Don't worry. I'll see you in a few hours.'"

I finish for him, fill in the rest. "The surgery went well. That's what the doctor said. But then you had another heart attack."

I don't want to be saying these words. This is not the conversation I want us to have. I move us along.

"Dad! You have grandchildren, even great-grandchildren. And my son is named Samuel Rodman—after your father, after you!"

He'll smile. Nodding, overcome, he can't speak right away.

Then, finally—"Jesus, honey, I've missed you guys."

It's my turn to nod, because if I speak, I might wail. Just as I did when I finally went to his gravesite. When I knew I had to accept that there was nothing I could do, it was too late, he was gone, and all this space and time—a world forever without him—was unimaginable.

I want to lighten this up. I don't know how much longer we have. "I made you a tuna fish sandwich." I hand it to him out of nowhere. "Remember when I was born you didn't have time to finish yours and I used to make you one on my birthday?"

He laughs, takes a big bite, and reaches for the Pepsi I have also plucked from the air.

A motorboat drives by in the distance, creating a time-lapsed cascade of waves. The water pulls at the shore, and my father looks off for a moment. Clearly some summer memory from years and years ago has taken hold, and he's fixed there. After a while, still looking at the lake, he says, "We had us some good times here. . . . So many wonderful days, didn't we, Poppsie?"

And then—"Are you happy, honey?"—his attention suddenly back to me.

He's caught me off guard. I hadn't anticipated that question. I hesitate, trying to steer my way into some coherent response that won't completely overwhelm and sadden him, but all I can come up with is this: "Well, sometimes, Dad, I'm lost."

He puts down his plate, reaches for my hand. He doesn't stuff the moment full of platitudes. He just looks at me in a way that needs no reply, fully aware that I hear him.

He's finished his sandwich and takes a last swig of his soda. I refill it a third time and give him dessert: Angel food cake, vanilla ice cream and chocolate syrup for him. Peppermint ice cream with a chocolate cookie crumb crust for me. Exactly what we used to order at Taughannock, our favorite summer restaurant by the falls.

"Delicious!" he says. "I haven't had one of these in years!" He reaches toward me and wipes away a bit of ice cream I feel dripping down my chin, though there's nothing on the napkin when he pulls it away.

I suddenly remember the lucky stone I've saved for him. I pluck it out of my pocket and set it on the table because he's picked up his soda again and his hands are full.

"Guess what? I see all our old dogs," he says between bites. "Beau, George, Maggie, Mike, and Heidi . . . they're all there. Still running away." We both laugh, remembering how he used to call them "the friendly travelers."

I'm wondering about his dad, his mom, his war buddies, his friends. But I don't ask. There seems a limit to what I can know. I'll tell him about the world today but not too much; it will distress him profoundly. He's put down his empty dessert plate and glass, listening intently; shaking his head, but perhaps not surprised that still so much has gone wrong. "Prejudice," he says—as he always did—"is our greatest evil."

And we'll be quiet again, looking out at the green, green water that has grown still. "You know what, Nanny?" he'll say after a while. "I'd count this as one of our best days ever. . . ."

At first I'll wonder if there's something wrong with my eyes—the way his face isn't quite as clear—and I'll rub them. Or, I'll think perhaps it's that the sun has set, the light is failing. Of course, that's it! And I'll grab a candle. But then, when I turn back, his chair is empty, rocking slowly from his departure. And I'll know—my father is leaving. Leaving incrementally. Leaving for good.

"Dad! Wait! Wait! Want to play Crazy Eights? Go Fish? Like before? Remember? Dad! We can't be done! There's so much more to say. . . ."

Frantically I'll search in the air, in the coming nightfall, waving madly for him, but there's nothing there.

In a choking, defeated, desperate voice, I tell him, "You can't go. Not again."

I wait. I listen. Please say something. And then, suddenly, from the edge of the porch, in the darkness—though faint, I hear him—this. This! "Honey, I loved your memoir."

At dawn, I'm still there, looking out at the new day and the early colors streaking across the sky. The lake is calm, with a few fishermen scattered in silhouette, their voices echoing quietly across the water, the sounds of their lines reeled in, a heron flying back to her nest. I'll have to go soon, get my things. I reach across the table, but it's empty. I look on the floor, on the railings, on the steps, feel in my pocket again. But it's not there. The stone for my father is gone.

I'll smile then, thinking again about that *Twilight Zone*, "Walking Distance," and though maybe it's just the wind, I'm almost certain I hear my dad, repeating those lines from the show: *"This is a wonderful time of life for you. Don't let any of it go by without enjoying it. . . . You've been looking behind you, try looking ahead."*

Anne Serling is the author of As I Knew Him: My Dad, Rod Serling *(Citadel Press, 2013). Her poetry has been published in the* Cornell Daily Sun *and* Visions. *The adaptations of two of her father's teleplays appear in the anthology* The Twilight Zone: The Original Stories. *She has had articles published in* Salon *and the* Huffington Post, *and appeared on NPR's* Snap Judgment. *Currently she is working on a novel:* Aftershocks.
Facebook: https://www.facebook.com/anne.serling
Facebook Book: https://www.facebook.com/AnneSerlingBooks

43

"Fill it all the way to the top, honey."

DAN ALLENTUCK (SON)
AND MAUREEN STAPLETON

Lunch with Maureen? In a restaurant? Where other people will be present? Invitation accepted with deep reservations. Even now, some eleven years after my mother's death, the thought—or rather, the memory—of lunching with her is enough to provoke the onset of unease and anxiety. You see, gentle reader, there's just no other way to say it: a restaurant lunch presented my mother with her first opportunity of the day to get stinking drunk, and once she had achieved that goal, Mumsy-kins was anything but a fun companion for a boy hoping to spend an enjoyable afternoon on the town, and after many (oh, so many!) searing incidents I won't dwell on here, I made a deep sworn vow that for the sake of my frail equilibrium, I would in future resolutely avoid all such occasions. To relax one's vigilance and allow oneself to be swayed by the prospect of a fabulous meal at a great restaurant or by winsome company ("Julie Christie will be there!") was to pay a price in public humiliation and private hurt that I eventually decided was too high. Before you brand me an ungrateful son or a spoilsport, I hasten to add that my not joining her party didn't mean that there *was* no party. A more convivial human being than my mother never lived, and where she went, the bandwagon was sure to follow. More often than not, she dragged it back home with her, horses and all. I grew accustomed to encountering strangers in our living room exhibiting varying degrees of alcohol-induced befuddlement when I returned from school in the late afternooons. So boundless was Mom's hospitality that more than one post-luncheon reveler ended up as a houseguest for days or even weeks. My point is that lunch with

Maureen was often a raucous free-for-all during which the customary rules of decorum were ignored and anything could happen. For one thing, there was never enough wine. Often, Mom stumbled or fell on the way out, either inside the restaurant or on the pavement outside, and since she insisted on taking her wineglass ("Fill it all the way to the top, honey") with her as she departed, these spills could be truly perilous. In short, lunching with my mother was a job for someone else. To this day, I tend to skip lunch entirely or make do with a sandwich. I'm much more of a breakfast and dinner man. But much to my surprise, when tasked by Erica to lunch with Maureen just one last time, I could not decline.

And mind you, it would be untrue to say that *every* lunch with Maureen inevitably devolved into a drunken saturnalia. Most did, but those that didn't were often memorable for many reasons, not the least of which was that when she was sober, my mother could be—and I don't exaggerate—the dining companion of one's dreams: endlessly playful and funny, deeply wise, kind and insanely generous to the help, from maître d' to busboy, a font of shrewd character analyses and sensible advice about my feckless love life, and my budding (or so I hoped) career as a writer. My sister, Katherine, and I cherish our memories of those golden occasions. Oh, but we laughed! Once, after the two of them had lunched together at a mediocre, faux-Polynesian restaurant in Lake George, New York, the waitress glanced at their empty plates and asked incredulously: "You *liked* it?" They laughed about this for the next twenty years.

When dining in restaurants, it had always been Mom's habit to wrap leftovers in a napkin that she tucked away in her purse for future consumption (often after "doctoring" the dish by adding chili powder, garlic salt, and ketchup until it bore no resemblance whatsoever to its original incarnation). On one particular occasion, temptation, as it frequently did, got the better of her, and she plucked from the buffet table what she thought was a freshly baked meatloaf, only to discover after she'd gotten home that she'd absconded with a brick by mistake. I suspect that my mother's impoverished childhood in Troy, New York, must have involved a certain amount of what is today called "food insecurity," and a corollary of this was binge-eating when the opportunity presented itself. Mom was a fat kid, and her fluctuating weight remained a lifelong concern; or to be more accurate, it did until her final years, when her appetite all but vanished. She avoided any food containing coconut because as a child, she'd sneaked into the pantry of her extended family's home on First Street and gorged on several cans of grated coconut, afterward becoming violently ill. Since Mom's Irish grandmother Mary did all the cooking, and since grated coconut is not, as far as I know, a staple of Irish cuisine, I suspect the cans had been purloined from a local grocery store by Maureen's mother, Irene, who was celebrated in the family (perhaps "celebrated" is not really *le mot juste*) for her light fingers.

But today is different, and I am looking forward with barely concealed excitement to having a perfect lunch with Maureen. Furthermore, since I am both the writer and director of this little scenario, the prospect of Mom spoiling the occasion by getting stinko is out of the question. I might even break one of my own rules and have a glass or two of wine with my lunch, for while I am very far from being a teetotaler, drinking even a single beer during the day makes me sleepy.

"Where would you like to go?" Mom would ask, generously leaving the choice to me. If this were a dinner date, I would seek out the most exalted restaurant I could find (Daniel? Le Bernardin?), one with acres of artfully arranged cut flowers in a spacious, elegantly appointed room. But since this is to be a luncheon date, and neither of us is accustomed to eating a large meal at midday (Mom rarely ordered anything more elaborate than a BLT sandwich), choosing a Michelin-starred restaurant would be inappropriate. For this occasion,

I have settled on a health-food restaurant called Vim and Vigor (alas, long gone) on West Fifty-Seventh, where we lived before my sister, Katherine, was born. We generally sat at the counter, where the female waitstaff, who had known me since I was a baby, always made a fuss over me and remarked how much I had grown since our last visit, even if this had occurred only a week before. We invariably ordered fresh-squeezed orange or carrot juice, which was served in cone-shaped metal canisters that held paper cups. The restaurant's pièce de résistance—and it was so delicious that we never ordered anything else—was a dish called baked cottage cheese, which Mom occasionally tried to replicate at home with unsatisfactory results.

Unless she was drunk, Mom was big on punctuality, a trait I have inherited with a vengeance. The prospect of my being late—even by a few minutes—for an appointment, is guaranteed to induce intense anxiety, and when others are late it's even worse, as my imagination goes into overdrive and I grow increasingly certain with each passing minute that they have forgotten about our date and are not coming. Nevertheless, old habits die hard, and today, as I often do, I make a point of arriving at the restaurant well ahead of time so I can scan the street outside through the plate-glass window for her approach.

Sure enough, my heart skips a beat as I recognize her approaching from half a block away. Long before I can discern her features, her gait and something else I cannot quite define proclaim unmistakably that it's Maureen. My wildly pounding heart all but bursts from my chest, and I spring from my seat, nearly upsetting the shaker of Vege-Sal on the table, and race outside to greet her. Hugs. Kisses. Tears. How often I have dreamed of this moment! After a suitable interval to allow the reality of our encounter to sink in, she cheerfully announces, "I'm starving! Are you?" "Not really " I reply, "but you know what's good here?" to which we both respond in unison: "Baked cottage cheese!"

The moment we step inside, the counter ladies and the waitstaff (all of whom are black, in case anyone is interested) erupt in a spontaneous torrent of greetings and "Lord have mercy!" This is a stark contrast indeed with the usual, frosty "Do you have a reservation? No? Let me check our book," that passes for a greeting among the giraffe-like eye-candy types who are often employed to guard the portals at loftier establishments. I had almost forgotten the guilty but gratifying pleasure of dining with a celebrity who is, by definition, the perpetual center of attention, and in particular, how quickly the murmurs of recognition and admiration one overhears come to be accepted as one's rightful due. ("That must be her son," "He looks just like her," "She looks smaller in person," and so on.)

For this occasion, no sooner had we both sat down, when Mom, wearing flip-flops and a sleeveless blue cotton frock, utters the words my sister and I know so well: "Anything we don't eat, we doggy-bag!" Evidently, leftovers are permitted in heaven or whatever afterlife she has been occupying for the past eleven years. Perhaps, that is the real meaning of "the angel's share"—the phrase distillers use to describe the portion of their product that is lost through evaporation. "I don't think there are going to be any leftovers," I reply. "You never know, ducky!" is her cheerful riposte. Before we can say another word, a beaming, middle-aged woman appears at Mom's side and says to her, "Oh, Miss Stapleton, my husband and I just loved you in *All in the Family*." To which Mom replies, "That was Jean Stapleton, honey, and we're not related. But you're right—she's great!" The woman looks perplexed, offers a weak, "Oh," and returns to her table, where she replays the exchange for her equally clueless friends. "If I had a dollar for every time somebody thinks I'm Jean fucking Stapleton, I could have retired in comfort." She says this with no animosity whatsoever. In point of fact, she receives (or used to) autograph requests in the mail just about every week with a photograph of Carroll O'Connor and Jean Stapleton in their Archie and Edith costumes. Never one to disappoint a fan—even if it's someone else's—she signed them anyway. With her own name, of course. No one seemed to notice. Taken as a group, autograph collectors are not the brightest of bulbs.

When our lunch arrives, I discover that I was hungrier than I thought, because I tuck into my vittles with relish—I haven't eaten Vim and Vigor's baked cottage cheese since the place closed, I don't know how many years ago, and it tastes every bit as good as I remembered. But I notice that Mom, who only minutes before had announced she was "starving," barely touches hers. Instead, after a few bites, she pushes it around with her fork, sculpting it into unusual shapes like a child toying with Play-Doh. This is a familiar sight. There is something about eating in public that never appealed to her.

"I guess you're going to doggy-bag it, huh?" I ask. "Yup. I'll finish it later," she replies. "It's no good cold," I venture.

"Oh, I know. We have a stove and hot plate. Don't you worry. I'll finish it."

You know what?

I know she will.

Dan Allentuck is a writer and documentary filmmaker who specializes in films about photography and painting. A lifelong New Yorker, he lives on the Upper West Side with his wife, the filmmaker Nina Rosenblum, and their Yorkshire terrier, Sasha. He loves to cook but has never tried to make baked cottage cheese.

44

"As I once said to your mother, it's a miracle you survived us."

TRACY TYNAN (DAUGHTER)
AND KENNETH TYNAN

The security guard confirmed that my late father was on his way up. I was nervous. I hadn't seen him in more than thirty years; thirty-seven years, to be precise. I'd agonized about what to wear. Being the daughter of a famously flamboyant dresser, the bar was high. I finally settled on a pale blue dress that showed off my long legs—my father's legs.

Choosing the cuisine for lunch had been a challenge. My father was a gourmet. He loved good food and had eaten at some of the best restaurants in the world. I decided to cook. When he was alive, I had cooked for him only once (roast lamb and potatoes, my go-to dish for many years), and I wanted to show him what a good chef I'd become. (Does one ever grow out of wanting parental approval?) Indian food was his favorite, but that was too far out of my comfort zone. Instead, I chose a recipe from a cookbook he esteemed, *A Treasury of Great Recipes*, by Mary and Vincent Price—not that he actually cooked himself, but he liked to read the book and tell my stepmother, Kathleen, what to make. I think another reason he was so fond of this book of famous recipes, from famous restaurants, written by a famous actor was that it was a perfect match for my father, a man who could never resist celebrity.

I made the classic Boeuf à la Bourguignon. It was a complicated recipe and required my husband—a writer, not a chef—to help me decipher some of the contradictory instructions, but I was proud of the results. It was simmering on the stove, giving off a delicious aroma. I also made new potatoes; no other veg: regardless of my father's sophisticated tastes, he was basically a meat-and-potatoes kind of guy. Hoping to impress the oenophile in him, I had splurged on an expensive bottle of French red Burgundy. It was open, and I was allowing it to breathe. Chilling in an ice bucket was a bottle of his favorite California champagne, Chandon Blanc de Noirs. I glanced around the room; it looked clean and tidy, the table was set with my best Russel Wright plates, but I was a wreck. I needed something to calm me down. I took a puff from my pot vaporizer to steady my nerves.

The doorbell rang. I opened the door. There he was, just as I remembered him: a tall, lean man with gray hair parted on the side, wearing the iconic white suit in which David Bailey had photographed him in 1968. We looked each other over. There was an awkward hug. We were never that physical with each other.

"You look good," he acknowledged.

"So do you, surprisingly."

First hurdle overcome. He surveyed my loft and complimented me on the décor—eclectic. I opened the champagne, and the pop of the cork seemed to release some tension in the air. The pink foam spilled down the glasses as we toasted.

"To us," he said.

"To us," I concurred.

Another awkward silence. Where to begin with someone who's been out of your life for over thirty years? Not to mention, out of his.

"Are you hungry?"

"Yes. Smells good. I haven't eaten in . . ." He waves the thought away with a grin.

"It's a recipe from the Vincent Price cookbook," I announce proudly. "From Le Pavillon."

He adds, "A great restaurant."

I serve the food. We sit opposite each other. My ginger cat jumps up on the chair at the end of the table, and stares at us.

"Who's this?" asks my father.

"Oliver. He likes to watch us eat."

My father laughs and reaches out to pet him. Oliver, not a particularly friendly feline, quickly falls under his spell and starts to purr. My father loved cats. Growing up we always had cats.

"He reminds me of Cagney," says my father. Cagney was his favorite feline.

"Once at a party, Dizzy Gillespie suddenly seized one of Cagney's front legs and plunged it into his mouth, right up to the shoulder. He then slowly extracted it. We all craned forward, expecting blood from claw scratches to come pouring from his mouth. Amazingly, there was none."

"It's hard to believe that a trumpet player would take a risk like that with his mouth."

My father shrugs. "You know what Dizzy said? 'That's how much animals trust me!' And that, in fact, is how much everyone trusted him. He was a cool c-c-at."

As he stumbles over the letter "C," I am reminded of the remnants of his stutter, conquered long ago, but still noticeable when he is nervous with certain consonants.

I see he has finished his champagne. I pour him a glass of the Burgundy. I feel it's important to keep us well lubricated. He lifts the glass and sniffs. "Mmmn, nice bouquet." He swirls the ruby red liquid and takes a sip. "Good choice. Good food, too."

Phew, so far, so good.

"So, what happened with you and Jim? Last time I saw him, he wasn't too eager to marry again."

"I finally beat him down. We just celebrated our thirty-fifth anniversary. You have two grandchildren, Matthew and Ruby. Matthew's middle name is Peacock, like you, and also like you, he loves clothes!"

My father smiles with slightly bewildered delight.

"Actually, you have five grandchildren. Roxana married Jim's son, Jesse, and . . ." (Roxana is my half-sister.)

"Wait a moment," says my father, mid-forkful, "Jesse, the little blond chap?"

"Yup. You know how you always said that incest was the last taboo to be conquered . . . ? Well, this isn't exactly incest because there's no blood. But it's close."

My father drains his glass of wine. He gulps. "Wow."

"Yeah, we were kind of surprised when they first started seeing each other, but actually, it's worked out rather well. They have two beautiful kids, Izzy and Jack." I refill both our glasses.

He tries to puzzle this out. "So, you're an aunt, or half-aunt, on one side, and a stepgrandmother on the other . . ."

"Yes, half-aunt and half-grandmother, they call me Grauntie." He's amused.

"And what about Roxana? Has she given up her ambitions for motherhood?"

"Hardly. She's the director of a nonprofit organization that works with unions to fight for economic equality and to raise the minimum wage. . . . She's also very beautiful. Looks just like Kathleen."

"And Matthew? I mean my son Matthew, not yours."

"He was a writer, like you, but he's become a lawyer and deals with entertainment law and intellectual rights. He's married to a chef and writer and they have a lovely daughter, Vebeke."

My father peers at me. "Such a big family. Rather unexpected."

"I know . . . I have sort of become the matriarch of the family. We are all quite close and spend holidays together, etc. . . ."

I can see he's not really paying attention. He was never much of a family man.

"Are you liking the Boeuf à la Bourg, Borgon . . . gonne?" I struggle to pronounce it properly; he corrects me.

"Yes, it's very tasty."

Does he really like the stew, or is he just being polite? I am never sure with him. He once wrote that I needed more confidence and clarity. Has nothing changed?

I try a different tack. "I saw tapes of you on *The Dick Cavett Show*. You were great."

"Yes, he was fun. Of course, they paid you nothing, well, practically nothing. I had to insist on getting more. He gave it to me. Out of his own pocket, I think. I reckon he knew how strapped we were for cash. Bit embarrassing."

"I was surprised to hear you tell that story of when Philip and I came to visit you in Italy." (Philip, the son of J. P. Donleavy, was my high school boyfriend.)

He laughs. "Oh yes. I was trying to be the progressive parent and put you in the same room so you could sleep together. And then afterward you told me that you weren't boyfriend and girlfriend. And I felt so stupid."

"But we *were* boyfriend and girlfriend; we just weren't fucking, because . . ." And then I stop. Do I really want to go into the saga of my vaginismus and how for many years my vagina was too tight to even get a tampon up it?

"Because?"

"Oh nothing," I say. "We just remember things differently."

"Well, anyway, the story really was about me, not you."

Wasn't everything? I think to myself.

"About me not being much of a parent, I mean."

I pour us each another glass of wine. The bottle is almost finished. I should have got another one, but at thirty-four dollars a pop, it seemed extravagant. I feel the need to turn the conversation more positive. I tell him how much I admire his writing, something I never told him while he was alive. I let him know that the diaries he had written in his later years, which he felt contained some of his best and most honest writing—although my mother insisted every word in them was a lie, including "and" and "but"—were finally published.

"Were they a scandal?" he asks.

The diaries contained some salacious revelations.

"Unfortunately, they were kind of ignored in the US. They came out after 9/11. . . ."

"What's that?"

What could I tell him? "You don't want to know. But the book did okay in England. The British press went to town on all the S-and-M stuff."

"Big surprise! Was Kathleen mortified?"

"You don't want to know about that, either." Kathleen had died before the diaries were published. "But we did manage to turn them into a one-man play that was performed at Stratford and later in London."

He perked up. "Who played me? Wait, let me guess. Jeremy Irons?" I shake my head. "Albert Finney?" I shake my head again. "He's too fat, anyway." He ponders and does that characteristic thing he does of pulling on his ear when he is thinking.

"What about Cecil Day-Lewis's son, what's his name? They lived with Kingsley Amis while Cecil was dying?"

"Daniel Day-Lewis," I offer.

"Exactly. I saw him in a National Youth Theatre production. He had talent. He's probably the right age by now, or he could be aged."

"Actually, he's recently retired."

"Okay, I give up!"

"Corin Redgrave . . . ," I say hesitantly, knowing that he will probably not be met with approval.

"That's an odd choice."

"I thought so, too, but Richard Nelson, who adapted and directed the diaries, was very insistent. He had worked with Corin before and had done a play about Oscar Wilde with him."

"You know I had Oscar Wilde's rooms at Oxford," my father interrupts.

"I know. So I thought that was a good omen. And Corin turned out to be terrific. He got great reviews. He had a wig made and lost weight. I designed the outfit he wore. I'm a costume designer, you know."

"Hmph, fancy that. I had a very unique style, you know. I hope you didn't take too many liberties."

"Do you remember that navy blue, double-breasted Tommy Nutter suit you had, with the red piping?"

"Good choice! That was a bespoke suit. I wore it a lot in the sixties."

"Did you know that some of your clothing is in a collection at the Victoria and Albert Museum?"

"That's bizarre."

"A PhD student is doing his thesis on writers and fashion, and you are one of his subjects."

"How did my stuff get to the V and A?"

"Kathleen sent a trunk of papers to the British Library, and at the bottom was a bunch of your clothing. They couldn't keep it, so they contacted the V and A, and they took it. I think it's kinda nice that it's wound up so close to where you used to live in Thurloe Square."

My father empties the last of the Burgundy.

"There's more champagne, if you want it. Do you want more Boeuf à la . . . ?"

"No, thanks."

I glance at the pot. We've barely made a dent. I will be eating beef stew for weeks. I clear our plates, and with great ceremony I bring out a plate covered in a napkin. I whisk away the napkin and reveal a large bar of Toblerone chocolate.

My father laughs. "You remembered."

"Well, it's not just for you. I like it, too." We sit there in silence, munching on our triangles of chocolaty almond nougat.

He glances at his watch. It's the gold Patek Philippe watch that my mother's father had given him when they married in 1951. Kathleen had given it to me when he died and then it had been stolen. I was glad to see it again.

"I should be going," he said. At parties, he was always among the last to leave, but with me, he would get impatient, ready to move on.

He gets up to go. He passes my desk and spots my memoir. Fuck. I meant to hide it. Or maybe I left it out on purpose, unconsciously wanting him to see it. See, Dad, I can write, too! On the cover are my father and mother circa 1958, both wearing leopard pants, sitting on a zebra-skin sofa; behind them, a huge black-and-white blow-up of Hieronymus Bosch's *Garden of Earthly Delights*.

"I couldn't resist using that photo. The matching leopard pants were really out there."

"Ocelot," my father corrects me. Shit, I can't even get the faux fabric right.

He flips through the book and reads. I hold my breath.

"Nice blurbs."

"Yeah." I take a gulp of air before I pass out.

"As I once said to your mother, it's a miracle you survived us."

I am gobsmacked. He's acknowledging that my childhood was . . . peculiar, different, a nightmare? I nod inanely. This is huge, but I am rendered speechless. Finally I find my voice.

"It wasn't so bad. I mean, compared to some other people. You did your best . . . considering."

He gives me a grateful smile and a pat.

"It was a delicious lunch. You're a good cook."

I positively beam. We embrace awkwardly. I watch him as he walks down the hall.

"Stop!" I shout.

He turns around. I go back into the loft, grab my book, and run after him.

"Here, I hope . . . I hope you like it. . . ."

He looks sadly down at it.

I say, "It might be a little rough about the early years. . . ."

"Thanks," he says. "Nothing would please me more than to read it. But I can't take anything back with me."

He reaches out to hug me again. This time it's a real one. I feel his body. I feel his essence: the faint smell of cigarette smoke that lingers on his clothing after all these years. He turns and disappears down the hallway, a ghostly white figure, surrounded by dark gray walls in a halo of light.

Tracy Tynan is a costume designer and writer living in Los Angeles. Her credits include Choose Me, The Big Easy, Blind Date, Great Balls of Fire, *and* Tuesdays with Morrie. *She is the daughter of renowned theatre critic Kenneth Tynan and novelist Elaine Dundy. Her memoir,* Wear and Tear: The Threads of My Life, *was published by Scribner in 2016. Each chapter is a personal story based on an item of clothing. The book follows Tynan's quirky trajectory from clothing-obsessed child to successful costume designer.*

45

"Fame is a horrible thing to do to someone."

MARK VONNEGUT (SON)
AND KURT VONNEGUT

I talk to Kurt all the time, probably more than when he was alive.

He's certainly much easier to deal with.

Fame is a horrible thing to do to someone.

Sometimes I see my father going along, handling things beautifully, especially for a vet with PTSD. He didn't drink himself to death or kill himself or anyone else. He was driving along, doing pretty well, and then there's a hairpin curve called fame; through the guardrail and over the cliff he goes. If it wasn't for art, for trying to tell the truth to save his own life, which he noticed made him and others less lonely, he would have ended up gone and I wouldn't exist. And no one would be asking what it would be like to have lunch with him now. I've never known a human who was less interested in food. He never cooked or seemed even a little bit interested in what things tasted like. His biggest concern with a restaurant was whether they'd let him smoke. He got away with stuff because he was famous, like smoking in restaurants. Who wants the job of telling an icon not to smoke?

I wonder if he'd tell me the truth about things, like doctors telling him he should keep smoking. I don't wonder that much; I think we both knew when he was lying. Mostly we'd talk about art and beauty and writing—how hard it is to try and how good it feels to get things right. I bought ten acres with my share of the royalties from *Slaughterhouse-Five*. I wander around sort of gardening the place, bragging a little about how much more land I own than he ever did and how beautiful I'm going to make it, and I thank him for what I learned watching him go from thing to thing to do gardening.

Dirt—Garden—Dirt.

I love how he gardened, but he's easier to deal with now that he watches over me.

And I amuse the hell out of him.

Mark Vonnegut has published two books, The Eden Express *and* Just Like Someone Without Mental Illness Only More So. *He's practiced primary care pediatrics for thirty-five years and is now taking care of babies of the babies he took care of when he started. He still writes, paints, and plays music. Life is good.*

46

"But there would be laughs, more than anything else on this occasion."

RICHARD BAUSCH (FRIEND)
AND EUDORA WELTY

I will have a late lunch with Eudora Welty, I think, and this will be the kind of serious fun you never quite let go of, since I had a late lunch with her for real, twenty-six years ago, at a Fellowship of Southern Writers' celebration. This was in Chattanooga, Tennessee, during the Tennessee Arts Commission Conference on Southern literature. I was being honored by the Fellowship, receiving the Hillsdale Award for Fiction. There was a brunch, made up of members of the Council and the members of the Fellowship. I went into that brunch feeling the effects of a good deal of socializing the night before, and I was desperately hungry. The first chair I saw was next to Eudora. I sat down, said, "Hello," quietly, and looked around the room. I saw Walker Percy, George Garrett, Mary Lee Settle, James Dickey, Reynolds Price. At the table with Eudora and me were Peter Taylor, William Styron, Shelby Foote, and Cleanth Brooks.

I knew Taylor, and Ms. Welty, but these others I had never met, and they were, of course, very high on my list of literary heroes. So I was nervous and knocked the table leg with a knee as I sat down. The water in the glasses wavered slightly. Eudora introduced me to the others, and I asked about her travel and arrival. I was starving. Someone set plates in front of us. Chicken Cordon Bleu. I picked up my fork and knife and set to cut a thick slice, sticking the fork deep into the breast, and in the same moment I realized that there was only one voice speaking in that large room. Someone was speaking a prayer of thanksgiving and an invocation at the podium, and everyone was sitting head bowed, hands in lap, silent. So I tried to lift the knife from the chicken, to sit back myself. The knife wouldn't come. It was too deeply embedded in the meat. So I had to simply sit back and leave it there, standing up in the chicken breast. Eudora leaned over slightly and murmured to me, "Richard, I believe it's already killed."

The rest of that speech, I had to control my laughter.

That was Eudora, to me: this quiet but wicked sense of humor. And a gentleness, too. She was eighty-two at the time.

I believe I would have us meet wherever she was most comfortable, and that would most likely be at a favorite restaurant; she would probably insist, given that we are in this world of allowing us preferences beyond time and space, that it be a favorite place of mine. So I would choose Pasta Italia, in Memphis, Tennessee. A quiet, café-like place, with a wonderful wine list and a big cheese wheel in a barrel as you come in the door.

I would go alone, and I imagine she would, too.

I think she would be feeling the slight strain of wanting to be entertaining and charming for this young man she has known only a short time, but with whom she shares several mutual friendships and a love of literature and good writing. I would walk over and kiss her cheek and sit across from her. She would already have her goblet of bourbon in crushed ice. I would order a glass of Barolo.

We would tell stories about our friends, adventures, triumphs, sorrows, losses. The last hard years, without help at times when it just wasn't there to be had. And the long nights, the dark. But there would be laughs, more than anything else on this occasion. She would remind me of that first time, when I sat next to her at Susan Shreve's house with my own bourbon on ice, and we realized that we were the only two people in that room drinking whiskey; and I told her that there is a line in her story "Petrified Man" that would work perfectly in Flannery O'Connor's story "Good Country People."

"What line is that?" she said.

And I said, "When that so-called Bible Salesman is going down the ladder with Hulga's artificial leg in his case, he should say, 'If you're so smart, why ain't you rich?'"

Oh, how we laughed then, and she said, "It would go there. You're right."

And then she said, "You know, I never liked her much."

And we laughed again.

We would talk about that kind of thing, and about the quickness of time, and we would eat pasta al forno, lovely wide folded strips of noodle, with prosciutto and fontina cheese and Béchamel sauce, and I would wonder aloud why she stopped writing stories as she got into her seventies—because I'm still writing them and will never stop until it's taken from me. And I imagine her saying, "It was taken from me. I couldn't do it anymore. I never felt I would have time to finish. I didn't want to leave anything undone."

And maybe I would tell her about a woman I knew who kept one closet in her house messy, for fear that if she ever finished with that, she'd die.

I wouldn't want the lunch to end.

And I would take it with me, a memory and a sweet thought; but then, we do have a version of this kind of thing. I can pick up one of her books and look in, and hear the voice again, and no matter when or where I or anybody looks in, there she is.

Richard Bausch is the author of twelve novels, eight volumes of short stories, and one volume of poetry and prose. He teaches in the writing program at Chapman University in Orange, California.

47

"A man with a thickly accented, high-pitched voice said,
'Dr. West, I would like you to buy a yellow moped.'"

CAMERON WEST (ACQUAINTANCE)
AND ROBIN WILLIAMS

The distinctive sound of the postal truck aroused the attention of our golden retriever, Baylie, from his mid-day snooze on the living room couch. I watched the mail lady, Irene, efficiently place the mail in a neighbor's box, then move to the next house around our cul-de-sac. I was pondering whether her name actually was Irene, or if I just thought it was Irene because the white pith helmet she always wore made me think of Hurricane Irene and how a person wearing a pith helmet looks prepared for anything. My cell phone's ring interrupted my speculation.

Not recognizing the phone number, I answered, "I'm hoping this isn't a sales call."

A man with a thickly accented, high-pitched Indian voice said, "Dr. West, I would like you to buy a yellow moped. Canary yellow— like Tweety Bird. *Twee-tee bird.* Guaranteed to not crash, probably, or to not attract hot women, definitely."

"Huh?" I responded, and my jaw actually dropped. I recognized the cartoonish delivery and eerily felt the presence of the owner of the voice. But it couldn't be.

"Hello?" the voice said. "Are you there? This is a call for Cameron West from far away, but closer than you think. Muuucchhhh closer, my friend."

I felt as though a chain had jumped off a sprocket in my brain onto another gear, and my mental feet were trying to adjust. *Robin Williams is on the phone?*

Robin and I became acquainted when, perhaps at the height of his fame, Disney purchased the rights for him to produce and star in a movie based on my memoir *First Person Plural: My Life as a Multiple*. Soon after we met, he shared the thought that, although our lives were very different, we were similar in that both our minds had many rooms. He promised to step gently into mine as he prepared for the role, and he hinted that some of his rooms were much darker than the ones he showed the public, which made him confident he could convincingly portray someone whose mind had been severely damaged by childhood trauma. The depth of Robin's inner pain was palpable to me, though I couldn't have guessed its physiological genesis at the time. The film was never made, and Robin's darkness, misunderstood and misdiagnosed, took him from us way too soon.

However, in that moment, on that perfect California day, he was, unaccountably, very much alive and on the phone in the persona of an Indian man who wanted me to buy a two-wheeled vehicle. Something shifted, and I felt a sense of excitement tingle my belly; a grin crept across my face.

"Yellow moped, Robin?" I asked.

"Who is this Robin? My name is Ahmed."

"Ahmed?"

"Yes, sir, that is me," he said. "Ahmed Abigmistake."

I laughed out loud.

He dropped the hilarious accent and said in his natural voice, which always hinted at mischief, "I know this is weird, but say you don't care."

"I don't care," I said.

"Great! Question . . . are your teeth bored?" he asked.

It took me a second to catch up. "Uh, yeah, I could eat," I said.

"I will come to you. I want to take a hike at Las Trampas and eat a burrito from El Balazo. With sour cream, black beans, and spicy salsa. Get it to go. I'll be there at one on the dot."

"One on the dot," I echoed.

Robin said, "Are we telepathetic or what?"

I laughed. "I don't know what the hell we are."

"It's okay! Bring Baylumps!" Robin said, using his pet name for our old hound. And then he was gone.

Baylie and I were stationed in the car in the driveway, drooling at the smell of Mexican food that wafted from the bag on the seat beside me when, at one o'clock, a black Lincoln Town Car came down the street and stopped in front of our house. The passenger door opened, and Robin Williams popped out—in the flesh. He did a shuffle ball change step and finished with a ta-daaa. He was wearing a gray T-shirt, green cargo pants, and the irresistibly impish grin on his face that I, and the world, had missed since he'd been gone. He ran over, yanked open the rear door of my car, and jumped in next to Baylie.

The dog squealed with joy and licked Robin's face. Robin clapped me on the shoulder and said, "Good to see me, huh? Let's go!"

I started the car and turned to back out of the driveway. The Lincoln was gone. We drove the short trip to the park in silence, and when pavement gave way to gravel and houses to rolling hills, I took a left into the empty parking lot of Las Trampas Regional Wilderness.

Disembarking, Robin surveyed the relatively steep switchback and suggested we eat when we reached the top of the hill. I gave him a water bottle and stashed the food in my old red backpack, and we started hiking at a comfortable pace. We walked in silence, but for the sounds of our exhalations, footsteps scuffing dirt, and a light breeze disturbing the foliage. Cresting the ridge in about twenty minutes, we found a shady spot under a coastal oak and sat down to eat. Robin tore the silver foil off his burrito and I did the same with mine, and we ate like savages, agreeing that the grilled chicken and the chips and salsa from El Balazo were perfection. Baylie sat nearby and got his share, of course, and things were comfortable and relaxed. When the feast was over, I put the refuse in my backpack and, under a cloudless sky, we headed south along the ridge trail.

Robin took a long sip of water and burped loudly—a good, long, multilayered belch.

"Good tone," I said. "Nice finish."

"Food is good. . . . I miss food. Except for one thing that I used to like that I can't eat anymore, not because I'm dead but because something bad happened."

"Do tell," I prompted.

"Well," he began, "I was at Juilliard in New York in '74, about this time of year. I was in the student union, last night of the term, nursing a beer and listening to the music, and Stevie Wonder came on the jukebox singing 'Blame it on the Sun.'"

"Beautiful ballad," I said. "He played all the instruments on that."

"Uh-huh, so when the song came on, this girl grooved up to me. She was maybe five-two, straight brown hair almost to her shoulders and kind eyes tucked into a nice face. Which was good, because that's the kind of face I have, except my eyes are mauve." He fluttered his lashes.

I fluttered back. "Her figure?" I asked.

He lifted an eyebrow. "Half Barbie, half Gumby. Gumby on the jeans half—no hips, flat ass. All Barbie under the peasant blouse."

"I remember those," I said wistfully.

"I remember *hers*," Robin continued. "Kathy . . . she asked me to dance."

He stopped walking, closed his eyes, and began to dance with an imaginary partner. He started singing the chorus of the tune, "I'll blame it on the sun, the sun that didn't shine . . ."

I joined in, "I'll blame it on the wind and the trees . . ."

Robin gave me a mischievous grin, threw down his water bottle, grabbed my hand, pulled me close, and, cheek to cheek, we danced and sang together, "I'll blame it on the time, that never was enough, I'll blame it on the tide and sea . . . but my hearrrt blaaaames it on meeee."

Robin bowed, stepped back, and grabbed his water bottle. We walked on.

"So after a few more tunes," he continued, "we went back to my room where my single bed awaited. You're a very stylish dancer, by the way."

"I'm not going back to your dorm room in this or any other world," I replied. "But Kathy did, and . . ." I beckoned him on.

"Well, for *all* of my solo practice, I was still a rank amateur at the finer points of sex, but Kathy, to my surprise and utter delight, had some heat in those Gumby hips and an ardent desire to perform what I perceived to be mouth-to-cock resuscitation, though the patient was very much alive and well at the time."

I let out a "Hah!"

Robin threw his hand up in the air and shouted, "Can Ah preach it like Ah feel it?"

"Amen!" I responded.

"Damn right," said the preacher, then Robin was back.

Softly, almost reverently, he said, "Seven, maybe seven-and-a-half seconds later, I'm in love."

I belly-laughed, almost pulled an intercostal.

"She spent the night," he went on, wiping a little sweat off his brow. "In the morning, as I daydreamed of a summer filled with CPR and sleepovers, Kathy told me that she had helped animate a short film that was going to be shown in two weeks at a small film festival and she was going and wouldn't it be great if I came along, and by the way it's in Switzerland."

"What'd you say?" I asked.

"I said I have a passport and three hundred and eighty-four dollars. I'm in."

"Very cool," I said.

"So a couple weeks and one flight later we're in Switzerland with backpacks, green cotton sleeping bags, and a matching green Michelin guide. We went to see the film the day we landed."

"Was it good?"

"No idea, but we walked to a park, got into my sleeping bag in broad daylight, and celebrated. My penis was as animated as the film. Afterward, we sat and watched a lady tell her dog in German"—Robin stiffened his body and said in a commandant way—" 'Rex, setz dich hin.' The dog sat down. I loved that. Rex, setz dich hin. Baylumps would have said, 'Huh?' "

We laughed and wound our way down the trail to an area where some cows were grazing and stopped to watch them.

I said, "Baylumps, setz dich hin." He wagged his tail and looked at the cows with his tongue hanging out. "Baylumps, sit," I said, and he automatically did, without taking his eyes off the heifers.

Robin laughed and went on. "We hitchhiked through the Swiss Alps down into Italy and over to Genoa. Then we caught a ride all the way into France past Nice with an old Italian guy in a watermelon truck, who spoke no English but had a big gapped-toothed smile and, inexplicably—or explicably in Italian that we didn't understand—dropped us off by the side of the road in the very late evening in what felt like the middle of nowhere."

We stopped on the path under some trees and had a drink. I gave Baylie a couple of smoky-smelling treats I had in my shorts pocket.

"I like today, Cam," Robin said. "Las Trampas, being with you and Baylumps, telling stories, saying 'setz dich hin, Rex.' "

I looked at him, and our eyes locked. I opened my mouth to tell him just how much I liked it, too, but, choking back a rush of emotion, all that came out was "I . . ."

Robin held me in his gaze and let the moment pass.

We walked on, and he continued. "It was a warm night, so we decided to sleep under the stars, and we walked a bit off the road and settled down . . . right near a damp, swampy area with *a lot* of mosquitoes—an entire French Foreign Legion of bombardiers!" He waved his arms and swatted the air and ducked imaginary attackers. "Buzzing and diving and biting and stinging . . . it was the worst night of the trip.

"The next morning, we hitched a ride into the nearest town, St. Laurent-Du-Var, to get some anti-itch cream and breakfast. Outside the market, Kathy and I slathered each other's bug bites with cortisone cream and ate two yogurts apiece. Mine were strawberry. After we ate, we were heading in single file down this narrow sidewalk and the street was winding and dug up in places from some roadwork. I was stepping around bricks—not bricks, but those old paving stones—and focusing on the sidewalk, and then I turned to ask Kathy if the itch cream was working and . . ."

He jumped a one-eighty and paused, clearly absorbed in the memory.

"And?" I prodded.

"And there was Kathy crawling out of a hole in the road about twenty feet back, and her mouth was all bloody!"

"Holy shit!" I said.

"Right! So I ran back and grabbed her face and looked closer, and there was a slice in her upper lip and it was big and gushing blood. She looked pretty stunned and opened her mouth and I could see that her left front tooth was broken in half on an angle and the missing half was gone. She'd stepped or tripped into the hole and smashed her mouth on the stone."

"That's terrible," I said.

"Terrible," Robin repeated, shaking his head. "I barely know this girl. I'm in a foreign country. She's hurt. She needs help, and I don't speak the language." Robin stopped and pointed off in front of us. "Aw . . . there's the parking lot. We're back so soon? That's sad."

"So what happened?" I asked.

Robin took a deep breath and let it out slowly. He turned to me, put his hands on my shoulders, and shook his head, looking very dejected.

"What happened is I puked up two strawberry yogurts," he said, with a double dry heave.

"Oooooh," I said.

"Yup. All over Kathy and my self-respect," he added. "Right there on the rue in St. Laurent-Du-Var in front of anyone who was looking. To the day I died, I couldn't eat strawberry yogurt."

He unscrewed the top of his water bottle. "Fortunately I can, however, still drink water . . . at least I can today." He tilted his head back and drank the last bit, swallowing with a lip smack and an "ahhhhh."

We made our way back to the car, still the only one in the parking lot. Robin opened the back door for Baylie, and the hound joyously hopped in, tail wagging and tongue hanging out. Robin followed.

Neither of us said a word for the five miles back to my house. I fought the overwhelming impulse to tell him how much he was missed and to acknowledge his pain and apologize for everyone who let him down. Instead, I looked in the rearview mirror every few seconds, just to take in the sight of his peaceful, rascally face and the puckish glint in his smiling eyes. And I savored the utter joy of having shared a perfect burrito, danced to Stevie Wonder, and heard one more wonderful story told by the funniest man I will ever meet.

Back at my house, the Lincoln was again parked out front. As I turned into the driveway, I glanced at the driver. It was our mail lady,

Irene. She wore her white pith helmet down low and stared straight ahead. In the back seat, Robin was hugging Baylumps. He looked up and caught my eye.

"Thanks for this, Cam," he said calmly.

Choking back tears, I managed, "Anytime, Robin."

He let himself out of the car and walked to the passenger side of the Lincoln. Irene reached over and opened the door for him, and he climbed in the front seat and fastened his seatbelt. She put it in drive and, just like that, my deceased friend and my mail lady eased down the street and out of sight.

Irene was back behind the wheel of her mail truck the next day, but I didn't see or hear from Robin again. On subsequent walks at Las Trampas, I did bring the subject up to Baylumps, who wagged his tail but didn't say a word.

Cameron West, PhD, is the author of the New York Times *bestselling memoir* First Person Plural: My Life as a Multiple *and the novels* The Medici Dagger *and* Futurecard. *An avid musician, runner, and dog lover, Cam and his wife, Rikki, live on the central coast of California, where they are currently writing a novel for young adults.*

48

"I would like to assure him that he is home, he is safe, he is loved."

JAMES GRISSOM (PROTÉGÉ, SUPPLICANT) AND TENNESSEE WILLIAMS

In the final years of Tennessee Williams's life, he referred to himself, mordantly, as the Flop King: he simply could not get a break—from producers, from the *New York Times*, from John Simon, from God, fate, whatever was in the air. Tennessee took some wry comfort in Joe Allen, the restaurant whose walls were festooned with posters of those shows that had closed quickly, and the brick walls, hung with what he called "[his] children." I would like to meet Tenn here today, with its brick walls much like the brick walls within which we first met in New Orleans, in the company of flops and me, his intrepid Boswell, trusted company.

I know that I would arrive first, because everyone tended to arrive first, and I would be seated and Tenn would walk in, boisterous, smiling, his face like moist marzipan, pink and full. "Baby! My favorite table!" A nice Southern lie to cover the rudeness of tardiness. There would be drinks. Tenn might flirt with the waiter by ordering a Negroni or some other cocktail that necessitated a recipe or an instruction or his hand on his arm. I, the designated driver still, would stick to iced tea, the house wine of the South. Food never much interested Tenn, unless Joe Allen could make a perfect pimiento-cheese sandwich with hospital corners on white bread, so he might settle for their perfect guacamole and chips—easy to pick up, easy to ignore, easy to throw down to make a point.

I know that Tenn would inquire about the theatre: Who was doing good work? Who was succeeding? Who was failing? He would mourn the losses of Edward Albee and Arthur Miller and Elia Kazan, men he loved and trusted and emulated. Tenn would then ask me about the "follies," the lovely women created by God to make the world and his life better, and he would offer a tribute, lovely and fulsome, to each one of them, because, as he often said, "Anger or loss is what most often leads me to create words, throw them up in the air." We would spend most of our time talking about Marian Seldes, the actress who vouched for me when Tenn called her from New Orleans in 1982 to ask if I was trustworthy, and of Maureen Stapleton, his "old shoe" and great friend. Tenn would take comfort—cold as it was—in having outlived them, since the death of Anna Magnani had unhinged him. "Loss of an angel," he had once told me, and would tell me again, "is the ultimate organ failure."

The theme of my lunch with Tennessee would have, I think, the same theme as the first: Did he matter? What was the word on the various streets about him, his work, his life? I know that he would delight in hearing about the many revivals, revisions to history, and adulation bestowed through festivals, biographies, emulations. Tenn had begged for me to be his witness late in his life, when he felt he had none, so I would take pleasure in all the many witnesses, not all of them well-meaning, who had rushed to place flowers at his feet. "My cold, dead feet," he would quip, but he would be thrilled. A sweet thought, a victory, often called for something sweet, and he would bemoan the fact that Joe Allen doesn't have a "supernaturally large" bread pudding, but he would order something to savor as he thought of his current placement. "When in doubt about your station," he might muse, "just die."

I would apologize to Tenn for not taking up his assignment immediately—for waiting too long. I know that he would wave away my apology and tell me that all had ended well. "You were a good witness," he would say, and I know that I would wonder if that were true, or if he were simply reverting to his innate kindness.

Deep within the comments Tennessee made to me in our earlier time together, I kept hearing the lament that plagues so many artists, so many people: Why isn't the work enough to satisfy me? If Tennessee Williams were challenged on the merits of one of his plays, he could defend it as a mother would her children, and his arguments were precise and intelligent, whereas his pleas for good reviews and kind words were disjointed and diffuse. Would the revelation of praise he had received after his death calm him? Satisfy him? Perhaps, but he would want to know, as he always had, if people had been moved; if people had recognized themselves within his works. "Work lasts if work connects," he had told me, and he would tell me again.

Tennessee asked me for witnesses, those who would say, loudly and in his presence, that he had mattered, and I would offer him the book I had written, the letters I had received, to show him just how many witnesses he had.

I would be aware of time passing, running out. Our lunch would be limited. Perhaps I should invest in a Ouija Board, as the poet James Merrill did, and try to contact Tennessee regularly, to re-create our lunches at the Court of Two Sisters, in New Orleans, in the evening, in that dark corner, with one of his special orders. Orders like Pompano en Papillote, an enormous fish baked in a large bag, which then billows and is punctured with a knife or fork, releasing steam and the fragrances of many herbs and seasonings. "It's a meal and it's theatre!" Tenn would exclaim.

Or at Joe Allen, with all the good news of how he was remembered and witnessed. I would apologize to Tenn for letting him down three decades ago, when I failed to quickly honor his assignment to trace those who might have been his witnesses. "Love is so often late," Tenn had once told me, "but don't forget it's love."

I would, however, better understand his need to know if a work had "landed," as he liked to put it. Had it been noticed at all? Plays are produced and fail; books are published and then pulled from shelves. Was it seen? Did it move anyone? I understand that fear now, as I could not when I first met him, but I know now that you harvest and love the feedback you do gain, and you listen to those who understand what you tried to do. Tenn often spoke of consummation with an audience, and it is out there, no matter how badly or indirectly your work might have landed. Would Tenn understand this now? With a list of all the things produced and written and said, would he finally believe that there had been consummation with audiences and readers?

Works surprise us as time goes on, as do the men and women who created them. Wayward children, Tenn called some of his plays, but sometimes they return home and care for their creator. I would want to talk about the care that has come home to Tennessee Williams. He spoke of finding a home, a safe place where one is loved, and I would like to assure him that he is home, he is safe, he is loved.

James Grissom has written for HBO, Showtime, and CBS, and his first book, Follies of God: Tennessee Williams and the Women of the Fog, *was published by Alfred A. Knopf in 2015. He is now at work on* The Lake of the Mind: Brando in the Night *when he is not suing Republicans.*

49

"He wasn't a big hugger, but I always hugged him,
never wanting him to die."

RICHARD LEWIS (CLOSE COMEDY PAL)
AND JONATHAN WINTERS

QUESTIONNAIRE

1. *Which pal would you choose to have lunch with?*
   Lenny Bruce is right up there, but in real life, Jonathan Winters
   was the man. He was like hanging with Picasso.

2. *In a sentence or two, describe your past relationship with this pal.*
   I worshipped him since I was twelve. Neither of us got much support growing up or entering comedy, and when each of us did, we
   were both crazy alcoholics. I'm close to twenty-three years sober
   now, and Jonathan was fifty-three years sober when he passed.

3. *Did he have a profession?*
   I don't know. Is being God a job? The man was a genius. Not just
   a brilliant fine artist, but *the* king of improvisation.

4. *When/at what age did he die?*
   Eighty-seven years crazy and young, in 2013.

5. *Where would you usually meet for lunch? At home? At a restaurant?*
   He lived near Santa Barbara in a gorgeous home with his painting studio about ninety miles from my home in Hollywood. I
   would meet him whenever he was free and felt up to it and I was

available. I usually picked him up, often with my wife, Joyce, and occasionally pals I introduced him to, and took him to the Biltmore Four Seasons, about five miles away. He loved to eat!!!!!! I must have treated him to about nine hundred thousand meals. Meeting him now, I'd try for Sunday brunch at the Biltmore Four Seasons in Santa Barbara. He was like a hysterical kid in a chocolate factory, but food wasn't important to me around Jonathan. I wanted as few distractions as possible while listening to his free-associating.

6. *Would you show up alone?*
Rarely, as I loved sharing his genius. Proud of his clean comedy after he retired from the stage, he was so R-rated afterward (when he wanted to be). Trust me, Pryor and Lenny would have sat at his feet like a guru, endlessly. He was that astounding.

7. *What emotions do you imagine would be felt on both sides at first seeing each other?*
Well, it'd be very emotional. I can only hope that I wouldn't collapse, weeping and wailing. See, he became a father figure immediately to me. My father died young and never saw me perform. Winters and I connected on a surreal spot in the universe. We both destroyed each other when we talked about real truths.

8. *Would you embrace?*
He wasn't a big hugger, but I always hugged him, never wanting him to die.

9. *What would you both order?*
I have crazy eating habits. Winters could eat an entire elk and octopus in three minutes. He loved to eat. I vowed to him that

he'd never pay for a meal with me and no matter how much he ate, he never did.

10. *What would the general mood at the table be?*

Total insanity. Plus, if the restaurant was jammed, oftentimes people loved seeing him and us together. But the killer was that he played the room like a nightclub. He would entertain fans for hours on end. And he loved women. His great wife was ill well before I met her, and he loved to flirt with chicks, and they loved it.

11. *Would you raise questions/issues you'd never expressed while he was alive?*

Are you nuts? For me, it was like talking to God! Two crazy, insecure drunks, now both sober, successful, and with thousands of stories and mutual friends. It was a dream come true. I'd often call him on a three- or four-way call and put on pals like Albert Brooks, who I swear didn't talk for sixty minutes, and when Winters hung up, Albert was blown away and wanted to make a documentary. But I felt the need to protect my buddy as he took pride in being remembered as a "clean" icon.

12. *Would there be laughing? Crying?*

We would scream with laughter. I would cry. He had a peculiar way of laughing at my jokes, which to me, was like hitting a home run out of Yankee Stadium. Imagine making an idol laugh.

13. *Bringing Winters up-to-date on your life in the interim, how would he respond?*

He loved me like a son. He helped me stay sober. Occasionally when he wasn't looking for laughs, he was deadly serious with advice. I called him from the road. He left me *thousands* of messages in different dialects. I cannot overstate how much of a genius he was!

14. *What would your overriding emotion during lunch be?*
Insanity. Every meal was like *Duck Soup*. I often brought along a few thousand dollars in singles and fives and poured it over his head. He laughed crazily. Although he had money, many from his generation treated money like a way to prove their success with jealous family members.

15. *Would recriminations be expressed?*
Absolutely none.

16. *Would you order dessert? If so, what would it be?*
He ate a bit of everything on the menu. Everything. He needed to leave the Biltmore oftentimes on a gurney. (Slight joke.)

17. *How long would lunch last?*
HOURS!!! Then afterward, sometimes, we'd go back and hang at his home. Occasionally, when he needed to come to Hollywood, he'd plan lunch at Musso and Frank's and invite some of our friends. It was complete bedlam.

18. *How would you say goodbye? Tearfully, with relief, with exhaustion?*
With terrible, overwhelming sadness that I'd never see this man again. I loved him so much, he was so precious to me, I can't even really describe it. But I'd also be thrilled that he was still a treasured best friend who respected me.

19. *Who would pay?*
Always me.

20. *Would the lunch reverberate in your mind for very long?*
Always. After hundreds of hours sharing tales both dark and hilarious but always the truth, looking back at having done this with a childhood idol felt like a surreal trip of pure joy.

21. *Would there be things you wish you had said?*
I *always* told him that I loved him profoundly and considered him the greatest, and this lunch would be no different. What more could I have said? Of course, I'd probably also attack my own self-esteem, secure in the knowledge that his respect for me was a true gift and an honor, and that he even considered me a part of comedy history. He had, really, a father's love for me, and also incredible pride.

22. *In summing up, how was the lunch?*
Worth every bit of the seven thousand dollars I spent. And much, much more.

Regarded by his peers as a "comic's comic," the New York Times *said, "This renowned comedian, often considered to be the heir to Lenny Bruce, is a master of long-form storytelling who turns his endless neurotic energy into brilliant comedy." Comedy Central has recognized Mr. Lewis as one of the top fifty stand-up comedians of all time. In addition to his outstanding career as a stand-up comic, this Renaissance neurotic has written books, appeared in major films, and starred in two home-run television series. His latest,* Curb Your Enthusiasm, *is set to begin its tenth season. The secret to his success? In his own words, "I go on a long tour and make people happy that they're not me." After a rocky beginning, Richard is especially grateful for being sober now for more than twenty-four years. Also, a great source of pride for him was when, in 2017, the historic New York City Friars Club named the men's room after him. He lives in LA with his wife, Joyce, and their dog, Luna.*

50

"I don't do children."

ERICA HELLER (DAUGHTER)
AND JOSEPH HELLER

Now I owe you a real lunch with my father, what would actually happen, so let's rewind, shall we? This time, I'll try to sift through a lifetime of unanswered wishes, scoop them out, and be pitilessly objective instead of losing myself in the healing, lapping waves of burnished nostalgia, which couldn't be less likely or appropriate.

In 1998, the year before my father succumbed to a massive heart attack, he gave an interview to Lynn Barber, a brilliant, gimlet-eyed journalist for the UK's *Guardian*. In the article, he boasted that "I don't do children," and he wasn't kidding. He didn't even "do" his own. In a different interview he explained that a particularly prized skill of his was that "I can feel things for people and then just make myself stop feeling them." Indeed he could.

Our relationship had always been strained, fractious, a purblind arabesque at best. When he died, suddenly, at the relatively young age of seventy-six (for someone who took such meticulous care of himself), we were not speaking. He'd always had a mile-wide bitter streak that I seemed to incite for as long as I could remember. As a verbose child, with my ringlets and dimples, I was his precious, chubby, precocious darling. He took me everywhere with him, like Edgar Bergen took Charlie McCarthy.

But then, according to a lifelong family friend, Dolores Karl, everything changed when I was about four. One night, at a dinner party my parents gave, loud shouting—my father's—could suddenly be heard coming from my room during dessert. Dolores and another family friend, George Mandel, rushed into my room to find my father poking a finger in my face and screaming, red-faced, about *what* it hardly mattered. It took the two of them to pull him away from me, with George pleading, "Joe, please, she's only four years old." After that night, nothing was ever the same. A vein of disdain, blackly bilious contempt, was unleashed that would only mushroom and burgeon exponentially for the rest of our days together.

Ours was not a happy household. My mother was an Olympian worrier; in fact, her reaction to a phone ringing, for her entire life, was "Uh-oh." From my fatalistic father, I got a near daily forecast of pain, disappointment, and horror as I grew up, and an in-no-uncertain-terms message that he had little if any expectations of me. I had a learning disability in school (alas, there was no such dignified name for it then) and remained a poor student all the way through college. To my father, this only meant that I was deficient, insubstantial, destined for nothingness. If I was ever proud of myself (extremely rarely), he would quickly douse my spirit. I was never permitted to be happy or hopeful. In college, I got pregnant the first time I'd ever had sex, and when my father found out, I got the silent treatment for one year (to the day), except for the many times he asked me, though I was visibly scared, miserable, and traumatized, how I could possibly have done this to *him*. He took all my clothes and belongings and tossed them out in our hallway, at the elevator. He was done with me.

While I was still struggling through high school, he was already trying to convince me to take a civil servant's job with a pension later on, telling me I was almost certainly going to grow old alone, unloved, without money. It was a forecast Cinderella's sisters would even have found brutal.

At my first ad copywriting job, at around twenty-three, I pessimistically mailed in an op-ed piece I had thrown together to the *New York Times*. When it was accepted for publication, I was beside myself with joy, an emotion quite alien to me. But Joe Heller had to rain on even *that* parade. Clearly proud and very excited when I called my parents to tell them, my father didn't miss a beat: "Well you'd better enjoy it the day that it's printed, kiddo, because the next day, someone else will be in that space." He was such a skilled and almost effortless voice of my very own apocalypse.

By then, I was so used to his need to dominate, I barely noticed it. There *were* exceptions, however. Somewhere along the way in high school, I met a dazzling, brilliant, beautiful boy who treated me like a goddess, made me laugh the way no one else could, and astonished me with his intelligence, intense warmth, frisky spirit of adventure, and abundant wisdom. We read each other's minds. I was uncharacteristically happy until my parents decided that my friend's skin was the wrong color, and they cruelly put an end to it. It was like surgery without blood. To this day, that boy, now a man who has accomplished an almost outrageous amount in his *various* fields, remains a fixture in my slide carousel of past delights, intermingling pleasure with a tingling, sorrowful, furious regret.

I remember one night when I was sneaking out of the family apartment to go to a party with this boy, before my father gleefully excommunicated him. All dressed up, I ran into my father as I was leaving the apartment and, looking me up and down, he said: "Well, I see you've found a way to mask all your defects." This was Joe Heller–speak for: You look pretty. Over the years he frightened away boyfriend after boyfriend, often without explanation or even alerting me. Whatever affection he had in him, seemed to go to the series of dogs our family adopted. To them he would coo and talk baby talk. (He didn't tell *them* they should take a civil servant's job, selling tokens down in the dank, gloomy subway.) He was often side-splittingly funny, I'll give him that, but his humor was perpetually laced with cruelty and almost always at someone else's expense.

When *Something Happened* was published in 1974, and an entire chapter was called "My Daughter Is Unhappy," I was hardly surprised but deeply, deeply hurt. Especially when he compared looking at his daughter's future to looking into a "cold, empty grave." My privacy, as well as my mother's and brother's, had been horrifically violated. Asking him how he could've possibly written about me in that way, his customary riposte was: "What makes you think you're interesting enough for me to write about?" Things went from worse to worst. When I was diagnosed with breast cancer in 1990, right after my parents' long, scalding divorce (he had treated my brave, witty, beautiful, and unfailingly loyal mother hideously for years), I ventured out to East Hampton one summer afternoon, where my dad was then living, to ask him for a five-hundred-dollar loan in order to get more tests done, see more doctors. "Can't do it, kid. It was a bad tax year," he offered, adding: "Get it from your mother," knowing full well (because he parsimoniously controlled her purse strings) that my mother didn't have it. But really, what could I expect from a man who, having gotten tired of his wife of thirty-eight years, actually pulled her in front of a mirror one day, counted her wrinkles out loud as the blood drained from her face, and asked her, chuckling, "See why everyone thinks you're my mother?" Heartless, but not quite heartless enough, the next day he presented her with a majestic, outrageously priced Russian sable coat. He kept her head spinning and the rest of her off balance until their only interactions were hostile manifestly untenable. When it finally became unbearable for him, meaning he was bored, tired of the game, and ready to go live with his mistress (the latest of many), he dragged my mother through a bitter, totally pointless, expensive court trial for their divorce. By then, I think he was at least just a tiny bit bonkers. Both before and after this marriage, years would go by with undiscussed, unexplained silences from my father, a cutting and sad, hurtful habit my brother seems to have unfortunately inherited, along with much of Dad's talent. Sadly, my brother is my own very powerful phantom limb. And so it happened that when Dad died, we were not speaking. I had always loved him just as much as I'd hated him, and I had worked tirelessly my entire life, begging for a few unconditional crumbs of acceptance, but they were never forthcoming. There was no trail home.

Near the time of his death, I was about to marry an Amsterdam-based Dutch artist. My suspicion is that Dad would've taken a brittle disliking to anyone who loved me, and the idea that I was happy now and optimistic about a cozy, productive, loving future with someone evidently enraged him. I was, after all, not playing the part he had so unfailingly groomed me for, the defeated, unloved loser. He instantly let me know that if I married this merry, puckish Dutchman, we would never speak again. We didn't.

Several weeks later, I took my vows on a blustery, chilly Nantucket beach (it was November), and I was uncharacteristically jubilant. The happiness didn't last, of course; the marriage was an absurdly convoluted and mostly ill-fated fiasco, but the point was, even if Father Knew Best about this (he *really* couldn't stand my husband), I never got a call from him on my wedding day, or the Sunday we were featured (at my husband's insistence) in the "Vows" column of the *New York Times*, which Dad had surely read. Instead, several weeks after my marriage, I got a middle-of-the-night call from his second wife (after calling just about everyone else in the tri-state area, including my brother), telling me that my father was dead. The show was over. The curtain had come down for the very last time. There would be no more doomed chances to try to patch things up, wrangle some affection, gain his respect, be friends. But as Robert Benchley famously wrote, "Death ends a life, not a relationship." My father has been gone many years now, but I still see myself at least partly as he saw me, and I can never forgive him for that. It is a battle I face every day and am determined to win, with or without him. Yet even now, I hold tender feelings for him. I see him as a tortured soul. How would you like *your* first book to have been *Catch-22*? Imagine the pressure put on him by himself and others to equal or surpass it? Imagine losing your father while still a small child, in a poverty-stricken household. Imagine completing eighty-six bombing missions in World War II and that when you've returned home, the horror of that war keeps you screaming almost every night in your sleep. It all makes sense to me now, with almost two decades of beneficial clarity. He did the best he could, except that with me, that turned out not to be very good at all.

So, in contemplating lunch with him now, my first question would have to be: Will he show? Does contempt and a lifetime of blistering anger and misguided disappointment carry on beyond the grave? Well, it's *my* fantasy, my realistic one, so let's assume he does in fact appear.

It's winter. We choose the new Union Square Café because of how much he'd loved the old one. I arrive early, nervous, with beads of sweat trickling down my back. After surrendering my coat, I spot my father at a table inside, talking animatedly to Danny Meyer. Dad is already eating. A long raft of empty oysters stretches across the table beside his empty martini glass. (He'd always had this annoying custom of starting to eat before I arrived, regardless of how early I did.) We greet each other without embraces. He looks good; tanned, healthy, and he's dressed impeccably. His customary tiny pack of Stim-U-Dents, his signature, sits near his elbow. He tells me to order, and I do. There is awkward silence. "So your marriage was a real mess, eh?" he has to ask, to which I nod sorrowfully. He laughs softly. Even now that fact strangely pleases him. We chatter about nothing, my building, my friends, my writing, but he is somewhere else, distracted. I order and my food is brought quickly, but I have little appetite. I leave my beautiful butter roasted monkfish pretty much untouched.

Carl Bernstein, lunching at a nearby table, comes over to greet my father. He stands there for fifteen minutes, engrossed in their conversation, with his back turned, never having been introduced to me. Annoyed, I eventually introduce myself. As he heads back to his table, I summon, with great courage, the nerve to ask Dad the only question that has ever really mattered to me. "Did you ever love me?" I inquire, knowing this is the last chance I will ever have to possibly find out.

Just then, a waiter brings us a complimentary dessert from the always magnanimous Danny Meyer; my absolute favorite, the 19th Street Banana Tart, with macadamia, honey-vanilla ice cream. I have been dreaming of having this for days.

The waiter sets it directly in front of my father and he dives right in, leaving me just a few sticky crumbs, in a matter of moments. "You don't need this," he offers, his explanation for appropriating it and gobbling it up alone, like some starved, ferocious bear in a Turnbull & Asser shirt. Steeling myself, I once again prepare to force myself to ask the most difficult question of the most difficult person I have ever known.

"Dad, come on, we're here. We have this last bit of time together to unscramble old animosities and make peace. Don't you want that, deep down?" He stares at me, dumbly. "Have you ever loved me?" I finally summon the courage to ask again.

He laughs a bit ruefully and says, a bit sternly: "You know I don't have discussions like that. If you asked me here to argue . . ." And those are his final words on the subject. The waiter brings the bill, and my father slaps down a mountain of cash and rises to leave. I am still flustered. "But you left all your literary properties to us [to me and my brother]. You must think *something* of me," I blurt out, while slipping into my winter coat and darting after him out the door. He says nothing. Instead, staring down at his shoes, he shakes his head with what seems to be impatience with a side order of despair. Outside it has begun to snow lightly. Standing beside him, shivering a little, I ask, "So, how do you get back from here to where you're going?"

"I take a taxi," he answers, hailing one and preparing to jump inside. Before he can, I stubbornly plant a dry kiss on his cheek.

"Let's see," I say, looking around me, as the snow is coming down harder, "how will *I* get home?"

He's already inside his cab, but the window's rolled down. He says, "There's a bus stop at the end of the block," rolls up his window, and is gone in the heavy profusion of swirling snow.

Death is irrevocable, but our fantasies are not. We can bend and shape them as we choose, again and again, polychromatically, as the years gallop by. We can change them one thousand times to suit a purpose, fill an emotional chasm, provide a powerful, poignant, and logical outcome.

Without question, ours has not been the happy or healing lunch I'd so longed for, the informative, loving, sentimental, long overdue rapprochement. But realistically, it's the only lunch the two of us could ever have. Sadly, to change anything at all, even imperceptibly, would require ten thousand lunches.

And two completely different people.

ACKNOWLEDGMENTS

Any acknowledgments here must begin with my extraordinary agent, Laurie Fox. (And Anne Serling, who kindly steered me to her.) I never met an agent more supportive and encouraging than Laurie. Her exuberance for this project and her willingness, no *insistence,* on throwing herself into it 10,000%, continues to astound me. Work with her, sit back, and then just let the fireworks begin. She isn't an agent. She's an experience.

There are no words that I can properly assemble here to adequately thank all the brave, committed, imaginative contributors to this book, as well as those whose lunches didn't quite make it. The task for everyone was not an easy one and was often painful, sorrowful, freighted with the burden of dredging up memories perhaps better left undisturbed. (Mine among them.) But everyone persevered. Even the merry, fun-filled lunches were tinged with a bittersweet *tristesse,* because, of course, there would be no more of them. But in each case, every lunch, we learned just a little something about the departed luncheon companion we might never have otherwise known. I hoped for these priceless nuggets at the project's outset, and lo and behold, they materialized. Also, for better or worse, each contributor *did,* in a sense, get to have one more lunch, with their imagination.

On then to the cavalcade of names; the loving friends, the strangers, the numberless battalion of unselfish souls who took the time to connect me with many of the writers featured here. Thank you.

My special thanks, then, go to David Cashion, Jamison Stoltz, Cynthia Tocman, Sue Held, Leslie Citron, Sara Giller, Mildred Marmur, Charlie Piccirillo, Rhonda Racz, Joe Winogradoff, Mary Bisbee-Beek, Ronald Blumer, Monda Wooten, Maija Veide, Emily Farrell, Carolyn Feigelson, Peter Shapiro, Iris Johnson, Ivy Heller, Joyce Lapinsky Lewis, Margot Olshan, Rikki West, Alicia Tan, Sarah Robbins, James Kim, and Enzo.

Noel Coward, that brilliant rapscallion, wrote that: "You live and learn. Then you die and forget it all."

As these lunches show, it is then up to the living to go on learning.